Lost Jews

The Struggle for Identity Today

Emma Klein

First published 1996 by
MACMILLAN PRESS LTD
Houndmills, Basingstoke, Hampshire RG21 6XS
and London
Companies and representatives
throughout the world

ISBN 0–333–61946–3 hardcover
ISBN 0–333–61947–1 paperback

A catalogue record for this book is available
from the British Library.

10 9 8 7 6 5 4 3 2 1
05 04 03 02 01 00 99 98 97 96

Printed and bound in Great Britain by
Antony Rowe Ltd, Chippenham, Wiltshire

Published in the United States of America 1996 by
ST. MARTIN'S PRESS, INC.,
Scholarly and Reference Division
175 Fifth Avenue, New York, N.Y. 10010

ISBN 0–312–12890–8

To
the memory of my father
Samuel Solomon
who made me the Jew I am
and to his grandson
Gabriel

Contents

Acknowledgements

I thank everyone I interviewed, whose contributions make up the substance of this book, and also many others who were willing to speak to me but had to be excluded for reasons of time and space. I am grateful to Marlena Shmool of the Board of Deputies Community Research Unit for helping me with statistics about Anglo-Jewry and to Dr Mark Tolts of the Hebrew University for his invaluable help in compiling demographic statistics of Jewish communities around the world.

This book might never have been conceived had not Andrew Harvey, one-time editor of the former *Saturday Review* of *The Times*, commissioned an article which focused my attention on some of the principal themes. Special thanks are due to Gloria Tessler who helped transform a journalistic nightmare into a realisable dream of authorship, and to Robert Wistrich who perceived the novelty of my field of interest and suggested I approach Macmillan. I have been fortunate to have Gráinne Twomey as my editor and am most grateful for her encouragement and enthusiasm. I would also like to thank her predecessor, Clare Andrews.

I appreciate the help and encouragement Martine and Peter Halban have given me from the earliest stages. Others who gave valuable guidance before the book really took off were Giles Semper, Richard Gollner, Neil Hornick and Hilary Rubinstein. I am indebted to Amir Nadel for his computer expertise. I thank Brigid Jackson for emerging at the eleventh hour to fill a domestic vacuum and enable me to finish the book.

Among the many people I barely know who were the source of interesting contacts, I thank genealogists Michael Honey and Nancy Burton and historian Kenneth Collins. Closer to home, I am grateful on that score to Judy, John and Flower Cooper, Monique Neumark, Diana Heller, Yvonne Cooke, Sally Margulies, Judy Cooper-Weil and my son Ariel. Louise Hidalgo and Simon Rocker also deserve thanks for helping me track down an important international personality. The concept of struggle, so central to the book, I owe to discussions with Mickey Yudkin and the chapter title 'The Promise Spurned' to my son Amos.

To Gordon Pocock, who all along has been unstinting with his encouragement, support and advice, I owe a special debt of gratitude. And without the constant love, support and dedication of my husband, Chaim, this book would never have been written.

If people I interviewed requested that their names should not be used, pseudonyms were substituted and have been marked with an asterisk at the first mention.

Prologue

Auschwitz 1992: a high ranking medical officer in the RAF contemplates the mass graveyard around him, the culmination of a series of pilgrimages to Nazi death-camps. Suddenly his anger is tinged with a certain elation: 'Hitler,' he declares, 'I'm a Jew and I'm here.' But his proud defiance conceals a sad irony. His wife is Christian and his children are not counted as Jews.

Air-Commodore Antony Wober is the heir to two venerable traditions. His mother's ancestors were Sephardi Jews from Spain and ancient Babylon. His father's family came to Glasgow at the turn of the century from Minsk. Though his Jewish identity had rarely been given expression in his married life, his journey through the lost world of east European Jewry was an experience in which he and his wife were united. Yet this reaffirmation of his roots is but a hiatus in another process. By breaking the chain through the simple choice of marriage partner, Wober seems fated to be the patriarch of a new dynasty of lost Jews.

I was profoundly moved by Air-Commodore Wober's story, moved by his emotion and by the fact that his own deeply felt Jewishness would be lost to the Jewish people. It was after that encounter that I decided to root out the people behind the statistics, to find out for myself who were the lost Jews.

Emma Klein

Forewords

Emma Klein is a very good writer and the stories in the book, like good pen sketches, come to life with a minimum of words and with maximum effect. So many of these stories could easily become full-length biographies, even novels and in some cases text books, on what it is like to be on the margins of life. Her book reflects enormous research and understated passion which I find both moving and appealing. The writing is non-judgemental but the reader cannot help form a host of value judgements. And if these value judgements themselves are not consistent it is because the people encountered in the book are not homogenous and each one stands in her or his own right with very distinct histories.

I find the book reflects very accurately the chaos in 20th-century Jewish life with the last century already serving as a background for it. Urbanisation, alienation and the process of secularising are almost universal features of 20th-century life. However, in the world of Jews there have been additional stresses and strains which come through so much of the interviews: those who become baptised to escape the fate of the Jews and those who were baptized simply to have an easier way through life; those in mixed marriages which is part of the price Jews are paying for a place in an open society; Jews for Jesus who somehow wish to have the best of two spiritual worlds but, as I see it, only heap gratuitous insult on both; 'God fearers', a fascinating and cherished part of the family of Israel since Biblical times who are still making their unexpected and exciting appearance in the pages of this book and, of course, refugees, those running away not only from persecutions but also from themselves. And so many discoverers of who they are in the new safety of Israel but with a sense that yet more complications will come.

This book is informative, fascinating from beginning to end and, best of all, highly readable. It is the kind of book that I will have no hesitation in recommending to Jews and those who ask questions about Jews and indeed to those who, for complicated reasons of their own, want to save the soul of Jews.

The proposal that comes through in a variety of ways *à propos* the matrilineal versus patrilineal question is very close to my heart and indeed it was part of the proposal I advocated when the RSGB and ULPS considered a merger some years ago, namely that where either of the parents is not Jewish there should be a *safek* - doubt - and there are very many ways in which this could be remedied.

Rabbi Hugo Gryn

Preserving Jewish identity has become a problem. In order to build her case for greater realism and flexibility on the part of Jewish officialdom, Emma Klein sets out to uncover the real meaning of Jewish identity - something ancient, enviable and inaccessible to non-Jews, often a cause of joy and pride and sometimes of anguish to Jews.

In doing so she reveals almost as many identities as there are Jews. But she also achieves something more remarkable. As she explores the many different and sometimes conflicting experiences of Jewishness, each showing a fresh facet of Jewish identity, there gradually and mysteriously emerges from the diverse detail a single picture.

Many people with some Jewish blood in them will find her book a revelation of themselves to themselves and an invitation to draw nearer to the core. Many without such ancestry will find their respect and admiration for this ancient faith and people redoubled, even if its ways can only be fully understood from within. Given the many pressures working to impede Jewish survival - in one age from persecution; in another from assimilation; in another, mixed marriages, the case for some radical rationalisation of the rules concerning Jewish identity seems unanswerable.

Clifford Longley
Religious Affairs Editor
The Daily Telegraph

1

Where Have all the Jews Gone?

THE DECLINE IN NUMBERS

Are the Jews a dying race? Is diaspora Jewry doomed to extinction? This is the question confronting the Jewish world at the end of a century which has witnessed Jewish martyrdom on an unparalleled scale and the fulfilment of the 2000-year-old dream of resurrected Jewish nationhood. It is not the skeletal remnants of the Jewish communities of continental Europe, decimated by the ravages of Nazism, which concern the prophets of doom, however. It is the dramatic decline in Jewish affiliation in much of the Western world in an era of unprecedented freedom.

At their post-war peaks, the Jewish populations of the United States and Britain were held to be 6 million and nearly half a million, respectively. In fact, it was only for a few years in the early 1970s that the figure of 6 million American Jews was recorded and maintained, while in Britain the magic half-million mark was never reached. The post-war high of statistically accredited British Jews was, according to a 1950 estimate, some 430,000, a number which has plummeted to barely 300,000 today. Put simply in the words of a high-ranking official in the Archbishop of Canterbury's court, 'Where have all those British Jews gone?' But Jewish emigration from Britain to Israel and elsewhere, reflecting the current trend in British society towards emigration rather than immigration, is only one factor of the striking erosion. My clerical friend's question is not so simple to answer.

Who is the Jew in the Statistics?

Nor is it simple to ascertain the identity of the composite Jew of the statistics. Since the official United Kingdom census does not include a question on religious affiliation, estimates of the size of the Jewish population are based on mortality:

> The traditional method for estimating the Jewish population in Britain has been to apply an age and sex-specific mortality rate per thousand

persons to the annual number of deaths of the given population. To this end the Research Unit of the Board of Deputies of British Jews collects statistics on the number of persons who are buried or cremated under the auspices of the various synagogal bodies in the United Kingdom.[1]

So to be counted as a Jew in Britain, a person has to die Jewish. How reliable is such a source of information? Since many people stray from their early affiliations but tend to return to them late in life or are buried by Jewish relatives, it is likely that more people die a Jew than live a Jewish life. But the burial statistics bear no relation to the *halachic* or orthodox Jewish definition which envisages as a Jew any offspring of a Jewish mother or a convert to Judaism under orthodox auspices. Given that intermarriage has always existed in a free society like Britain, there must be a number of people born to a Jewish mother and a gentile father who have never identified themselves as Jews and would never request a Jewish burial.

In the United States, where recent estimates record a Jewish population of some 5,575,000, self-definition plays a more direct role, as indicated in the National Jewish Population Surveys of 1970 and 1990 under the sponsorship of the Council of Jewish Federations. According to the most recent survey, approximately 4.4 million Americans define themselves as 'Jewish by religion', another 1.1 million admit to being Jewish but have no religion and some 1.3 million declare themselves to be 'of Jewish descent'. The latter figure, of course, testifies to the striking prevalence of intermarriage. Where the 1990 survey focuses on intermarriage, it reveals that since 1985 more than 50 per cent of marriages contracted by Jews have been to gentiles who have not converted to Judaism.[2]

If 'Jewish by religion' is the prime criterion for defining 'who is a Jew', then the dramatic assertion by the British Chief Rabbi, Dr Jonathan Sacks, that 'American Jewry is disappearing faster than any Jewry since the lost ten tribes',[3] might well be valid. In New York, however, I heard two diametrically opposed reactions to Sacks' statement. Not surprisingly the British Chief Rabbi was supported by orthodox rabbi Dr Jacob Schacter, whom I spoke to at the Jewish Center in New York's Upper West Side. The same day, however, I heard Sacks' perspective demolished as 'rhetoric' by the British-born demographer Dr Barry Kosmin, at the City University Graduate School.

Assimilation or Transformation?

These conflicting reactions represent different sides of the argument engaging many thinkers concerned with the future of American Jewry. Summed up as 'Assimilation or Transformation', it focuses on the erosion of the traditional Jewish family and the new, and much more fluid, demographic phenomenon which is taking place in the Jewish world, particularly in the United States. Those who support the orthodox view that American Jewry is doomed to disappear through assimilation perceive the Jewish family unit of the intramarried couple who pass on the Jewish tradition to their children as the only means of preserving Jewish continuity. To the adherents of this perspective, intermarriage is the harbinger of communal death.

The opposing viewpoint recognises the inevitability of intermarriage in an open society but sees it as a challenge as well as a threat. To support their case, those who argue that American Jewry is not dying but undergoing a transformation often refer to the remarkable number of converts to Judaism or 'Jews by choice' as they prefer to be known. Striding like a colossus across his spacious office high above midtown Manhattan, Barry Kosmin contends:

> Of all the Jews by choice that have been produced in the last 1500 to 2000 years, the majority are alive and well and living in the United States today. There are around 200,000 Jews by choice – that's a social revolution. The idea of Jews becoming non-Jews through apostasy or assimilation is by no means a unique phenomenon of our times. The unique phenomenon of our times is gentiles becoming Jews.[4]

The 'voluntary, tolerant, pluralistic society' which has produced this phenomenon is a double-edged sword. Feared by proponents of the assimilation scenario, the open society can also be viewed as a free market where Judaism may strive to gain adherents in the same way as other religions and ideologies. The market analogy is particularly relevant in face of the inexorable rise of intermarriage.

> We are long past the stage where we can invoke effective religious, communal or familial sanctions against marrying those born into other faiths. However, we can be successful in outreach to these Jews and conversion of their spouses and children if we can get 'equal time' with the Christians and new religions. The demographic imperative for outreach and conversion necessitates our competition in the free marketplace of ideas; the challenges of the 1990s offer American Jewry no other realistic alternative.[5]

With the emphasis in the United States today on the individual's freedom to choose a cultural and/or religious identity, the 1.3 million Americans who acknowledge that they are 'of Jewish descent' must be prime targets for communal outreach if American Jewry is to weather the threat of intermarriage.

Not all that number would be open to the Jewish option. Some are born Jews who have converted and others are adults who currently hold a different religious identification. But the largest group, some 700,000, are children under 18 ostensibly 'being raised in other religion'. From my experience of children of mixed marriages I have found that many have had no real religious upbringing and are likely to have minimal religious identification or none at all, even if they have been exposed to some rudimentary form of Christianity. As an American woman who had grown up celebrating Christmas and Easter explained: 'In America Christmas is Christmas trees and Santa Claus and Easter is bunnies and eggs and Easter baskets. People who are Jewish don't do that but the fact that you do doesn't mean you're Christian.' When British Chief Rabbi Sacks speaks of '1,325,000 Jews who, whether through conversion or upbringing, today identify themselves as Christians',[6] he is virtually writing the whole lot off.[7]

Small is Beautiful, or do Numbers Really Matter?

Does it really matter how many Jews there are? Those who equate the methods for successful outreach with Christian evangelism[8] obviously believe it does. Surprisingly, not only disaffected Jews but some of the pillars of orthodox Judaism would disagree. Jacob Schacter is not one of them.

> I wouldn't proselytise but I would very much like there to be more Jews in the world. I think we're in big trouble and the more Jews we are the better we are. Converts have enormously helped and infused the Jewish people with a great deal of insight, sensitivity, intelligence and strength and wisdom and I would love to see that continue.

As well as sincere and properly converted gentiles whom he would welcome as 'full-fledged members of the Jewish people', Schacter would be happy to witness a return to the fold of 'lost Jews' of Jewish descent, but fears that the trend is very much in the other direction.

Dayan Isaac Berger, formerly of the London *Beth Din*, sitting in the study of his Stamford Hill home crowded with learned books, declares passionately that as a Jew, he has the duty 'to reach out to every Jewish soul'. His definition is the *halachic* one and would include persons of matrilineal Jewish descent and converts who observe the highest standards of orthodoxy. Numbers, as such, do not concern him, however.

> If God Almighty in his infinite wisdom decides that a third of the Jewish people ought to be burnt at the stake at Auschwitz, it's His

judgement and I'm not going to cut corners just to make up those numbers.

Many other orthodox luminaries are equally indifferent to numbers but, unlike Dayan Berger, would be less interested in proselytising to a Jewish periphery. In Britain, for example, there are those who view the current Jewish drop-out rate with equanimity. Rather than see the Jewish heritage diluted by indifference and lack of observance, these Jews are willing to relinquish anyone who is born a Jew but does not live up to the stringent requirements of extreme orthodoxy, and they envisage a tiny but intensely committed orthodox Jewish community surviving into the future.

A PERSONAL PERSPECTIVE

So what if diaspora Jewry disappears? What is there worth preserving? Why do I, personally, feel so strongly about the shrinking of diaspora Jewry and the desirability of Jewish continuity?

I have come to understand that my priorities are somewhat different from those of the mainstream Jewish establishment. Whereas the Jewish establishment is primarily preoccupied with the active core of the Jewish people, I have an almost obsessive interest in those on the outside edge. Clearly it is the periphery – Jews who mingle mainly with their gentile fellow-citizens, young Jews alienated by communities they perceive as too narrow, people with one Jewish parent or more remote Jewish descent – that is most likely to be lost to the Jewish people. It is not so much the diminished numbers that concern me as the fact that without this periphery diaspora Jewry would be little more than an inward-looking ghetto that I would find quite alien.

This book aims to explore the periphery, to find representative voices of a wide range of Jews lost to the mainstream community, with a particular emphasis on people of Jewish descent who may not be identified, by themselves or by others, as Jewish. These are people who, in the past, would have been content to disappear, to be absorbed into the wider culture and forget their Jewish ancestry. In recent years, however, this trend has been reversed and thousands of lost Jews are seeking out some testimony of their Jewish heritage, many going so far as to assert a Jewish identity denied them by parental or ancestral negligence or by the rigours of Jewish religious law. I find this phenomenon profoundly moving and would wish to actively encourage people of Jewish descent – and gentiles who sincerely wish to convert to Judaism – to become part of the Jewish people.

A New Approach to Jewishness

Fifty years after one-third of world Jewry was destroyed, I believe, unlike Dayan Berger, that the time has come to take a fresh look at the entry points into Judaism or Jewishness. It is widely held that in the earliest biblical period, women of a different race who threw in their lot with the People of the Covenant were readily absorbed as wives and mothers within the House of Israel. Prominent examples are Zipporah, the wife of Moses, and Ruth, the great-grandmother of King David.

One popular belief is that the conditions for determining 'who is a Jew' were tightened after the trauma of the Babylonian exile when Ezra and Nehemiah, who led the people of Israel back to their native land, set the seal on the law of matrilineal descent by deciding that the offspring of Jewish women raped[9] in captivity should be accorded Jewish status. By the same token, they forced the men who had married outside the House of Israel to abandon their foreign-born wives. This interpretation is usually challenged by orthodox scholars who argue that the Talmud indicates that matrilineal descent was an established tradition well before the exile and that the post-exilic prophets were reaffirming this tradition rather than enacting a new law.[10]

Another interpretation dates the matrilineal ruling on Jewish status from the Roman period. Rabbi Rivon Krygier, the scholarly young leader of the *masorti* congregation in Paris, argues that throughout the Biblical and Apocryphal periods Jewish descent was patrilineal and that *halacha* was influenced by Roman law.

> The Romans considered that if the mother was a Roman citizen, the child was too. If a Roman citizen married a woman who was not a citizen, their child was not a Roman citizen. If a Roman had children by a slave, the children were slaves. But if a Roman woman married a foreigner, her children would be Romans. All this corresponds exactly to the *Mishna Kiddushin.*

Irrespective of how and when it originated, this book will challenge the long-standing religious law that accords Jewish status automatically to the descendants of maternal Jewish grandmothers, a birthright that is so often squandered. While most orthodox figures I have spoken to invariably justify the *halacha* by emphasising the crucial role of the mother in the child's upbringing, I was surprised to hear a contrary view from the magisterial former Chief Rabbi of Paris, Alain Goldmann.

Often when the father is Jewish and the mother is not, the father wants all the same to assert some religious pressure, whilst when the mother is Jewish and the children are automatically Jewish we have noted that the children practise nothing. Because of a husband who is not Jewish, except in very rare cases, there is pressure from the non-Jewish element which discourages everybody. Reality shows that the mother cannot have any influence unless she already has influence over her husband.

Wise words indeed, *pace* the feminists. And if Goldmann feels that it is not his place to challenge the *halacha*, Maharit Algazi (1727–1802), a renowned *kabbalist* and *halachist*, did indeed take this ruling to task.[11] Algazi's view, very radical from the *halachic* standpoint if perfectly reasonable to the outside observer, was that a child born of Jewish and non-Jewish parentage has a mixed inheritance, 50 per cent from his father and 50 per cent from his mother, and is therefore equally balanced. The true status of such a child is not determined at birth but depends on education and how he or she turns out. If the mother is Jewish and the father is not Jewish, it does not automatically mean that the child is Jewish. If, subsequently, the child adopts a Jewish life-style and behaves like a Jew, it could be said that the Jewish side has triumphed. If the child chooses differently, the non-Jewish side would have triumphed. From this perspective it would be logical to assume that the same criteria should be applied to the child of a Jewish father and a non-Jewish mother, but it should be stressed that Algazi does not touch this hot potato!

What I wish to emphasise is the element of adult choice in determining whether or not the offspring of mixed parentage is Jewish. Of course, this can backfire, as in the case of a young man studying in an ultra-orthodox *yeshiva* who suddenly discovered that he was not *halachically* Jewish. After pondering this dilemma, he did not choose the option of an instant conversion,[12] as others in his situation had done, but renounced any pretensions to being Jewish.[13] In his case, evidently, the non-Jewish side had triumphed, despite the strictly orthodox upbringing to which he had been exposed or, as some sceptics might have it, subjected.

In researching this book, I have found support for the changes I propose not only from lost Jews who have suffered directly from lacking the requisite maternal ancestor but from the children of Jewish mothers who have taken up the option of being Jewish but feel it is not their exclusive prerogative. An American woman who was not brought up Jewish feels she has no right 'to have it so easy':

> To me the fact that my mother's Jewish is theoretical and it means I don't have *halachic* problems but to say that I can be Jewish but someone whose father is Jewish and who might know the Torah inwards and outwards isn't Jewish is crazy. So I feel almost apologetic, I don't feel I deserve that status automatically. It's what you're raised as, what you know, those are the important things to me. It doesn't matter what my mother's blood is – that to me is not what counts.

In a similar vein is the reaction of a young Frenchwoman who had some Jewish upbringing to the rejection suffered by her cousin in front of a synagogue congregation. This cousin, whose father is Jewish, was called up to the Torah together with other members of the family after their grandmother's death, only to be told by the rabbi, 'You're not Jewish. You can't stay here.' She says: 'Even if your mother is not Jewish, if you feel Jewish it's more important. We need someone to help us, to show us the way. Afterwards, if you need to convert, okay, people should try to explain to you "why", not throw you away like that because your mother is not Jewish.'

A Sense of Kinship

While many orthodox rabbis liken being Jewish to being pregnant and argue that 'you can't *feel* Jewish. You either are or you aren't', Chief Rabbi Sacks has always believed that 'Jewishness is something, to use the modern idiom, in the software rather than the hardware.' Where others would encourage persons of Jewish descent without *halachic* credentials to content themselves with being 'righteous gentiles', Sacks has a more sensitive appreciation of their value to the Jewish people:

> To enter fully into the *halachic* community, somebody who is not a Jew according to *halacha* must undergo conversion. But that doesn't mean to say that even prior to that stage we cannot recognise the genuine value to the Jewish people of their friendship and kinship. There is a sense of identification with the State of Israel, . . . with Jewish suffering in the Holocaust, . . . with Jewish persecution wherever it happens. Those senses of identification move many. Sometimes they can feel connected to Jewish ethics, sometimes to Jewish culture, sometimes to Jewish history. We shouldn't try to dimishish the centrality of the *halachic* definition of Jewishness, but at the same time there is a wider sense of family we cannot ignore.

What Does it Take to be Jewish?

What should be the guidelines for any proposals for change? Upbringing? Learning? What you feel? How you live? How you are perceived by other people? How you die? I make this latter point in tribute to a Russian immigrant soldier killed in a terrorist incident in Israel. Because his mother was not Jewish, he was buried apart from his other fallen comrades. The outrage expressed by the majority of Israelis, from the Prime Minister downwards, ensured that the orthodox officer who supervised the burial was dismissed from his post and that the Russian soldier will be joined in his final resting place by other Israeli soldiers who fall in the line of duty.

The matrilineal ruling has been challenged by the most progressive wing within the Jewish spectrum – the Reform movement in the United States and the Liberal movement in Britain – which has taken steps to recognise the children of Jewish fathers and gentile mothers as Jewish, provided these children are raised as Jews. One reservation I have is that such a stand by one segment of the Jewish world is inevitably divisive and spawns what could be seen as a 'second-class Jew', accepted in one camp but not across the board.

Another reservation concerns the conditions which determine whether these children are accepted as Jews. In the past, certainly, acceptance was based on the child's attendance at a synagogue religion school. This may be a stepping-stone towards the adult adoption of a Jewish identity and life style. Equally, it may not. Like the young man with the strictly orthodox upbringing cited earlier, the half-Jew raised in a progressive environment may choose to turn his back on Judaism. Because of his ancestry, every half-Jew or part-Jew is granted a unique option: whether or not to connect up with his Jewish past.

My own proposals are geared to the individual lost Jew who seeks to make a commitment to the Jewish people. In line with the secular Israeli ruling inscribed in the Law of Return which accords anyone with one Jewish grandparent the right to Israeli citizenship, I would propose that the same applies to Jewish status. In order to qualify as 'Jewish' for religious purposes an adult of matrilineal, as well as patrilineal, descent would need to acquire, either through upbringing or through study and participation, some 'ground rules' of Jewish cultural and religious experience.

It is impossible to prescribe what these should be. Beyond a basic introduction to synagogue worship and the cycle of the Jewish festivals, Jewish experience is so vast and indefinable that each lost Jew who is drawn to the Jewish option will find something different that will challenge or resonate, give meaning or hark back to an ancestral past. My own Jewish feelings are evoked, all too rarely, by a blend of religious music and liturgy with an age-old, mantra-like quality, by the sea of prayer shawls in the synagogue on the Day of Atonement evoking a vision of timelessness. But while months or even years may pass without these feelings being stirred, some special service or ceremony in a synagogue may suddenly leave me in floods of tears.

Conversion or Something Else?

Should the lost Jew who undergoes this process then be entitled to an automatic conversion to Judaism? The very term 'conversion', to someone with Jewish parentage or ancestry, may seem off-putting or demeaning. As the American woman cited above explains:

> Conversion sounds terribly daunting and difficult, so maybe there needs to be another process that is positive and gives someone an opportunity to declare what they are and be recognised for it, some sort of affirmation, a ceremony or ritual. To convert sounds like going from being one religion to being another. If you've never been one and you're simply bringing out something that's always been there it should have a different name.

A radical proposal along these lines, for children of Jewish fathers, was put to me by orthodox Rabbi Josy Eisenberg, the popular 'télé-rabbin' and leading member of a rabbinical governing committee working with French Chief Rabbi Joseph Sitruk. Eisenberg would rather the term 'conversion' was changed and suggests that these children should have a solemn ceremony of 'reintegration'. 'From the moment they show a very strong desire to be Jewish, they should be reintegrated immediately.' As well as circumcision for a man and a ritual bath, Eisenberg's only condition would be 'a commitment to remain faithful to Judaism and the Jewish people'.

An alternative term non-*halachic* lost Jews who have led a Jewish life may accept is 'regularisation of status'. This was suggested by a young man in Jerusalem who had converted under orthodox auspices and also by Paris-based Rabbi Rivon Krygier. 'If someone whose father only is Jewish comes to me, I tell him that what he is going to do is not a real conversion, it is a regularisation. He is regularising his situation.' Although Krygier will not act outside the *halacha*, he would, ideally, prefer to extend the process of regularisation to the children of Jewish mothers as well.

Some lost Jews may wish to undergo a conversion process; similarly, there will be offspring of Jewish fathers who are converted to Judaism as infants or children. My proposals cater for people of Jewish descent who, as adults, choose to identify as being Jewish. They should be able, if they prefer, to undergo a ceremony of *affirmation* – or *reintegration* – which symbolises their commitment to the Jewish people.

DO STATISTICS TELL THE WHOLE STORY?

According to statistics, over 100,000 Jews in Britain have 'disappeared' since the war. While several thousand have emigrated to Israel since the state was founded in 1948 and as many or more to other countries, there have been thousands of immigrants from Israel and elsewhere, in particular South Africa. Wild claims are often made about the number of Israelis in Britain, with figures between 30,000 and 50,000 bandied about. The latest count based on the 1991 census made by the Community Research Unit of the Board of Deputies revealed some 12,060, but these findings are limited to people actually born in Israel. Whatever the real number, the loss through emigration has been largely offset.

More serious is the falling birth rate among Anglo-Jews, except among the ultra-orthodox communities. The tendency of many young Jews to marry late or not at all may be seen as a typically Jewish hyper emulation of the prevailing pattern of late or non-marriage in British society today. Chief Rabbi Sacks has bewailed the 'declining and ageing community' he was called upon to lead,[14] which has shrunk drastically in the last decade from 390,000 to 300,000. In the same vein Dayan Berger told me, 'We bury more than we bring into the world.' How characteristic is this situation of diaspora Jewry as a whole?

Communities in Decline

While nowhere in the diaspora is there a Jewish community that shows any encouraging sign of natural increase, British Jewry since World War II provides a peculiarly striking example of a downward population spiral of deaths exceeding births which has not been offset by the artificial boost of high Jewish immigration. The decline is proportionately greater than elsewhere in the diaspora, with the exception of the former Soviet Union where an equal or wider gap between Jewish births and deaths has been exacerbated by mass emigration.

Nowhere else in Western Europe has there been so dramatic an erosion. In France, in contrast, a greatly reduced post-war Jewish population of some 180,000 has been boosted by waves of immigration, primarily from North Africa, to 350,000 in 1960 and 535,000 in 1970. Modest natural increases of up to 30,000 were recorded in the decades 1950–9 and 1960–9, while from 1970 to 1980 the population figures remained stable. The most recent figure of 530,000 (1991) indicates a slight decline. The smaller communities in Western Europe have remained more or less stable, with some fluctuations.

The British decline is most closely reflected in Argentina, the country in South America with the largest Jewish population, where a community of fewer than 15,000 at the turn of the century expanded through immigration and natural increase to some 285,000 after World War II. While there have been wildly fluctuating estimates, some showing an Argentinian Jewish population of half a million in 1970, revised estimates indicate a peak total of 310,000 in 1960 which declined steadily to some 242,000 in 1980 and 213,000 at the latest count. The volatility of political regimes and substantial emigration to Israel have obviously contributed to the diminution of Argentinian Jewry. Elsewhere in South America, the Jewish populations remained more or less static from the post-war count until 1980, showing some decline in the last decade – in Brazil, for example, from 110 000 to some 100 000. In Chile (25,000 to 15,000) and Uruguay (40,000 to 24,000), the erosion has been more dramatic, due quite possibly to political factors, while in Venezuala, in contrast, with its oil-based business boom, a tiny post-war Jewish population of 3000 increased to 17,000 in 1980 and 20,000 at the latest count.

The newer countries of immigration like Canada and Australia have seen steady if undramatic rises in the Jewish population since the end of World War II. Canadian Jewry has increased from some 180,000 to 310,000 today, though an increase of 2000 in the last decade is obviously minimal, while Australian Jewry's increase has been more evenly staggered, from 40,000 after the war to 70,000 in 1980 and approximately 90,000 today. The situation in South Africa, where post-war pro-apartheid regimes led to a large measure of Jewish emigration, is particularly interesting. Where a rather drastic reduction in the Jewish population might have been expected, the post-war population of some 104,000 in fact increased to 118,000 in 1970, since when there has been a very gradual decline to some 114,000 at the latest count. While there has obviously been a measure of Jewish immigration from the former Southern Rhodesia, Israel and returning émigrés, the figures suggest a remarkable communal solidarity and a relatively low level of intermarriage.

Facing up to the Statistics

Unlike American Jewry which is seriously attempting to confront the challenge of intermarriage with numerous surveys, seminars and programmes for conversion and outreach, some officials in Anglo-Jewry have, in the past, displayed a sadly ostrich-like attitude and refuse to attribute the erosion in numbers to factors other than emigration and a low birth-rate. I recall being present at an 'Any Questions' evening in a London synagogue when the chairman virtually vetoed questions relating the plummeting population statistics to the way intermarried couples and their children are perceived by the Jewish community, as if the subject was somehow too subversive. And no statistical surveys of intermarriage within Anglo-Jewry exist, ostensibly because of a lack of funds.

The only statistics which have any bearing on this question are those on synagogue marriages. Since the Second World War, these have drastically declined. 1947 was the post-war year with the largest number of synagogue weddings – 3768. In 1994 there were 914 synagogue weddings, the lowest number on record and 101 fewer than in 1993. Alarming, perhaps, but predictable. Only once since 1985 has the figure exceeded 1100. Taking into account the post-war factor, the prospects for Jewish continuity based on the traditional Jewish family are dismal. Even more depressing is the comparison between Jewish marriage rates and rates of marriage of the general population. In 1947 synagogue marriages were 9.8 per thousand as compared to the general rate of 9.3 per thousand. In 1965, the last date recorded for this particular comparative statistic, when there were 1765 synagogue marriages, the Jewish marriage rate was *exactly half* that of the general population: 3.9 per thousand as compared to 7.8 per thousand. Other methods of comparison used subsequently indicate that the synagogue marriage rate has continued to be half the marriage rate of the general population.[15]

Of course there are always a few marriages among born Jews that take place without any Jewish officiation. The well-known journalists John Diamond and Nigella Lawson are a couple in question. And with marriage out of fashion, there are obviously live-in partnerships which are exclusively Jewish but unlikely to lay the foundations of Jewish families. More prevalent are the many 'thirtysomethings', too busy, too successful, too choosy, to get the marital act together, leading to the desolate picture of wasted Jewish females in their forties, rejected by their male counterparts who are still seeking the perfect Jewish nymphette of child-bearing age. To what extent, one wonders, has difficulty in finding a compatible Jewish mate contributed to this state of communal barrenness?

Not all officials in the Anglo-Jewish establishment are blind to the intermarriage factor. Yes, they say, the decline in numbers has largely been caused by intermarriage and assimilation. End of story. Chief Rabbi Sacks has spoken with a certain finality of 'a generation that marries out' as the inevitable result of previous generations missing out on a Jewish education. In order to secure a future for Anglo-Jewry, he has launched an ambitious venture, *Jewish Continuity,* which will resource a variety of innovative projects of Jewish education and outreach. On more than one occasion, he has linked a propensity to marry out to the despair evoked in young Jews by excessive exposure to the Holocaust. Jewish Continuity aims to imbue Jewish youth with a sense of pride and involvement in the hope that this will lead to a substantial increase of marriages within the faith. The outreach it speaks of will target disaffected and non-Jewishly educated Jews rather than the intermarried and their progeny.

Not the End

Need intermarriage be the end of the Jewish story? Many Jews who marry out of the faith retain a distinct sense of Jewish identity which may be religious, cultural, ethnic, Zionist or defy description. This may indeed be intensified by the act of having 'married out'. Take, for example, a family in Paris of first-generation immigrants from Tunisia. All nine brothers and sisters 'married out', but they have preserved the structure of a large, extended Jewish family; the younger generation, products of the intermarriages, are in fact more Jewishly involved than their elders. Such a family strikingly confirms an observation of Todd Endelman, an American professor of Jewish history and a specialist in trends of assimilation.[16] As he explains: 'There's a very high intermarriage rate in France today, also among North African Jews, and yet there's also a revival among young people of things Jewish across the board.' Evidence of this is the high number of applicants, over 1500 per year, who wish to convert to Judaism under the auspices of the Paris *Consistoire*, the established French orthodox Jewish body. Former Chief Rabbi Goldmann of Paris, responsible for conversions throughout France, accepted, in general, only 10 per cent of applicants. A large majority of applications are from people with Jewish ancestry.[17]

Even where the link with Jewishness is more tenuous, children with one Jewish parent often cling to their 'half-Jewishness' as a way of defining themselves in today's secular, pluralistic society. As American poet Sylvia Plath once told a friend: 'Everybody today seems so rootless. Only the Jews seem to be part of something, to belong to something definite and rooted.'[18] Todd Endelman would concur: 'People don't want to be nothings. As the world becomes more alike and people are uprooted more in various ways, they want to have roots, they want to have some sort of identity.' This is one explanation, Endelman believes, for the radically new phenomenon of people who have some kind of Jewish background finding their way back. It also has to do with the change in society's attitude towards Jews everywhere. It's got to be more positive, otherwise people wouldn't do it and I don't know that it ever happened before. The best thing is for people like that to be reincorporated into the Jewish community.

Response or Rejection?

Rather than finding a place for these people within the Jewish community, where their particular Jewish sensibilities can be nurtured and encouraged to develop, the official response of orthodoxy world wide has been to ostracise Jews who, by choosing a non-Jewish partner, are seen to have 'betrayed their heritage'. Some go further and claim that Jews who 'marry out' are doing Hitler's work for him. This somewhat crude interpretation of the statement by the Jewish theologian and philosopher Emil Fackenheim that Jews are forbidden to allow Hitler 'posthumous victories' is common currency in certain Jewish circles.

Not only the traditionalists have taken Fackenheim's credo on board, as Barry Kosmin explains:

> A highly secularised New Age Buddhist of Jewish descent who also wants to deny Hitler a victory is going to say 'I'm Jewish' even though there's very little Judaic about him except that he's of Jewish descent and has transformed his Judaic consciousness into some kind of universalist creed.

The Fackenheim *diktat* in its traditionalist guise has also caused anguish for many young Jews who find it difficult to live up to. In a sensitive article in the Canadian newspaper *The Globe and Mail*,[19] Leonard Stern, who lives in Ottawa, agonises that 'Fackenheim . . . is making my life difficult'. Like many young Jews who have refused to be 'ghettoised', he is about to 'marry out'. Nevertheless, he never wants to have a Christmas tree or go to church while his girlfriend is 'looking forward to Passover *seders* and *Chanukah* candles'. Rather than condemning Leonard Stern outright, an imaginative Jewish leadership might see him and his future wife as a couple meriting some attention.

Kosmin himself, not surprisingly, sees the Hitler analogy as 'rhetoric'.

> If half a million Jews go out tomorrow and marry a non-Jew, that does not make them cease to be Jewish, even under the most harsh *halachic* ruling, except maybe in the eyes of these people who regard intermarrying as treason and the renouncing of citizenship.

Past or Future?

If Jews who intermarry are according Hitler a posthumous victory, what of the people who ostracise them? Ostensibly, these are committed Jews with a concern for Jewish continuity. By failing to come to terms with the realities of today's open society, are they not exhibiting a mindset steeped in the ghetto or *shtetl*? Rather than putting an end to intermarriage by their stance, are they not contributing to the outcome they are fighting: the diminution of the Jewish people in the future?

THE LAYOUT OF THE BOOK

Following this introductory chapter, Chapter 2 provides examples of radical assimilation in the history of Anglo-Jewry, an example of a community in the Western diaspora marked by immigration, integration and assimilation. This chapter is based both on primary and secondary sources, while Chapter 3 is based on interviews with 'lost Jews' who represent a particular historical context, including descendants of later immigrants, refugees from Nazism and Holocaust survivors, and descendants of prominent old Jewish families.

Chapters 4–9 focus on a wide spectrum of today's lost Jews, those who have 'married out', children and grandchildren of mixed marriages and those of Jewish birth who have chosen an alternative affiliation. These chapters include stories of lost Jews who have returned and lost Jews who have never been 'lost' in terms of commitment but only in terms of being denied Jewish status; there are also abstracts from numerous interviews with lost Jews of all orientations, including a new breed of lost Jew, the expatriate Israeli, whose Jewish identity is tenuous. These chapters form the heart of the book.

Chapter 10 discusses the attitudes of young 'marginal' Jews on the fringes of the community who have not yet married 'out' or 'in' and concludes with a depiction of the 'self-imposed ghetto' created by many Jews in Britain and elsewhere as perceived by both marginal Jews and lost Jews. A response to charges of 'ghettoisation' is provided by a well-known Jewish personality.

Chapter 11 investigates the attitudes of a wide cross-section of the Jewish establishment in Britain and other countries to the questions raised in the book, while Chapter 12 assesses some conclusions that have emerged in the course of the book and attempts to show a way forward.

2

Immigration to Assimilation

The development of Jewish communities in the Western diaspora is a paradigm of radical assimilation. In Britain, France and the United States, successive waves of immigrants settled, became absorbed and, all too frequently, disappeared as Jews within a relatively tolerant society which afforded them opportunities undreamed of in their countries of origin. The Second World War wiped out the traditional reservoirs of immigration from Central and Eastern Europe and the rise of a Jewish state drew immigrants from remaining pockets of persecution as well as from the West itself. Of the large-scale Jewish communities in Western countries, only French Jewry has grown from an influx of immigrants, drawing the cream of north African Jewry in the wake of France's colonial demise. The Jewish communities in Britain and the United States have suffered an inexorable decline.

The American historian, Todd Endelman, has made a seminal study of radical assimilation which forms the backdrop of any discussion on lost Jews today.[1] Rather than duplicate his findings, this chapter will highlight certain episodes of radical assimilation in the history of Anglo-Jewry, based primarily on accounts provided by descendants of families that assimilated.

THE SEPHARDIM

The first Jewish settlers readmitted to England under Cromwell's Protectorate in 1656 were Sephardi Jews, descendants of the Jews expelled from Spain in 1492 because of the Spanish Inquisition. In Spain, Jews had mingled with their Christian and Muslim fellow citizens and contributed significantly to the culture and society in which they lived. The year 1701 saw the opening of Bevis Marks, the Sephardi 'cathedral synagogue' in the City of London, which is still in use today, although the majority of families in England during the synagogue's early days are no longer Jewish.

The tendency of Jews from well-established families was to intermarry and assimilate. Between 1740 and 1800, the annual number of marriages celebrated at Bevis Marks fell by 43 per cent.[2] Several well-to-do Sephardi

Jews who made their fortunes in the City in finance and trade aped the country-loving habits of the English landed gentry and bought themselves country estates. The next step, inevitably, was to socialise more freely with their English neighbours. Well before the mid-eighteenth century, the grandchildren of some of the original immigrants were marrying into genteel English circles and baptising their children even if they, themselves, did not formally convert to Christianity.[3]

From Riches to Rags

A slightly different example of radical assimilation is the Brandon family of Portuguese origin. David Brandon, a tobacco importer from the West Indies, arrived in England in the 1720s. His great-grandson, Joshua (*c.* 1780–1863), was the great-great-great grandfather and last wholly Jewish ancestor of Robert Barrett, an investigative journalist and genealogist. A descendant of Joshua's younger brother is Lord Brandon of Oakbrook, a Lord Justice of Appeals. 'The Brandons were Sephardic leaders, they had quite a bit of money, they were a family of note in the eighteenth century and married into the most extraordinary families,' Barrett recounts. These included some of the great Sephardi names of Anglo-Jewry, the Mocattas, the Montefiores, the Costas and the Lindos. Joshua's first wife, Jessie, was the daughter of a prominent Jew from Switzerland, Baron Leon de Simons, a corn factor with several children. Another daughter married into the Mendes da Costa family.

Joshua Brandon had a family house in Barnes, as did the de Simons. The Brandons also had a house near Paris, where a lot of the extended family were living. However, Joshua died a resident of Church Street, Bethnal Green. He had two children with Jessie, a son who became an architect but died young and a daughter who married a Jew. When Jessie died, he married a Marianne Hunter from Scotland and all the children of the marriage were baptised. Barrett is descended from the third daughter, Laura.

Joshua Brandon's 'marrying out' is clearly linked to the decline in his fortunes: 'He was always described on the records as "gentleman" or "esquire"', Barrett explains, 'but he died in poverty. From the wills and letters of administration you see he didn't leave much money. I think he was probably the "remittance man" of the family after he married out. He was the first one to leave and was more or less cut off.'

This did not detract from his children's prospering in the gentile world. His second son, Joshua Arthur Brandon, was an architect like his half-brother and, like him, a member of the Catholic Apostolic Church. Joshua Arthur became quite famous – his work is recorded in the

Dictionary of British Architects – but suffered from manic depression, a genetic problem, and committed suicide. 'He did some pretty good work throughout London and was a man of some note,' says Barrett. 'I know the family was desperately upset when he committed suicide.' Laura, a beautiful woman like her sister, Celestine, married John Fleming, a landed proprietor, but died in childbirth in 1869.[4]

A Royal Connection

Radical assimilation is very apparent among the descendants of Zaccaria Levy, believed to have come to England from Venice towards the end of the eighteenth century. The Bevis Marks marriage register records his wedding in October 1786 to Simha Hannah Montefiore, from a distinguished and well-connected Sephardi family also of Italian origin. After a successful career as a merchant, ship-owner and Lloyds underwriter, Zaccaria Levy died in 1828 and was buried in the Spanish and Portuguese Jewish Cemetery in Mile End Road. Records show that he was granted a coat-of-arms. His wife's fate was very different. None of the couple's eleven children remained Jewish and the family name was changed from Levy to Laurence. When Simha Hannah died 10 years after her husband, she was not buried in the plot reserved next to him in the Mile End Cemetery but as Mrs Selina Hannah Laurence in Stoke Newington churchyard.[5] Deprived of his spouse in his final resting place, one wonders how Zaccaria Levy might have reacted to the celebrity accorded his lineage over 150 years after his death and the knowledge that he would be the ancestor of a son-in-law of the Queen of England. Commander Timothy Laurence, RN, who married the Princess Royal in December 1992, is Levy's direct descendant.[6]

A fresh perspective on Zaccaria's origins is shed by Robert Barrett, the genealogist who unearthed the Levy connection.

> It is written that he was from Venice and his family were settled there for many years before. When I went to research the Jewry in Venice, there was no reference to Zaccaria, not even in another part of Italy. From a blanket search of all the Jewish communities throughout the world I was able to discover that he came from Baghdad. There were two Levy brothers and they stole monies in Baghdad and went on to make an enormous amount of money there.

Barrett obtained this story from a descendant in New York of Zaccaria's brother and backed it up with documentary evidence. The brother also came over to England for a while but then went to France. His descendants, dispersed all over the world, retain the name Levy and for the most part remain Jewish.

The coat-of-arms granted to the Levy/Laurence family was in fact the work of Zaccaria's son, Joseph, the ancestor of Timothy Laurence, who had the arms he was granted backdated to his father so that it could pass to all Zaccaria's descendants. Like the so-called Venetian origins, 'all this adds to the glory of the family', Barrett explained. The name Laurence came, in fact, from the maternal grandmother of Joseph's first wife, Penelope Jackson from Walthamstow. In her will Penelope's mother had written 'It is my wish that my daughter, Penelope Goodchild Levy and her husband Joseph Levy should take my maternal surname of Laurence.' All Joseph's brothers followed suit, but it was not so easy to conceal their Jewish origins. As Penelope's mother told her daughter after making her will: 'They may be able to change the name but they'll never be able to change that nose!'[7]

A Community on the Wane

The Montefiore family, though no longer pillars of Anglo-Jewry, were nonetheless more resilient to radical assimilation. Simha Hannah's nephew, Sir Moses Montefiore (1784–1885), remained a devout Jew and much of his long life was consecrated to the concerns of his less-fortunate co-religionists. His seat at Bevis Marks is reserved today for distinguished visitors. Claude Montefiore (1858–1939) was the founder of Liberal Judaism in Britain, while the recently retired Bishop of Birmingham, Hugh Montefiore, was not baptised at birth but embraced Christianity himself while at school.

By the end of the nineteenth century, the influence of the Sephardim had declined considerably. According to Dr Moses Gaster, their *Haham* or spiritual leader from 1887 to 1919,

> the Sephardic community had become a very insignificant body. So little was known of it that the world outside did not even know that Sir Moses Montefiore was a Sephardi. It had practically disappeared from the consciousness of Jewry in spite of the fact that the people here (in England) considered themselves to be the very centre of the world.

Gaster, a brilliant young rabbi and scholar from a distinguished Jewish family in Rumania, who had immigrated to Britain in 1885, had been advised against accepting the position of spiritual leader of a community 'who live upon a past which they do not understand'. What tempted him to take on the role of *Haham* was precisely the glamour of that romantic past in Spanish history.[8]

EARLY ASHKENAZI SETTLERS

The majority of Ashkenazi immigrants from Holland, the German states and elsewhere in Central Europe, who started to arrive in England from about 1690, came without skills and possessions and from communities that were isolated from the gentile world. Relatively few of these Ashkenazi families were as upwardly mobile socially as the Sephardim and assimilation was rare in the eighteenth century, though it increased as the families became more established.[9]

There were, of course, exceptions. The Harts from Breslau, who came to England at the end of the seventeenth century, were prominent in communal affairs, but also socialised with the country gentry in Richmond and Isleworth where they took up residence. Moses Hart, an observant Jew, established himself as a stock and commodity broker, with the help of his wealthy cousin Benjamin Levy and secured the appointment of his brother, Aaron, as the rabbi of the Ashkenazi synagogue, which he rebuilt at his own expense in Duke's Place in 1722. The Hart brothers, Moses, the magnate and philanthropist, and Aaron, who could be said to be the first Ashkenazi Chief Rabbi, dominated the affairs of the Great Synagogue until their deaths in 1756.[10] Their sister, Zipporah, married Meir Waage, an immigrant from Frankfurt, who held the post of synagogue treasurer.[11] By the beginning of the nineteenth century, however, few descendants of the Harts, the Levys and the Waages – changed first to Waag and later to Wagg – remained Jewish, though the reasons for their assimilation may not have been the same.

A Distinguished Loyalist Ancestor

The Waage or Wagg family can be traced today to Christine Wagg, a member of the Jewish Genealogical Society of Great Britain and the great-great-great-great granddaughter of Meir and Zipporah's son Abraham. The name Waage was taken from the sign of the golden scales – 'Goldene Waage' – outside their house in Frankfurt's *Judengasse.* One of nine children, Abraham was born in 1718 and apprenticed in 1738 to a London jeweller; he also held a seat in the Great Synagogue. At some unknown date he emigrated to America and was successfully pursuing the trade of grocer and chocolate manufacturer in New York when, in 1770, he married an heiress thirty years his junior at the Mill Street Synagogue, then the only synagogue in the city. Rachel Gomez, his wife, was from a wealthy Sephardi family prominent both in Jewish life and in the commercial life of the city.

The youngest of Abraham and Rachel's ten children, Matthias, born in 1788, is Christine Wagg's last wholly Jewish ancestor. He married a Charlotte Brook and their children were baptised in the Church of England. But the journey towards assimilation taken by this branch of the Wagg family is very different from that of their cousins.

Abraham Wagg and his family were still in New York in 1775 when the American War of Independence broke out. 'Abraham was a loyalist. He swore an oath of allegiance to George III. He joined the militia, he did firewatching and he got his leg injured, as a result of which he was permanently lame,' Christine Wagg recounted. With defeat of the loyalist cause imminent, Abraham fled back to England in July 1779 with his wife and children and settled in Bristol.

Abraham Wagg's heroic stance 'for king and country' wrought havoc with the family fortune. 'He'd lost money by being a loyalist and had left behind in America all his own goods and chattels and money, and anything Rachel had inherited,' Christine Wagg explained. Abraham made a claim for compensation, accompanied by proposals he had drawn up for peace between the warring sides, which gained some influential support but was ultimately unsuccessful. Since the family returned, they had been living on the charity of Abraham's cousin, Judith Levy, a daughter of Moses Hart who married the son of Benjamin Levy and was left a wealthy widow in 1750. When Mrs Levy died intestate in 1803, it was a blow to the Wagg family and Abraham himself died a few months later.

Christine Wagg takes pride in her distinguished ancestor:

> It does seem to me that through Abraham's impulsiveness, supporting the British cause in the American War of Independence to his own detriment and having to flee back to England leaving all his property and everything behind, he impoverished his whole family. Had he kept his head down, he and his children might have been a great deal more prosperous. But he must have been a man of some sort of principle. What I find so curious is that he went overboard in becoming loyal to Britain and the king when he was only a first generation Briton himself.

Abraham was also a man of some piety. In the *Family Memorandum* he left, written partly in English and partly in Hebrew, he writes for his sons 'May God think me worthy to bring him up to *Torah* and *chupa* and *ma'asim tovim'* – in accordance with Jewish law, to Jewish marriage and good deeds. His wish was not to be posthumously gratified.

Of his surviving children, Matthias became a cabinet maker in Shoreditch and Michael, formerly Myer, a publican in Bristol. In line with the assimilatory pattern, perhaps paradoxically hastened by the reversal in the family fortunes, Frederick, the eldest of Matthias' seven children and Christine Wagg's great-great grandfather, was baptised at St Leonard's, Shoreditch, in June 1817 and was married himself in 1840 at St John's, Bethnal Green.

The March 1851 census provides a surprising revelation. Three months after the death of Matthias' wife, Charlotte, his two youngest children, Charlotte and Henry, were recorded at the Jewish Boarding School in Bethnal Green. 'It may have been that Matthias couldn't cope with the children on his own and he couldn't find a home for them as he was a lodger in somebody else's house. If he wanted a roof over their heads and an education, perhaps going back to Jewish roots was the way to do it,' Christine Wagg surmised. 'I had assumed the Jewish identity more or less went as soon as Matthias' mother, Rachel, died in 1809.' After this final flurry of Jewish identification, however, there were no more manifestations of Jewish adherence in the Wagg family.[12]

A Growing Community

The majority of the Ashkenazi middle class was immune to assimilatory trends during the eighteenth century, probably because few were wealthy enough to qualify for admission into the landed gentry. In 1800, the young Nathan Mayer Rothschild, the founder of the English branch of the dynasty, arrived in Manchester with £20,000, sent by his father to purchase and ship English textiles to the family warehouse in Frankfurt.[13] His arrival coincided with the emergence of a new class of prosperous Ashkenazi merchants and brokers.

Within the same family, some members would intermarry, have their children baptised and assimilate fully, while others would continue to play a role in Jewish communal affairs.[14] The descendants of the Goldsmid brothers, Benjamin, Abraham and Asher, provide an apt example. While the seven children of the enormously wealthy Benjamin were baptised together with their mother, Jessie, after their father's death, the children of the equally wealthy Abraham were already suitably married before their father died and some of their descendants remained active within the Jewish community well into the twentieth century, as did most of the descendants of Asher.[15]

A Remarkable Return

Benjamin Goldsmid's posterity was not completely lost to Judaism. More than sixty years after his great-grandmother, Jessie, formally abandoned the Jewish faith, Albert Goldsmid, a military man like many of his ancestors, rediscovered his Jewish origins and 'returned triumphantly to the old faith and became an ardent Jew'. At a dinner of the Maccabean Society in 1902 he summed up his devotion to both his country and his religion: 'Loyalty to the flag for which the sun once stood still can only deepen our devotion to the flag on which the sun never sets.'[16]

Albert Goldsmid was distinguished both in Jewish communal life and in his military career. He founded the Jewish Lads Brigade and was concerned with the settlement of Jewish refugees in Palestine. He headed the Golden Jubilee Procession in 1887 as Deputy Quartermaster-General and became the first practising Jew to rise to the rank of colonel. His sympathy for Jewish national aspirations led him to encounter the Zionist visionary, Theodore Herzl, who looked on his meeting with Goldsmid as very encouraging and prophetic. Goldsmid is believed to have told Herzl that he was the original for Daniel Deronda, the hero of George Eliot's pro-Zionist novel which might well have been 'inspired by a lost Jew who returned'.[17]

Albert Goldsmid married a very distant cousin, Ida Stewart Hendriks, the granddaughter of General Sir John Littler. She also reconverted to Judaism and the eldest of their three daughters, Gladys, married Louis Samuel Montagu, the 2nd Baron Swaythling. Some of their descendants remain Jewish today.

Expanding Horizons

Although Jews were not admitted to parliament until 1858, they had earlier begun to enter spheres of activity from which they had previously been excluded. In 1833 Francis Henry Lyon Goldsmid took the oath before being called to the bar without the need to profess the Christian faith.[18] And while only a handful of Jews entered Oxford and Cambridge before the 1870s, the new University College in London, established in 1826 on a non-sectarian basis, afforded Jews opportunities for further education not previously available.

A Forgotten Luminary

One of the early graduates of University College was John Zachariah Laurence, otherwise Lazarus (1829–1870), who founded the Royal Eye Hospital, now an annexe of St Thomas'. Laurence, the only Jewish eye specialist considered worthy of mention by the author of a history of Jews in medicine and renowned for his treatment of cataracts and for identifying a genetic condition known as the Laurence/Moon/Beadle syndrome, was the great-grandfather of Sabine Doust, another member of the Jewish Genealogical Society. An article in the *British Journal of Ophthamology* in 1932 mourns him as 'One of those forgotten luminaries who shone brilliantly in his own day but whose career was so brief that he has all but been forgotten today.'

John Zachariah Laurence, the son of Samuel Lewis Laurence otherwise Lazarus and Amelia Levy, was the great-grandson of Isaac Zachariah, an immigrant from Bohemia who was buried in Portsmouth Jewish Cemetery in 1779. The Zachariahs would appear to have been members of the provincial Jewish middle class. Isaac's daughter, Elizabeth, John Zachariah Laurence's paternal grandmother, married Lewis Lazarus, a naval agent and one-time President and elder of the Portsmouth Hebrew Congregation, while her sister, Phoebe, married another naval agent – her cousin, John Zachariah. The family did not remain rooted in Portsmouth – Lewis Lazarus moved to Bath and later to Ireland – and there were no early signs of assimilation.

John Zachariah Laurence enjoyed an education and a professional status beyond that of his immediate family, due, to some extent, to a quirk of fate. His father was declared bankrupt and it would appear that the future eye specialist was fostered by his prosperous and childless great-aunt and -uncle, Phoebe and John Zachariah, whose name he bore. Phoebe left £8000 on her death in 1861 and both her will and that of her husband contained a proviso stating that John Zachariah Laurence would only inherit the money due to him, 'as long as he didn't marry out of the Jewish faith'.

Laurence duly married Miriam, the daughter of Nathaniel Solomon, and had three daughters and a son who died in childhood. However, none of his surviving descendants through his daughter, Blanche Mcleod, Sabine Doust's paternal grandmother, remain Jewish. It is possible that the early deaths of their parents – Miriam Laurence died in her thirties of a miscarriage – expedited their daughters' outmarriage and assimilation.[19]

Anglicisation

By the mid-nineteenth century, Anglo-Jewry had, for the most part, shed its immigrant character as, with the passing of foreign-born parents and grandparents, the majority of the community were native born and raised. The economic and social status of the Jewish population as a whole had also changed. At the turn of the century, the community has been depicted as predominantly poor. According to George Rigal of the Jewish Genealogical Society who has researched extensively into insurance certificates as a source of genealogical investigation, it was not uncommon for a peddlar or second-hand clothes dealer to own several hundred pounds of stocks.[20] By 1850, when the Jewish population of London was estimated at about 20,000, over one-third were classified as upper or middle class, while by the 1880s well over 50 per cent of London's estimated 46,000 Jews had attained at least middle-class status.[21] Further evidence of Jewish prosperity is the number of Jews who had their wills proved at the Prerogative Court of Canterbury, the senior court for making a will, before 1858.[22]

Jews were now free to enter Parliament, the universities, the professions and even the London clubs and to receive honours and titles. Indeed, for many Anglo-Jews seeking the glittering prizes, Victorian England was a social nirvana. But with the increasing anglicisation and embourgeoisement[23] of Jews in England, other factors contributed to estrangement from Jewish life. Among these was the parochial and inward-looking nature of Jewish communities, particularly in predominantly Jewish neighbourhoods such as Maida Vale in West London, which alienated Jews with wider horizons, a trend which has continued to this day. Jewish Maida Vale was the focus of critical novels by Jews in the late nineteenth century,[24] in the same way that Golders Green was to become in the 1950s and 1960s.

Before the Flood

The Jewish community in mid-Victorian Britain in 1870, estimated at 60,000, may well have counted itself the most fortunate in the world. Despite the persistence of antisemitic stereotyping of which Charles Dickens' Fagin is an example, it was comfortable to be Jewish.

The mass immigration of a very different kind of Jew from Eastern Europe which started during the 1870s and continued unrestricted until the end of the century and with some restrictions until the outbreak of World War I, brought the number of Jews in Britain to a quarter of a million. It was a shock from which the native Jewish community would not recover.

FLEEING THE POGROMS

> A considerable proportion of them speak a foreign tongue; while in religion, in character and in habits . . . they are marked off from their neighbours by peculiar features. . . . They have completely transformed the character of whole neighbourhoods until they are overrun by foreigners. They are self-assertive and loud and their women are idle, wasteful and extravagant. . . . The tide of immigration has brought to

this country a race of strangers with a sleuth hand instinct for gain and an indefinitely low standard of life.[25]

These words are not part of some racist or antisemitic tract but from a sociological study of East End Jewry published in 1901. Significantly, one of the authors was a Jew. But these ancestors of the bulk of today's Anglo-Jews, who fled pogroms and persecution, were as alien to many of their co-religionists in Britain as to the gentile population. For established Anglo-Jewry at the turn of the twentieth century these immigrants were an embarrassment and, for the most part, they were cold shouldered.

The numbers and ethnic cohesiveness of the new immigrants made them largely immune for some time to assimilatory pressures, although in religious practice many were notably more lax than the Jews left behind in the Eastern European Pale of Settlement. They were active in the nascent Zionist movement and in radical political causes like anarchism and socialism, much to the disquiet of the established community.[26] The 'old guard' were opposed to the Balfour Declaration of 1917 approving the establishment 'in Palestine' of 'a national home' for the Jewish people. The first draft of the document had, in fact, been watered down largely in response to the pleas of Edwin Montagu, the only Jew in the Cabinet.

Like many Jews of his standing, Montagu feared the accusation of 'dual loyalties'. Imputations of this kind have given rise to the 'contract theory' of immigration, adopted by contemporary Anglo-Jewish historians, which presupposes that as long as Jews and other immigrants adopt the culture of the host country and keep their particular religious practices to themselves, they will be accepted as loyal citizens. Clearly the new immigrants with their 'foreign' speech and habits did not pass muster.

It was not only Anglo-Jews from established families who distanced themselves from the immigrants. Michael Brandon, of the Bevis Marks Synagogue Trust, recalls how his father, born Arnold Pokrasse in 1905, acquired an honorary Sephardi identity. Arnold's father, Hyman, whose family were Russian immigrants in America, came to England to seek his fortune and married Esther Mindel, from a wealthy and more established Anglo-Jewish family. By 1915, Hyman had made his mark in business and changed the family name to Brandon. He was now Henry Brandon and his son was Ernest. In 1916, Ernest was sent to Clifton College, one of the few public schools which had a Jewish house but was placed in 'School House'. Not long afterwards Henry was boasting to a business associate that his son was at Clifton in 'School House, the best house'. The business associate was not impressed. 'Either your son transfers to

Polacks' (the Jewish house), or our deal is off,' he told Brandon. The move to Polacks' was the first intimation young Ernest had that he was Jewish. Many of his housemates were from Sephardi families and so, 'ready made with a Sephardi name', Ernest took on a Sephardi identity.[27]

The changed face of the Anglo-Jewish community was also reflected in the readership profile of the *Jewish Chronicle*, the community's principal newspaper established in 1841. George Rigal of the Jewish Genealogical Society, who traces his ancestry in England back to the eighteenth century, recounts that his family placed advertisements regularly in the *Jewish Chronicle* until 1890. By 1910, however, no middle-or upper-class Jews were placing advertisements in the paper known as 'The Organ of British Jewry'.[28]

The presence and continuing arrival of hordes of Jewish aliens sparked an antisemitic backlash, resulting in the 1905 Aliens Act which restricted immigration. After World War I antisemitism took on a political and ideological character rarely manifested in Britain though not uncommon in other countries in Europe; outbreaks of organised violence against Jewish targets became increasingly frequent from 1935 to 1937, when Oswald Mosley's British Union of Fascists took to the streets of London's Jewish East End.

While increasing numbers of Jews from varied backgrounds felt uncomfortable about their origins, the sons and daughters of recent immigrants had their community to fall back on and were, in any case, psychologically attuned to perceiving gentiles as antisemitic. Acculturated Anglo-Jews suffered more from gentile slights and defections from the older community became more prevalent during the interwar years. During this period, too, intermarriage became commonplace in many of the older families that had previously been pillars of the community, for example the Rothschilds and Montefiores. Defection and intermarriage also occurred among the families of recent immigrants, often when young people felt stifled by the parochial and somewhat philistine character of their Jewish environment.[29]

But the continuing incidence of intermarriage failed to pose any immediate threat to the Jewish community in Britain which continued to grow steadily if not dramatically to about 300,000 in the early 1930s, until it was boosted by yet another wave of immigration, this time from Nazi Europe. Jewish marriage rates were first recorded in 1901, a year when they were substantially higher than the marriage rates of the general population. For nearly fifty years, with obvious annual fluctuations, they matched the general rate. It was only five years after the end of World War II that they started to plummet.[30]

3

Intimations of Decline

SEMI-SUBMERGED

The late cartoonist, Mel Calman, who had a non-Jewish partner and two non-Jewish ex-wives, gave me this definition of 'lost Jews': 'Most of my Jewish friends are nearly lost or very lost, semi-submerged. We're more like icebergs where the tip is showing and there's probably stuff underneath but it doesn't show and one doesn't think about it unless you're having this kind of conversation.'

A Truncated Childhood

Calman was born in 1931 in Stamford Hill, then a petty-bourgeois Jewish area; his parents, immigrants from Lithuania, arrived in England a few years before World War I and met and married in the new country. Calman was raised in a traditional Jewish home, with his mother observing *kashrut* and the festivals; he hardly saw anyone who was not Jewish. When he was 6, with Blackshirt violence at its height, he was rudely introduced to the world outside.

> I was standing at the gate of our house and a little boy came along who was not a Jew – a cockney bloke about 2 years older than me. He was carrying a pair of gym slippers and he stopped and we said 'Hello' and then he suddenly said, 'Are you a Jew?' No one had ever asked me that and I said 'Yes' and then without another word he took one of his gym slippers and hit me right across the side of the face. That was the first, very dramatic intimation that people somewhere out there didn't like you.

His mother, familiar with pogroms and the sight of her own mother fleeing stones in the streets of Vilna during Easter week, remained unruffled by the episode and calmly consoled the stricken child. The daughter of a successful Vilna midwife, she was an educated woman, sharing a taste for music and the theatre with her husband, a frustrated writer, before he was taken ill and hospitalised. Calman was then eight and soon experienced another upheaval when his mother and he were evacuated to Cambridge after war broke out. Mrs Calman found a kosher butcher and maintained a Jewish home but later returned to London, pragmatically absolving her son from observing the dietary restrictions.

Alone in Cambridge, Calman effected a 'curious compromise', eating whatever he liked while continuing to attend synagogue. At the Perse School, which had a Jewish boarding house, he was a day boy on a scholarship, finding himself 'slightly outside a little group of outsiders', but making lasting friendships with several Jewish boys. 'Theologically, it was quite Jewish,' he recalls. But when he was 18 or 20 the 'gradual process' of losing the religion began: 'You start doing less, you still think of Passover and then you stop thinking about that and then . . . I married out.' Calman's brother, 13 years his senior, has remained a practising Jew.

Calman's Jewishness was perceptible in his attachment to Jewish culture and his sensitivity to antisemitism. As a Jew during wartime bombing raids he felt particularly vulnerable and his perception of himself as a first-generation Englishman was tempered by his awareness of being a Jew and the son of immigrants. This other persona was evoked by incidents like a discussion about pacifism he had with a colleague in advertising: '"If there hadn't been a war," this guy said, "If people hadn't fought, the Nazis would have made you into a lampshade!" So somebody says something which completely pulls the rug from under you.'

Calman recollected his childhood with nostalgia:

> I have nothing but warm feelings about my background except that it was so short. It was truncated by the war, the evacuation and my father's illness. Possibly in different circumstances I might not have been so 'lost' as a Jew.

But that did not mean, he added, that he would have married 'a nice Jewish girl'.

Who Wants to Marry a 'Nice Jewish Girl'?

The 'nice Jewish girl' was anathema to many young second-generation Jews, who found their frustrations and aspirations voiced in Brian Glanville's *The Bankrupts*, published in 1958. They resented the pressure to conform to received values which, as far as the opposite sex was concerned, meant 'You met a nice Jewish girl, you got engaged, you got married and then you went to bed.' Independent-minded young Jews like Nigel Harris* and his friends, who believed in sexual liberation, found the Jewish community and its outlook 'oppressive and threatening', not least the perception of gentiles as 'inferior', 'antisemitic', 'drunks' and '*shiksas*' and the idea that 'the only suitable person to marry was Jewish'. For them, the foreign au pair girls with their more liberal-minded attitudes represented a desirable model of womanhood. The most attractive Jewish girl, in contrast, was heavily disadvantaged. As Harris explains: 'I might have been attracted by a girl and got to know her and learnt that she was Jewish and she would immediately lose part of her allure for me – because it was too close to home.'

Harris, a literary agent and lecturer, and a group of his childhood friends, all professional men from traditional Jewish homes, represent a microcosm of the Jewish intelligentsia growing up in the 1950s. All abandoned their adherence to the Jewish faith, even Harold* from an extremely orthodox background. Several suffered a crisis of identity during adolescence and young adulthood, in some cases leading to a nervous breakdown; John*, who 'had fallen in love with the traditional idea of Englishness' and whose 'great sensitivity was and is being identified as a Jew', has condemned himself to virtual exile from Britain because of his inability to accept his background. But such Jewish self-loathing, which can only be kept at bay by playing the Englishman abroad, is certainly not shared by Harris and the other members of the group, who would never deny their Jewishness.

Not one of the group married an English Jewess, or even an English gentile. Sidney* excited Harris's envy and admiration: 'He really pulled it off! He married a Black, gentile divorcée with a child. Imagine the effect on his family!' Harris, himself, married in his thirties, 'having sown many wild oats'; his wife is a Yugloslav gentile. Simon*, a consultant psychiatrist, married a French gentile, while Daniel*, a computer expert, married an American Jewess. All three chose wives who are six-foot tall, 'in reaction', as Simon pointed out, 'against the little Jewish mother type'. For the rest, John has had two continental gentile wives, while Henry*, an accountant, married a Danish gentile. After a shaky start, during which he suffered a nervous breakdown, the marriage revived after Henry pursued his wife to Israel. There she converted, becoming 'more staunchly Jewish' than he. Unlike the others, Harold, a distinguished professor of law, led 'a rather inhibited life', a residue, perhaps, of his orthodox upbringing. He was in his forties when he was introduced to a suitably mature Israeli.

Harris and his friends exemplify the effect on Jewish marriage patterns of the sexual revolution and increasing secularism. In contrast, his elder brother, who had also experienced identity problems during adolescence, found his feet in adulthood by becoming a pillar of the community. But sexual freedom was not a strictly masculine preserve. A gentile friend, who confessed to Harris how sexy he found Jewish girls, ended up one. Some, at least, of the rejected 'nice Jewish girls' sought ιon outside the community. Intermarriage was a two-way street.

REFUGEES FROM NAZISM

The Nazi takeover of Central Europe in the 1930s created a new wave of Jewish refugees, often highly acculturated Jews who identified more strongly with their country of residence than their Jewish origins. Many were Jews by default; some were even baptised Christians, thrown back to their ancestral roots by the harshly racist Nuremberg Laws.

Reminders of Jewishness

In a personal *mémoire*, Will Halle*, a psychologist raised as an Old Catholic in Vienna, recalls his transfer after the *anschluss* in 1938 from his *gymnasium* to a Jewish school:

> I was almost equally unwelcome as Jewish but a Christian – the only one in my form. The few weeks there were the one time when I was consistently ostracised, even by teachers. I was an outsider . . . I was not bullied: I might simply not have existed.

On leaving Vienna on a 'Quaker transport', Halle left his Jewish origins behind. He was met at Harwich and taken to a small boarding-school in Sussex where he soon felt very much at home. 'Fundamentally, I never looked back,' he writes. 'I had been very lucky.'

John Daltrop's memories of childhood disruption are more familiar. A lawyer like his father, he was raised in an assimilated Jewish family in Bielefeld, Westphalia.

> As forms of persecution increased, we became more and more aware of our Jewishness, but in an absolutely lay sense. When schools were closed to us the cantor took us for lessons which were fairly hectic. The kids in classes consisted of anything from six to sixteen-year-olds; it was not a very successful teaching environment and we ragged him.

George Clare, author of *Last Waltz in Vienna* and *Berlin Days*, from a family of 'Austrians of the Jewish faith who didn't take much notice of their religion', was seventeen when he experienced the trauma of the *anschluss*: 'Suddenly one was proscribed without any legal protection whatsoever. Everybody was your enemy from the copper I'd known all my life.'

In Britain, knowledge of the persecution of Jews in continental Europe and Blackshirt violence nearer home sometimes evoked recollections of an often distant Jewish past. Sidney Tuck, who is vaguely aware of Jewish ancestry on both sides, explains:

> We were brought up never to think that Jews were bad at all but that Jews were good and in fact that we probably came from them ourselves. It probably started with the Blackshirts – I can only just remember them but I think that's how the subject always came up.

Sabine Doust, the great-granddaughter of John Zachariah Laurence, also discovered her Jewish ancestry at that time:

> My mother said during the war, 'You wouldn't have had much of a chance when the Germans came with a Jewish grandmother.' That was when I first knew. Perhaps it was the time of the invasion coming up. We were living in the south of England, in the target area.

In contrast, Robert Beecham, grandson of Sir Thomas Beecham, the conductor, suggests that the war triggered off his mother's reluctance to acknowledge her origins. She was a Jewess from India who came to Britain during the 1930s.

> My mother lived through the war. Her elder sister had to get out of Paris as the Nazis were approaching. I think my mother till her dying day feared that acknowledging she was Jewish would be a liability in the circles in which she moved.

Enemy Aliens?

It was not only their Jewishness that refugees from Nazi Europe had to contend with but the status of 'enemy aliens'. This led to the wartime internment of many immigrants from Germany and Austria. Those who endeavoured to contribute to the British war effort were also branded with this label, as George Clare explains. Clare had managed to leave Vienna in 1938 by obtaining immigration papers for Ireland and hoped to volunteer for the RAF. At the British High Commission in Dublin, he asked to see the air attaché: 'The whole idea that an enemy alien – the Jewish thing never penetrated – wanted to volunteer for the RAF and had done something about it so impressed him that I got permission to go to England.' Despite Clare's energy and initiative, he was packed off, like the majority of 'enemy aliens', to the despised Pioneer Corps. Further enterprise on his part, this time in alerting 'William Hickey' of the *Daily Express* – in real life the MP Tom Driberg – to the plight of 'enemy aliens', was instrumental in enabling people like him to transfer to other regiments.

John Daltrop, who emigrated from Germany on the last *kindertransport* in 1939, experienced discomfort with his ambivalent status during his schooldays.

> At Clifton, I was also a German. Not only was it uncomfortable but it did impinge on one's consciousness. I was called 'Hans' and that gave me a certain amount of embarrassment, as if I was called 'Fritz' or 'Adolph'. And a French Jewish boy showed a bit of hostility. It was after the invasion of France so he wasn't sure whether, to him, I was more Jewish than German or more German than Jewish.

The Jewish Reception – History Repeated

The majority of refugees and Holocaust survivors who found their way to England were absorbed somewhere within the Anglo-Jewish spectrum. The list of those who made valuable contributions to virtually every area of British life is too vast for inclusion here.[1] But the Anglo-Jewish community has little cause for complacency in this regard. In his book, *The Journey Back From Hell*,[2] Anton Gill brings up the attitude of the Jewish community to the survivors who arrived in England. In some cases, including that of Auschwitz survivor Kitty Hart, who has appeared in many documentaries on the Holocaust and helped to make the film *Sophie's Choice*, the reception was decidedly negative.

Bohemian-born André Doviner* had survived Terezin, Auschwitz and a forced labour camp when he found himself on a train back to Auschwitz. He made a daring escape, jumping, 'as coincidence and fate would have it', within 5 miles of his home. 'I was collapsed in a gutter and was found by people I knew intimately and they hid me and fed me and then the war finished,' he told me. His reception in England some 2 years later was not so propitious.

> The response of the Jewish people in England was lousy. I went to try and be among my people and the reception I got was anything but helpful. I was hoping that if I came among my people there would be some sort of welcome considering what I had to go through, some sort of human help that would have cost them nothing to extend.

Doviner's father, who was to become the first foreign Royal Academician, had arrived in England before the war but was in no position to help his son. Doviner asked a member of the Birmingham Jewish community for advice about finding a job and was directed to the labour exchange down the road.

> Now that was a classic response. There was a lot of hoo-hah about the good the Jewish community in Birmingham did for people. Not for me anyway. I thought, 'Let them go to bloody hell if they think they are helping me by telling me the labour exchange is 5 minutes away!'

At times, Doviner confided to a Christian lady active in Jewish communal affairs who befriended him years later, he felt treated like a leper.

> When you go to a communal hall and say, 'My name is Andre Doviner and I'd like to be friendly and civil', and they say, 'Well, we're busy at the moment,' you feel like slinking out of the room.

Doviner's experience may be extreme and, partly, as he himself would confess, self-generated. In recent years, as I learnt from his Christian friend, he has often been invited to community functions and would sometimes show up but turn away at the door. The original slights had wounded him too deeply. But the chilly reception from Jews he complains of is by no means unique. Ruth Weinberger, the child of a mixed marriage and now an ultra-orthodox Jerusalem housewife, told me about her mother, who came to England before the war as a refugee from a traditional Jewish family in Vienna.

> My mother lived in Golders Green with a *goyische* family where she had to keep home for them. I, of course asked her, 'Why didn't you go into a Jewish home?' and she just said, 'The Jewish people did not want to let us in, the welcome was coming from the *goyim*.

Families Fractured

If family loyalties are important for Jewish continuity, the disruption of family life, a common casualty of the Nazi years, took its toll. Will Halle put it this way: 'People were evacuated away from their families. Families were broken. There was no father with whom to identify or who was telling you what to be.' For himself, Halle believes, this was no bad thing.

André Doviner was not so fortunate. He was preparing for his bar mitzvah when 'the whole thing collapsed, my father went to England and my mother and I were stuck in Bohemia.' He was booked on the last *kindertransport* but that, too, fell through. At fourteen he was a baker in Terezin. John Daltrop and his sister, who did catch the *kindertransport*, were 'shipped to a family in the Cotwolds'. 'They made absolutely no attempts – on the contrary – to divert us from our Jewishness although they were very firm Christians.'

This was not the case with many children who arrived as refugees and were taken into Christian families. Some remain ignorant of or wish to suppress their Jewish past. Rose Cameron from Scotland cancelled her appointment to speak to me because her mother, a Holocaust survivor, did not want her to 'rake over old coals'. Others, like Suzy Stocken, have been sustained by their Christian faith, but have made contact with Jewish relatives. The need to spare their own, gentile, families too much disruption has often inhibited them from exploring their lost Jewish identities more deeply.

A Sense of Identity

George Clare is clearly a citizen of the world. Immaculately dressed and striding along a country lane in the Suffolk village where he has retired, he greets passers-by with jocularity and ease. A car passes with a friendly hoot. 'You see,' he says, 'he hooted at me.' 'There's no antisemitism here. We're the only Jews here,' he adds, although his second, German-born wife is not Jewish. Clare speaks of being Jewish as

> a community of fate which I have shared to some extent. It tells me, more than tells me, that I am a Jew, that I was in danger, that my parents were murdered (in Auschwitz) because they were Jews and that is a bench-mark that remains for ever. There is an inner belonging to the Jewish people without my being able to analyse exactly what is there. It's just there, inborn.

Clare has never been afraid to stand up for his rights as a Jew. At 15, on a route march in Austria, some classmates were singing the Horst Wessel Liede .[3] 'I complained about it to somebody and then went next day and complained to the headmaster although a lot of my Jewish chums said "For God's sake, don't."'

Where Clare admits to 'a certain pride' in achievement by Jews, balanced by 'a certain discomfort if you've got a Jewish fraudster', John Daltrop feels 'almost sad, certainly desperately embarrassed by the Saunders and the Maxwells and so on'. By the same token Mike Goldmark, the English-born son of refugees from Vienna who runs a bookshop in Rutland, stresses the importance of correct behaviour: 'Locally people see me as a Jew because of my name and the fact that I haven't at any time denied it. Therefore I feel a necessity to behave well because I am still carrying that particular banner or label.' André Doviner, who ran an antiques business in the Cotswolds for some time, also felt it important to 'keep his nose clean'.

Daltrop believes there has always been 'a strong streak of Jewishness' in him, sometimes more latent than active, and he expresses some regret that he didn't emigrate to Israel rather than Britain: 'I think by and large I would have felt more comfortable out there.' Clare, too, confesses to feeling 'a bit guilty that I didn't go to Israel, that I didn't fight for Israel.' To compensate, he sent his son to a kibbutz. Daltrop's sons also volunteered to work on kibbutzim, 'and that was important to me'.

Will Halle was over sixty when he considered in what sense, if any, he could be regarded as a Jew.

> Whatever religious background I have is solidly Christian, genetics I cannot take seriously, so I'm in a curious position. I'm sometimes recognised as 'not English' but only some 25 per cent of non-Jews identify me as Jewish. But the majority of Jews probably think of me as Jewish.

Halle sees his relaxed approach to identity as typical of his generation. 'One of the effects of the war was a mélange of humanities. Your identity was defined in very gross terms. You were on the allied side rather than the axis side.' This, no doubt, has made him reject exclusivity. Mike Goldmark also takes a stand against separateness and grouping.

> Most of the pain I had seen was caused by people forming themselves into groups, whether that be a religious thing or a nationalistic thing. It may well be that subconsciously I was thinking: 'Had my parents not been Jews and these other people what they were they wouldn't have gone through what they went through.'

Goldmark defines himself as being born of Jewish parents. 'I always thought that made you a Jew until I had a discussion with a philosopher who suggested that actually I'm not a Jew because I don't practise the religion.' That criterion would eliminate many who identify themselves as Jews. Clare finds that religion provides no bridge between himself, 'a typical central European Jew stamped by that particular devotion of the Jew to German culture with a fairly strong overlay of English culture' and many other kinds of Jews with whom he has nothing in common. His adult experience of synagogue on *Yom Kippur* was profoundly alienating: 'I looked at the prayers and all this "Oh you great King, oh the greatest, oh the all-powerful, oh the Almighty" reminded me so much of Goebbels talking about Hitler. I just couldn't stand it. It put me off.'

And What of Continuity?

Halle became interested in genealogy after the birth of his first grandchild 'to put down a link between the English or British family which stems from me and the Austro-Hungarian part of the family from which I am descended'; he would have no satisfaction if one of his descendants was Jewish. Clare's first wife, his childhood sweetheart, was Jewish, but none of their three children married Jews. He professed some satisfaction that two of his grandsons had 'become aware of a Jewish atmosphere in the wider family and the feeling that this is also part of their past, of their genetic structure', but is not particularly concerned about the Jewishness of his grandchildren. 'One Jewish son-in-law I would have liked, though,' he confessed. Daltrop, too, would be 'slightly better pleased than not' if one of his sons were to marry a Jewish girl, although his wife is not Jewish. 'It wasn't relevant at all when we got married. I think maybe it should have been and with hindsight I think I would have preferred it if she had been.' As far as his children are concerned, it was important to him that 'they should be conscious of their half-Jewish parentage, that they should have sympathy and never deny it'. André Doviner, with two broken marriages to non-Jews behind him, is resigned to his sons' indifference to their Jewish heritage: 'I tried to instil into my sons that their father was a Jew and their mother was a Christian, but if they didn't want to follow the religion, so be it.' However, Mike Goldmark, whose wife converted to Judaism almost against his wishes, made a conscious decision not to bring up his children with any specific religious belief.

No Place

Goldmark is conscious that he has embraced universalism at a price.

> The downside of the way I've chosen to live may be the rootlessness I live with and I don't know whether it's because I'm a first-generation immigrant. Had I stayed within a community, I might not have felt this rootlessness. It's not so much a sense of isolation, more a feeling of not belonging in any particular place and I sometimes think of the phrase 'the wandering Jew' and wonder whether that's what I am.

Similarly Masha Gardner, a beautiful *mischling* who survived the war in Germany and came to England as the bride of an English serviceman, does not really feel very English. 'I feel nothing and sometimes it worries me when misfortunes happen and I think "Oh God, I wished I belonged somewhere", but normally when all goes well I don't feel any need to belong.'

Masha's brother who remained in Germany is quite different. He feels strongly that his place is in Israel with the Jewish people.

DESCENDANTS OF THE GRANDEES

While few descendants of the illustrious Anglo-Jewish families are still Jewish today, many people in all walks of British life, not least the royal family, have Jewish antecedents. Indeed, one of the secrets of the *Almanac de Gotha,* the finest book on European royalty and nobility, was that the father of Queen Victoria's consort, Prince Albert, was Jewish.[4] As well as Commander Timothy Laurence, the husband of the Princess Royal, whose ancestor was Zaccaria Levy, the late Lady Edwina Mountbatten had Jewish ancestry, as does Lord Snowdon, ex-husband of Princess Margaret. The marriage of Princess Margaret's son, Viscount Linley, to the former Serena Stanhope, whose maternal grandmother had Jewish ancestry, is an intriguing union of two lost Jews. And to push the Jewish connection in royal romances still further, a strongly fancied girlfriend of Prince Edward, the queen's youngest son, has a certain Rachel Abrahams of Bethnal Green among her maternal ancestors.[5]

Who are My Ancestors?

The interest in recent decades in 'roots' and genealogy has spurred many to seek their Jewish origins. Approximately one-quarter of the nearly 300 members of the Jewish Genealogical Society of Great Britain are 'no longer Jewish'. Henry Roche, dark-haired and bearded and easily passing for Jewish in Jewish company, is a specialist in the history of Portsmouth Jewry. He had three Jewish great-grandparents and is connected to many old Anglo-Jewish families, including the Waleys, the Henriques and the Montagus. Roche's colourful and cosmopolitan Jewish connections include his direct ancestor, the classical pianist, Ignaz Moscheles, born in Prague in 1794 and resident in London from 1825 to 1846; the ancestors of the Lehmanns, novelist Rosamond, poet John and Beatrix, the actress; and a daughter-in-law of Charles Dickens.

Raised as a Protestant, Roche feels 'very English. All my Jewish ancestry has been in England from the early 1800s or earlier. I don't think anyone who knew my family had any knowledge that we were descended from Jews.' He has become 'obsessed' by genealogy: 'It's a combination of pride, interest in history, the detective chase and in the case of Portsmouth, of uncovering and recording for posterity things which could very easily be lost.' In the course of his researches, he taught himself Hebrew to read synagogue registers and feels 'a sort of soulmate companionship' with many of the distant cousins he has discovered, most of whom are on the Jewish side.

His oldest brother's marriage to the daughter of a convert to Judaism has produced a renaissance of Jewishness in the Roche family, with both children of the marriage growing up as committed Jews. Roche's nephew, a student at London University, has become ultra-orthodox and wears the black apparel of the Lubavitch chassids.[6]

Robert Barrett, the genealogist responsible for many of the royal Jewish 'scoops' and a descendant of the Brandon family, prominent Sephardi Jews in the eighteenth century, remembers walking into his grandmother's kitchen when he was a child and noticing the different chopping boards. 'I understand that's a very kosher thing; she did all sorts of funny little things like that. My mother said that my grandmother was aware of the family's Jewish background and that explained how she had her kitchen just so.' Some years after his grandmother's death, when he was in his teens, Barrett started to put together material gleaned from members of the family and found out about his Jewish origins. This he was able to substantiate by delving into the Bevis Marks records.

Intriguingly, Barrett talks of 'marrying out', even for family members whose Jewish origins are now remote. It was an expression, he says, that his grandmother used. His reminiscences of her kitchen habits were reinforced when he witnessed the 'koshering' of the kitchens of the banqueting house in Whitehall in preparation for a Jewish function:

> They had the rabbi in to bless the kitchen and certain foods before. They laid this plastic sheeting and cellophane and greaseproof paper throughout the kitchen and you weren't allowed in certain quarters after they had cordoned it off. It was a wonderful introduction into preparing food the Jewish way. I have an enormous respect for the Jewish faith and feel there's so much to be learnt from that way of life.

Barrett looks forward to visiting Jerusalem which his sister found a very moving experience.

He has no relations in this country who are still Jewish but there are Jewish Brandon cousins in Australia and New Zealand and a few in the United States.

Three Women

Among the remnants of some of Anglo-Jewry's prominent families are three women of mixed parentage who represent a spectrum of Jewishness from non-practising identification to a committed orthodox life-style. Two other young women from very assimilated backgrounds also told me their stories; one had returned to orthodoxy, the other to a committed progressive Jewish life-style. In both cases the parents were unhappy with having the stories published so they have had to be pulled out.

Facing East

Irene Samuel, small featured and petite, is descended from Emanuel Samuel, who came to London from Poland in 1775 and heads a dynasty which includes Viscount Herbert Samuel, the Liberal politician and first British High Commissioner in Palestine. She was five when her father and her non-Jewish mother divorced. It was not until her father remarried and her stepmother was rather more observant that Irene, then about six, had any awareness of being Jewish. From then onwards, her identity was fixed: 'From the minute I knew there was something called "being Jewish", it's been very simple to me, no question at all. It's just like "Is my hair dark or fair?"' 'This Church of England stuff' in contrast, had 'left her cold': 'You get prayers and stories in school and even at the age of five it seemed totally impossible to relate to.'

The family attended the New London Synagogue under Rabbi Dr Louis Jacobs, who had broken away from the orthodox United Synagogue because of a theological dispute with the then Chief Rabbi. Irene went to a private teacher for Hebrew lessons and basic religious instruction. When she was fifteen, she told her father she wanted a bat mitzvah. He was very concerned. 'Nobody chooses to be Jewish. Wait till you see who you want to marry.'

> I thought that was sacrilege. I always felt I belonged in that synagogue. There wasn't any problem. Louis Jacobs had always known I'd been brought up by a Jewish stepmother and the home I'd been brought up in. I did a conversion at the same time as the bat mitzvah. The result is he considers me Jewish and the orthodox rabbinate of course don't.

Irene had just started university when the Yom Kippur war broke out in 1973. 'I seriously thought, "Well, the war's going on. Maybe I should go out there and do something."' It was some years later that she actually went, at a stage when 'I was sort of falling apart and not enjoying life at all and my doctor said "You need to go away," and, because of some friends he had, within 20 minutes he'd fixed up for me to go to a kibbutz.' Asked at the time if she was a Zionist, Irene had no idea what that meant.

Hebrew had always enchanted her:

> I've always felt an instinctive something about Hebrew, a kind of gut feeling about hearing it. When my stepbrother was having Hebrew lessons for his bar mitzvah, I used to like sitting and listening while he was having them. I don't know why. It's like something from a previous life.

Israel, too, was a watershed. 'The first day I arrived, I thought, "This is right." Going on the bus up north you see all that rugged landscape with all the rocks and I just think, "This is it, this is where I want to be."'

Circumstances and her own ambivalence brought Irene back to England. She now teaches music and lives with her cats in a charming house in Barnes. Israel remains a vital ingredient in her sense of identity:

> I sort of belong in an El Al plane somewhere between the two countries. Here I'm not the same as everybody else, I'm Jewish and I'm very involved in Israel, and in Israel I'm not the same as everybody else because I live in England and even if I speak Hebrew and I visit often I'm not an Israeli. The best thing I think I ever did was to live away from England, to live in Israel, and probably the worst thing I did was not to stay, but I value both and it means you get a very interesting view of both places, of both cultures, from seeing them partly from the inside, partly from the outside.

At her Mother's Knee

Lydia Howard, a broadcaster, with gentle, intelligent features and a humorous glint in her eyes, is the great-granddaughter of *Haham* Dr Moses Gaster, former spiritual leader of the Sephardi community. Her late mother, the writer Marghanita Laski, was the daughter of the *Haham's* eldest daughter, Sissie and Judge Neville Laski, from a leading Manchester Jewish family. Brought up 'dead orthodox', Marghanita became a convinced atheist and married John Howard, a gentile, at the British consulate in Paris. 'They couldn't get married in this country,' Lydia explained. 'It would be too shameful. The *Haham* was still alive.'

The loss of her Jewish first name, Rebecca, 'for no very good reason' – actually, she had been put off it after reading Daphne du Maurier's novel – in no way reflects her attitude to her Jewishness:

> My mother was very interested in religion and wrote and argued and broadcast about it so religion was always an issue for us; she was very

> interested in things Jewish so I grew up knowing a lot about things Jewish. I feel I am Jewish, although I don't practise and I don't believe in it. I don't feel I have a choice about it. I wouldn't have wanted a choice but it would never have occurred to me not to be Jewish.

Lydia's Jewish identity is entwined with her Gaster connections. Numerous photographs in her Kentish Town living room reveal how the finely etched, almost soulful features of her great-grandmother Lucy, the *Haham's* wife, have been stamped on her mother Marghanita and her younger daughter, Hannah. Anecdotes abound of the *Haham's* numerous offspring, 'the first lot, the older ones', very orthodox, very obedient and conventional, and the younger ones whose nursery her mother shared in her early years – Bertha, Theodore, Jack and Lulu, who 'reacted like hell'. 'They all grew up talking about religion and rebelling against Judaism together.'

Despite her atheism, Marghanita Laski was a strong believer in tradition and taught Lydia Hebrew: 'It was like something passed from mother to daughter. If religion is handed down at your mother's knee, she felt it was part of her maternal duty towards me.' Having forgotten it herself, Lydia sent her elder daughter, Esther, to Hebrew classes, in the teeth, ironically, of 'vehement' opposition from her mother and her great-aunt Bertha.

Although she jokes about 'awful Friday night suppers' at her grandparents, she recalls with nostalgia Passover *seder*-night gatherings at her grandmother's or her great-aunt's where the orthodox members of the family were outnumbered by the lapsed rebels and their '*goy*' spouses and offspring. She feels 'the family's Judaism didn't so much drift away. More there was a fight and people chose to break it' and the loss saddens her:

> I hope to learn Hebrew again but I doubt if there will still be family things to go to. I hope there will still be somebody to help me with it. I've got lots of Jewish books and inherited lots of Jewish things I would have liked to have gone through with relations who understood them. I feel they're part of my family's culture and heritage but I am myself so ignorant of them that for my children they'll be no more than curios they could have found in an antique shop.

The Rules of the Game

Sarah Montagu, a midwife with a down-to-earth, open look and three lively children in tow, is very much the mother. The great-great grandaughter of Colonel Albert Goldsmid, the lost Jew who returned to his ancestral faith, she is descended from Goldsmid's eldest daughter and Louis Samuel Montagu, the second Lord Swaythling. 'There was a bit of a hoo-hah when great-grandmother Gladys married great-grandfather because the Swaythlings were querying whether Albert Goldsmid's conversion was good enough.'

Much of Sarah's life as a Jewess has been a pragmatic, self-motivated process leading to a conversion that is 'good enough'. 'I'm the most converted person, I've had two orthodox conversions,' she quips. Her mother had converted in the liberal synagogue and Sarah was raised in a committed liberal Jewish home. 'I got a huge amount of my Judaïsm from my mother because she had made a commitment to learning about it. She taught us Hebrew and I learnt Jewish cooking from her and acquired a feeling of Jewish commitment.' The Montagu children attended religion school, went to synagogue fairly regularly and celebrated Friday nights and the festivals.

A turning point came when, at a liberal Jewish youth weekend, Sarah met an orthodox Jew who pointed out that the founders of liberal Judaism were brought up orthodox and had chosen from orthodoxy to become liberal. 'People who are brought up liberal have a fairly watered-down form of Judaism, so if you're choosing, it's not from a position of having experienced full observance.'

Sarah and her siblings started to become more observant. 'In my case it was a gradual process – I worked myself into it, as it were.' Cutting out pork and shellfish was a first step. 'My mother was quite receptive and stopped buying things we didn't want to eat. My parents never minded us being "more Jewish". They would have been upset if we had been less Jewish or didn't care at all.'

At Cambridge she read Hebrew and joined the progressive Jewish student's society, graduating to the more traditionally-orientated 'J soc' after spending the summer vacation of her second year in Israel. At the 'prog soc' she met her future husband, from a reform Jewish background but in a similar situation: his maternal grandmother was a reform convert. They married under the auspices of the reform synagogue and went to live in Germany where her husband worked on his doctorate. Proud of the family tradition, Sarah kept her name.

In Essen the couple led an orthodox life style, observing *kashrut* and the Sabbath. They went several times to Dusseldorf, the nearest town where there was a rabbi, and he talked about the level of their observance and their knowledge of Judaism and Hebrew. Their orthodox conversion with the *mikveh* ceremony took place in Frankfurt – 'the only place in Germany you can get three rabbis together' – followed by a *chupa* or marriage ceremony. After 3 years they returned to England with their two older children.

Applying for synagogue membership in Birmingham, they discovered that the London *Beth Din* wanted them to convert again.

> They didn't accept the German conversion just like that but they didn't put us through exactly the same process as they would someone coming to them out of the blue. They were aware of the family history and asked us how we got to where we were. We went to a rabbi in Birmingham for a few sessions and then up to London to do the *mikveh* – the kids had to be dunked as well. If you accept the orthodox premise, the principle of *halacha* is that these are the rules of the game. If you buy the package, you buy the package!

4

Who Says I'm Lost?

GRANDMOTHER IN THE CLOSET

Can the *halachic* definition of Jewishness still impinge on people's lives? Can the need to conceal matrilineal ancestry that is not unadulteratedly Jewish lead to secrecy and denial? As far as the United States is concerned, Barry Kosmin, the British-born demographer, dismisses the idea of any external authority checking on the status of a would-be Jew.

> The state is totally disinterested and actually forbidden to turn round and say what the Jewish group is. That's why there's no Chief Rabbi in the United States and Canada and there's no *Judenrat* and no Jewish police. It's a completely voluntary system.

Individuals whose Jewish status is *halachically* dubious may proclaim themselves 'ethnic Jews'. When it comes to the religious option, however, the nirvana of open-door access to communal and religious life is still to come. Many American Jews inhabit the interface between the large and powerful American Reform movement which accepts persons of patrilineal Jewish descent as Jews and the other influential non-orthodox Jewish body in the United States, the Conservatives, which adheres to the *halachic* ruling. An individual who passes the Jewish litmus test in one community may find themselves not accepted in another. One example of this discrepancy on New York's Upper West Side is the Chavura School, which accepts children of Jewish fathers, working in tandem with the Ansche Chesed Synagogue, a conservative congregation which does not accept patrilineal children as candidates for bar mitzvah.

How Dare There Be Anybody Who Tells Me I'm Not Jewish?

Jane* was about eleven or twelve when she suddenly discovered she was not Jewish, as Jerry Raik, director of the Chavura school, explains:

> Before I met Jane, she had recently been told that she was not eligible to have a bat mitzvah because she wasn't Jewish. Her grandmother had converted to Judaism only after Jane's mother was born. This was told

> to Jane and her family by the rabbi of their community (not Ansche Chesed) after Jane had been in Hebrew School for a while. It was a shock to everybody. Jane's mother had considered herself to be Jewish all her life. She had had an active Jewish life as a child, her parents had been very active and well-known in the Jewish community and it had never occurred to her that there was any problem about this. The family's response to this shock was anger at the situation and at the rabbi who had presented it to them. Then Jane's parents immediately had her converted in the most widely accepted fashion, to take her to a *mikveh* and to have a *Beth Din*. Jane was very confused and very very angry, not just at the rabbi but also at her parents for making her do this, for suggesting that she wasn't Jewish.[1]

Jane was brought to Raik at the Chavura school. They spent 'a remarkable couple of years' together preparing for her bat mitzvah and, more importantly, 'working through this anger she had at everyone involved'. Her mother still refused to undergo the *mikveh* conversion ceremony herself, arguing that she was an adult and nobody could make her go. 'This was an issue between her and Jane. Jane's mother's attitude was "We're going to make you do this so that you can be spared the anguish that I'm going through now and any further anguish that you're going through." ' At the age of fifteen, Jane eventually had her bat mitzvah in the Ansche Chesed Synagogue and made a speech, telling her story. 'It really knocked the synagogue for a loop!' said Raik. 'Everybody was stunned and incredibly impressed with the presence of this girl and very moved by her story.' Raik acknowledges that plenty of people would be outraged by what Jane had to go through, but is convinced that 'the ongoing establishment of orthodox and conservative Judaism in America would affirm that what happened to Jane was rightfully done and probably they would say: "The outcome of it proves that we are right." '

Jane's situation illustrates the nebulous status of children born to a mother who converts to Judaism after marriage. It is by no means unique and all the more likely in countries like Britain and France where the orthodox establishment is far more dominant than in America. Within weeks of hearing her story, I came across two similar cases. Michèle Charkham, blonde, girlish and a grandmother for the first time, lives in north London, while Déborah Lévy is an attractive Parisienne. Both had suffered the trauma of having an identity they had taken for granted brutally withdrawn.

When Michèle learnt that she was not the Jewish girl she thought she was, it was another step in a saga, punctuated by secrecy, that had started with the rejection of her parents, an intermarried couple, by her father's family. Married in secret in 1935, her parents went off to Havana, where her mother had a sister. Her father was one of 11 children from a prominent and respected orthodox Jewish family. Contact was briefly resumed with the father's family when the couple returned to England but before long they were cut off. In 1939 Michèle's father was called up to the army and left for India in 1942, with his wife 3 months pregnant. He did not return until Michèle was 3 years old. By then he had become one of the youngest majors in the British army in India. After reading of his son's achievements in the *Jewish Chronicle*, Michèle's grandfather took some steps towards reconciliation.

'I always thought I was Jewish,' Michèle recalled.

> My parents moved to Muswell Hill and my father joined a small Jewish community there. Later we moved to Hampstead Garden Suburb and he joined Norrice Lea *shul*. I assume no-one asked any questions. It must have been a matter of omission. They were probably much less formal than they are today with the paperwork and the assumption must have been that my mother was Jewish. For me, my mother's relatives were non-existent. Her parents were dead, one sister lived in Havana and she had a brother and sister in England I had never met so it was easy for me not to feel any non-Jewish input. I went to Hebrew classes from the age of about 10, sometimes twice a week, and I went to *shul* on *Shabbat* with my father. I sat upstairs (in the ladies' gallery) and I was involved with some quite religious girls. There was never any question about my Jewishness.

Unbeknown to Michèle and her younger brother, their mother, now more accepted within her husband's family, had decided to convert to Judaism. Although she approached an orthodox rabbi, the conditions for converting under orthodox auspices were too stringent – she would have had to live away from home – so she had a reform conversion. When Michèle was eleven and her brother six, they were packed off to tea with friends one afternoon while her parents remarried in a synagogue, in the presence of her grandfather and all her father's family.

'We knew nothing about all this,' Michèle told me.

> Then when I was sixteen we were coming back from holiday when my father said: 'By the way, Michèle, we'll be changing *shuls*. We won't belong to Norrice Lea, we're going to a reform synagogue.' I said 'Why?' and he said 'Because your mother wasn't Jewish.' That was the first time I was told and I was very very angry and I told him: 'My grandfather's quite right. How dare you marry somebody who wasn't

Jewish?' I knew it made me different and at sixteen I didn't want to be different. I didn't realise the full implications but I knew I would have to leave a community where I was happy. I think that did have quite a bearing on my feelings about Judaism.

An incident shortly afterwards exemplifies Michèle's hypersensitivity. 'I had this boyfriend who was quite *frum* and I was round at his house. His parents were lovely, always made me very welcome, they were going out and his mother opened the fridge and said "Help yourself, Michèle. It's all right, you won't find any bacon there." ' Convinced that she was referring to the fact that 'I really wasn't Jewish,' Michèle rushed out of the house and went home. Meanwhile the boyfriend's parents were so bemused that they turned up at her parents' house, knocking on the door and asking what they had done!

Worse was to come. Michèle's family settled down at the reform synagogue and she later met the boy who was to become her first husband.

As it was nearing the time to get married, we went to talk to the rabbi. 'I've got some news for you, Michèle,' he said. 'Your brother and you are not technically Jewish and if you want to get married in the *shul* you'll have to go before the *Beth Din.*' I said 'I don't want to do that. I don't believe in a God who's going to look and say I'm Jewish from a certain date and give me a piece of paper. It's absolute nonsense. I'll get married in a registry office.'

Although the rabbi was very understanding, he explained that if Michèle married in a registry office, her children would never be able to marry in a synagogue.

I calmed down a bit and my brother and I went to the *Beth Din*. It wasn't a problem for me. I could read Hebrew. I knew the prayers and all the questions they asked and I didn't have to do any studying. Even so I considered it an indignity and I have a piece of paper which says I'm a proselyte of righteousness from a certain date. It's extremely archaic and it made me feel very bad.

Now an active member of her local reform synagogue and of a women's prayer group, Michèle looks back on the anomaly which caused her such anguish:

I was left with the feeling that I never quite fitted in anywhere. I've been in a group for people who've converted and I didn't quite fit into that but on the other hand I can't quite fit into the category of someone who's always been Jewish though I have always been Jewish – it's the 'not Jewish enough'. I understand why it's passed down through the mother but it wasn't always like that in the Biblical period so why should they draw a line in this way which excludes me? *How dare there be anybody that tells me I'm not Jewish?* I believe that God doesn't want to pick and choose about who's mother is what and who's father is what, but if you're committed to God then God accepts you. I'm very proud of my Judaism, I live my Judaism. I wonder what my grandfather would have thought about the fact that a grandchild who is so committed to Judaism has come from the mother who wasn't born Jewish. Judaism has been a wonderful part of my life and it could all have been lost. I would have been totally lost to Judaism, no doubt about it, if I had been excluded from an orthodox community and had no other Jewish option.

Michèle did explore the option of converting to orthodox Judaism but did not pursue it as it would have meant that her mother, a reform convert, would not have been allowed to stand under the *chupa* at her wedding. For Déborah Lévy, to marry in an orthodox synagogue and to raise Jewish children who will be spared the problems of status she has had to confront are such strong priorities that she is prepared to undergo the rigours of converting under the auspices of the Paris *Consistoire*. As I discovered when she first came to see me, 22 year old Déborah is the only member of her family who isn't accepted as Jewish.

Making her Pay

The second time I met Déborah, it was shortly after the remarriage of her parents at an orthodox synagogue near the République in Paris. Her mother had just received authentication from the *Consistoire* for a conversion process successfully completed 4 years earlier.

All my family were there. It was a traditional wedding and my parents were very, very happy. The rabbi mentioned that now my two sisters are converted – they went to the *mikveh* with my mother – and that my brother had already converted earlier, so they were all Jewish. After my parents were married under the *chupa*, they called my two sisters and my brother to go under the *tallit* for a special family blessing. My little sister, she's five, asked: 'Why aren't you coming too?' I said, 'No, go, go and see *maman*,' but she kept looking at me, she didn't understand.

I felt quite bad really. I felt happy for my parents but it was difficult to stay smiling because when all my family were under the *tallit* I felt, 'I'm not part of them.' I don't think anybody realised how I feel. I didn't want to say anything because for my mother, it was the fulfilment of a dream, she had wanted this for so many years, and my grandmother, too, was so moved, she was just looking at my parents. I don't like to show my feelings, especially that day. I couldn't tell them I felt left out, excluded.

It hurts me a little because now all my family is very happy because they are all Jewish and I'm not but I don't feel like I'm not. For the *Consistoire* I'm not Jewish. I feel it's not fair because my mother brought me up in the same way, but what can I do?

Déborah's attitude reflects a mature acceptance of something that caused her outrage some years earlier:

I went to see a rabbi and he told me 'You're not Jewish' and I said 'I am. You can say everything you want but I am!' And he said 'No, in my eyes you're not.' I was seventeen or eighteen and I came back and said to my father: 'I don't want to do my conversion. I am Jewish and I don't mind if they think I'm not.' I was very angry but now I understand more and I don't look at the same points I was looking at before. Before I was just thinking 'I am Jewish' and it's not important to have a card with my name and 'Jewish' on it. Now I realise that even if it is silly to do it, the conversion can have a lot of repercussions on everything.

Two weeks after the wedding, the older of Déborah's sisters celebrated her bat mitzvah. This had finally propelled the *Consistoire* to validate her mother's conversion. Déborah was never given the opportunity to have a bat mitzvah. The family attended an orthodox synagogue in their suburb, St Maur, but Déborah was not allowed to continue with Hebrew classes at the synagogue's Talmud Torah. Her father explained this away, saying it was not important for a girl to have a bat mitzvah, but Déborah feels he made a mistake.

I am sure it was very difficult for my father to talk about this when I was young, but as he wants me to be Jewish and my children to be Jewish, why didn't he tell me before, when I wanted to do my bat mitzvah? He wants me to marry a Jewish boy and if tomorrow I want to, I can't, and maybe no Jewish boy will want me because I'm not Jewish. My father could have explained the situation to me, explained what I had to do if I wanted to be Jewish. Perhaps at the time I would have done it. It would have been better.

Déborah's story has many similarities to Michèle's but also some differences. For example, her parents were first married in the well-known liberal synagogue in Rue Copernic in Paris, which suggests that her mother had undergone a liberal conversion. Her father was one of seven children of an immigrant family from Algeria and her grandmother, an orthodox Jewess, was none too pleased with her son's choice of bride. Within the greater openness of the Sephardi tradition, the grandmother soon appreciated the daughter-in-law's desire to learn Jewish ways and taught her how to be a Jewish wife and mother. 'I never felt like I'm not Jewish,' Déborah recalls. 'When I was born my mother did everything for me to be Jewish, all the food at home and all the celebrations and festivals, we did everything.'

As in the case of Michèle, the situation came to a head when the time came for Déborah's brother, who is five years her junior, to have his bar mitzvah. To enable her son to do this, Déborah's mother undertook to convert to orthodox Judaism. Déborah's brother completed his studies successfully, took an exam and was converted at the same time. The mother continued her studies and regular synagogue attendance and then took an exam. Then the four-year wait began.

Had Déborah been allowed to prepare for a bat mitzvah, she would have been able to convert at that time. Now she is an adult, she was excluded from the family conversion undergone by her mother and young sisters. She feels there is nobody she can trust as far as her Jewish status is concerned.

> Maybe my father doesn't look at me as Jewish. After all, I wanted to do my bat mitzvah but he didn't want me to do it. It's not my fault if my mother wasn't Jewish. I didn't have anything to do with it and now I have everything on my head.

Undeterred, Déborah is determined to go ahead with her own conversion.

> I want to do it for my grandmother and for myself. I am 22 and the rabbis will make it very difficult for me because they don't want a young woman or a young man to do a conversion in order to get married. I think they want me to feel like I'm not Jewish. So it's up to me. It's a test in a way. They don't look at me like a Jew and I want to prove to them that I am, even if they are hard with me and even if they try to stop me.

Is She or Isn't She?

These cases exemplify inconsistencies and anomalies which may result from the conversion process. A rather different phenomenon is the continuation of Jewish family life where the maternal grandmother of the family is not Jewish and no conversion has taken place. It is as if the grandmother's 'non-Jewishness' has been hidden in a closet, in dramatic contrast to scenarios throughout Jewish history where the threat of persecution forced people to conceal their Jewish ancestry.

I visited a family with such a history in the United States. Despite their kindness and hospitality, they refused to be interviewed, doubtless because of the sensitivity of the issue. I will give the bare outline of the story, withholding their names and even the town in which they live.

The grandmother, from a prominent and respected gentile family, had met her Jewish husband abroad. They had one daughter and later returned to her home town. There the family joined a reform Jewish temple where the grandmother became an active and welcome member. The daughter – now the mother of two sons – grew up and fell in love with a Jewish man from an orthodox background who was an active member of a conservative Jewish congregation. The couple married in the reform temple but maintained their membership of the conservative synagogue where their two sons had their bar mitzvahs and where the mother also took part in a bat mitzvah ceremony for mature women. The family, including the grandmother – the grandfather has now died – are respected and well-loved members of the town's Jewish community. It is unlikely that the two grandsons are aware that their grandmother, who clearly merits the title of honorary Jewess, is not, in fact, Jewish.

In London, I had been contacted by twenty-three-year old John Davies*, a tall, good-looking postgraduate student at Oxford, when I was researching the opinions of young marginal Jews (Chapter 10). I had expected to interview him as a 'marginal Jew' when he disclosed that his maternal grandmother was not Jewish. It appears that John's younger brother is not aware of this, as I learnt several months later.

John's parents had been married in a liberal synagogue but he was brought up in a reform synagogue, where he attended Sunday school and had his bar mitzvah. His family mixed in exclusively Jewish circles, but as far as practising the religion was concerned, they were 'twice a year Jews', putting in an appearance at synagogue on the Jewish New Year and the Day of Atonement. John was sixteen when his Jewish identity was called into question.

'At that time I often went to visit my grandmother. She seemed to get depressed a bit – it was the beginnings of Alzheimer's disease – and I used to have long conversations with her over a cuppa after school.' This grandmother had seemed an exemplary Jewish mother who had brought up three children in the Jewish tradition. In fact, as John's paternal grandmother was to tell him later, she was 'more Jewish than all of us'.

It was then that my grandmother told me that in fact she wasn't Jewish after all. I can't remember how it came up but the long and the short of it was that she wasn't Jewish. I was quite surprised, of course, and I was aware of the matrilineal question, so technically then I was not what I thought I was.

Am I or Aren't I?

John broached the subject with his parents, who acknowledged that what his grandmother had told him was correct. While they seemed happy to continue with 'some sort of Jewish veneer', John was forced to question what being Jewish was all about. Unlike Michèle and Déborah who responded to being told 'You are not Jewish' by insisting all the more that they were, John's reactions were more complex, a basic wound overlaid with indifference.

For me, the main point is: what's it all for? I can't see the reason why people should want to be or stay being Jewish. Learning about the 'closet' situation has made me think more of these matters. To some extent it was the question of my identity. For many young Jews who are just brought up in the tradition, it's neither here nor there; being Jewish is just a label, take it or leave it. I've thought about it more than if it had just been a label, because I question the point of the label in the first place and why it's felt we need it.

Still searching for an answer, John left for university where he came into contact with 'marginal Jews' whom he found more interesting than 'the run of the mill Jewish people' he had known at home. Unlike most marginal Jews, however, he accepted the hospitality of the local Lubavitch rabbi. 'I found the rabbi very interesting but nevertheless my conclusion was these people are far too enclosed, narrow-minded, parochial and that really put me off.' Significantly, John asked the rabbi if he was 'kosher'.

He said, 'If you want to be "kosher", you'll have to go to the *Beth Din* [in this case the Chief Rabbi's court] and become like me and pray three times a day.' That put me off. It's hypocritical that they demand that you be more Jewish than the run of the mill Jews.

For all his professed detachment from his Jewish upbringing, John admits to having been hurt:

Of course I have. It's difficult, it's upsetting actually because if you're brought up to believe you're such and such religion and then, in fact, you're not, then there are implications for you. You feel that, strictly speaking, you don't belong on paper.

The whole question of whether John considers himself Jewish is fraught with confusion and denial: 'I thought I was Jewish, I'm not Jewish, sorry, I'm not Jewish – no, I'm not Jewish from the orthodox perspective. It doesn't bother me, I think it used to bother me, but now it doesn't.'

'Do you feel you're Jewish?' I persisted. The answer was a heartfelt *'Yes, yes.'*

Who's a Jew?

Kanika is five years old. Her father is an English gentile and her mother . . .? Laila, Kanika's mother, has an ancestry as mixed as you can get. Her father was a German Christian . . . and her mother? Laila's 'Jewish' mother was the daughter of a Jewess and a Muslim. And her grandmother? Laila's 'Jewish' grandmother was, in fact, the daughter of a Jewess and a Hindu. And so it goes on. Young Kanika's ancestry is certainly not run of the mill. Yet as far as *halacha* is concerned, she is Jewish. Kanika would be permitted to marry in any synagogue.

I met Kanika's mother, Laila, a charming young woman with a slightly exotic but essentially indefinable aura, together with her first cousin, Rahel. Although bonded in an intimacy that made them seem like sisters, superficially the two couldn't be more different. Rahel's mother and Laila's mother are sisters. But Rahel's father was an American Jew of Russian origin. From the outset Rahel struck me as an American Jewish girl. Which, in fact, she is. Who says fathers don't count?

NOT LOST BUT EXCLUDED

The greatest rift in the Jewish world centres around the definition of 'Who is a Jew'. Since 1983, when the American Reform movement reaffirmed its long-standing policy of recognising children of gentile mothers and Jewish fathers as Jews, provided they are brought up Jewish, the gulf between orthodox and progressive Judaism has been accompanied by cracks within the non-orthodox ranks. In America, the non-orthodox but affiliated Jews who form the large majority of the Jewish population are divided between the Reform, the Conservative and the smaller Reconstructionist movements, while the two progressive movements in Britain,[2] the Reform and the Liberal, are a relatively influential minority.

In France there is barely more than a handful of non-orthodox congregations but three separate groupings; only one challenges the *halachic* ruling on Jewish status.[3]

Officially, the American Conservative movement and its affiliates worldwide, including the Reform movement in Britain, maintain the *halachic* line. But a national Jewish leadership survey conducted in 1990 by the Jewish Outreach Institute, an American think-tank on issues of intermarriage, revealed widespread acceptance of the concept of patrilineal Jewish descent among lay conservative Jews, as well as among reform Jews; even a minority of the conservative rabbis who responded to the survey indicated that they would consider a grandchild born to a gentile daughter-in-law as Jewish. And while the Reconstructionists officially endorse patrilineal descent, some prominent reconstructionist rabbis oppose it.

In Israel, 'Who is a Jew' has been an ongoing battle between the religious and secular communities, with the *halachic* status quo preserved by the wheeling and dealing of orthodox political factions within the various government coalitions. Popular attitudes on the subject emerge from the responses to a question asking 'Is it clear to you what the definition of a Jew is?' included, in 1970 and 1982, in a survey on the Jewish identity of Israeli Jews carried out periodically by the Israel Institute of Applied Social Research, now known as the Gutman Institute. In both years approximately two-thirds of the respondents said it was either 'definitely clear' or 'clear'.

There was a distinction between the two categories, however. According to Dr Shlomit Levy of the Hebrew University[4] who extrapolated various conclusions from the surveys in her doctoral thesis on Jewish identity (1985), those who responded 'definitely clear' – about 28 per cent – had the *halachic* definition in mind. These are the people for whom religious conformity is the dominant component in their Jewish identification, as opposed to factors like national feeling. All the other respondents, Dr Levy concluded, were confused and did not feel strongly about the *halacha*. Even those who responded 'clear' were split between *halachic* and non-*halachic* definitions because the religious component in their Jewish identity is not always very strong.

One can assert fairly confidently therefore that the majority of non-orthodox Israeli Jews would have no hesitation in accepting a person of patrilineal Jewish descent who nailed his colours to the national mast and that the majority of rank-and-file Jews worldwide see Jewishness in other than *halachic* terms.

In Britain, however, it is only the Liberal movement that officially accepts as Jewish the child of a Jewish father who is raised as a Jew, a stand which goes back to the early days of the movement but which has received less than fulsome support from some liberal rabbis. The issue of Jewish status has also provoked considerable tension between the Liberals and their progressive partners, the Reform Synagogues of Great Britain (RSGB), with the Reform claiming to adhere to *halacha* in the interests of wider Jewish unity, while nevertheless accepting members of liberal synagogues within their ranks. Since the majority of British Jews are ostensibly orthodox in affiliation if not practice, in contrast to the United States, the supporters of patrilineal descent are outnumbered by those who pay lip service to *halacha*.

A pamphlet on Jewish identity produced by the British-based Union of Liberal and Progressive Synagogues (ULPS) in 1993 clearly demonstrates how Jewish identity may be determined by the transmission of Judaism rather than the fact of birth and contains a clause which coincides to some extent with my own approach to the affirmation of Jewish identification and commitment in adulthood.[5] While it will make no impression on committed orthodox Jews who virtually sanctify the *halachic* ruling on Jewish status, it deserves to be considered by objective-minded opinion formers in an age of rampant intermarriage.

Clan or Club?

> The danger with the Jewish people, a terrible danger, is that we are getting to a situation where Jews will not be able to marry other Jews.
>
> Eldred Tabachnik, President of the Board of Deputies, London

> Who cannot see the danger hovering over our future? It's the 'citizenship' within the Jewish people which is at stake. All these children who have Jewish names, attend Jewish schools and frequent Jewish circles, will fall in love with other Jews and want to marry them, only to find themselves in a *halachic* no man's land, denied the capacity to marry 'according to the laws of Moses and Israel'. We are going to have ethnic, non-*halachic* Jews who will be able to marry non-Jews more easily than Jews.
>
> Shmuel Trigano, journalist, Paris[6]

> Say there's a young man with a Jewish father who wants to convert to Judaism and the reform community or the reform rabbi helps him to be Jewish. Afterwards there's really a problem. He will be a Jew here in this place, it'll be okay, but the moment he may want to go to Israel and get married, suddenly he won't be Jewish.
>
> Rabbi Karel Sidon, Prague

> There is a strain in Jewish thought that says that there is a special Godly something or other that is passed down in a certain genetic line which confers a special quality on people and Jewishness is a special quality. I call that metaphysical racism.
>
> Rabbi Mark Solomon, ULPS, London

The creation of a breed of Jew who is not 'lost' but excluded, the inevitable by-product of intermarriage and varied approaches to Jewish status, takes no account of the natural affinity between Jews, irrespective of background, which may also extend to half-Jews with no formal Jewish identification. Tanya Alfillé, who has a Jewish father, recalls her schooldays:

> The moment I came into the class, the Jewish girls knew that I was Jewish or that there was something Jewish about me they could relate to. I felt comfortable with them too. I've always tended to get on well with people who have something foreign or Jewish about them.

Whether such affinity between people who share Jewish ancestry is racial, ethnic or the bonding of outsiders is totally immaterial as far as the marriage market is concerned. This is of crucial importance in France, where non-orthodox Judaism is marginal, and in Britain, where the preoccupation with preserving the marriage market for those of unsullied *halachic* lineage also determines the policy for entry to Jewish schools. Dayan Isaac Berger, who has 'tried to bend the rules as much as I could', recognises the anomaly of refusing entry even to children of Jewish fathers who have been brought up as practising Jews.

> Here we are waiting for these children, if you like, to come of age and convert to Judaism yet we shut the doors in their face and say 'No Jewish school'. The rule is that children are not Jewish who are not eligible to marry in *shul* and should not attend a Jewish school so as to protect the other children.

The situation is exacerbated by the fact that there is no facility for the conversion of minors within Anglo-Jewish orthodoxy.[7] In France, in contrast, there is a practice of converting minors at approximately the age of bar mitzvah or slightly after that.[8] Any prospective applicant for conversion may also apply to enter a Jewish school. With the strict standards demanded of converts, however, the applicants invariably outnumber the successful candidates.

The Anglo-Jewish obsession with who is marriageable is equally prevalent outside the orthodox community. In RSGB circles, for example, comments have been heard to the effect that children of non-*halachic* status involved in activities within the reform synagogues should wear badges to warn the other children that they are not marriageable.

In contrast to the orthodox, however, the RSGB facilitates the conversion of patrilineal Jews and has recently introduced a procedure whereby children of Jewish fathers may be converted in infancy by immersion in the *mikveh*, provided the mother takes the course of study demanded of a convert, even if she decides not to convert.[9]

But a non-orthodox conversion only offers a limited solution. A poignant example was given me by an orthodox Israeli girl who fell in love with an English boy with a Jewish father. 'It would have been worse if his mother had had a reform conversion,' she told me. 'He would have believed he was Jewish and I would still have had to refuse him.' Ineligible to marry under orthodox auspices, non-orthodox converts – and their children – are restricted in their choice of Jewish partners. Shades of the *mischling* experience in war-time Germany, as Masha Gardner recalls: 'There were these incredible meeting-places of nubile *mischlings* – it was quite revolting, so totally artificial. *Mischlings* were only allowed to marry *mischlings*.' Had the beautiful Masha succumbed to the sighs of one of her Aryan admirers, it would have been the end for her and her whole family.

While the involvement between one of today's Jewish *mischlings* and a *halachic* Jew can lead to nothing worse than a broken heart, the non-negotiability of credentials required for marriage and the need to prove them might suggest that what's at stake is a matter of life and death. Kim Kraft from America got off relatively lightly. For her marriage at one of London's orthodox Sephardi synagogues she was required, among other things, to produce her grandmother's *ketubah*, lovingly framed by her non-Jewish father and hung in the family's Seattle home. In the event a photocopy was eventually accepted. Nevertheless, the procedure did impinge on her joy at the occasion: 'In getting married through the synagogue, when you have to prove all these things and get all the papers, it takes the joy out of it and Judaism becomes a burden rather than something to celebrate.'

For a young woman I spoke to, the wholly Jewish descendant of two old Anglo-Jewish families, the search for credentials to enter the north London orthodox marriage market was far more taxing. The fact that her parents were married at the West London Reform Synagogue, as were two previous generations of maternal ancestors, failed to help her case in the eyes of the orthodox authorities.

> What the *Beth Din* needed were birth certificates of both my parents and then all the way up my mother's female line. And then the marriage

> certificates of everybody going back as far as we could. I got all those going back quite far; it involved writing to Germany. My father's side was fine. My grandfather got married in Bevis Marks.

That was insufficient to satisfy the authorities of her Jewish lineage.

> What saved the investigation was the fact that we had an invitation to my great-great-grandmother's wedding. They had to prove by examining probate that everyone was related and to go through the historical records and get evidence from Germany that there was only one synagogue in that town at that time and it was orthodox.

This is by no means the only case where the *Beth Din* have invested so much time and effort.

If you have the audacity to remark that an investigation of this order seems excessive, the orthodox have their response ready: 'It's just like having to satisfy the membership conditions for a golf club!'

Which Claudia can Play Golf?

Claudia S and Claudia L are both students at London University. Both study French and both spent their third year in France. Both went to boarding schools where Christianity and church attendance were part of the curriculum. Both have one Jewish parent. Only one is entitled to join the club.

Claudia L never knew a Jewish mother gave her automatic membership: 'My mother feels she's Jewish but I don't think she'd consider her children that. The first time I realised Judaism goes through the mother was when a friend at college told me. I never considered myself Jewish, not at all.' Because of her experience of Christianity at school, she sees herself as 'more that side'. Like many children of mixed marriages, however, her religious identification is virtually nil.

Claudia S, in contrast, made a choice between being Jewish and being Christian.

> I chose Judaism because I really can't believe in Christ. But it's more that I feel Jewish. Judaism is a way of life as well as a religion and I was brought up in a Jewish environment with a Jewish sense of humour and a Jewish way of doing things. I feel very at ease with it. I never felt at ease with Christianity.

She is well aware that a Jewish father is no entry ticket. 'I know I want to marry a Jewish man and I will convert one day, so that I can have a Jewish wedding and Jewish children.' 'Most of the time my mother is more

Jewish than my father,' she adds. 'Judaism has just rubbed off on her so much.' But of course this does not make her Jewish under the *halacha.*

Claudia L is ready to let her membership slide while Claudia S is determined to join the club. A strange situation indeed. But then, as Dayan Berger once told me: 'Every club must have its own rules!'

5

The Struggle Towards

The majority of individuals of part-Jewish descent neither identify totally with their Jewish past nor totally reject or ignore it. Theirs is that vast grey area ranging from some vague, nagging awareness of a heritage they might like to explore, to a deeper yearning to embrace that heritage, often obstructed by ambivalence, inertia or fear, as well as constraints of *halacha*. Some of these lost Jews may be groping towards a degree of acceptance or knowledge; others may express a more ambitious desire to belong but lack the will or energy to see the process through. Still others may have experienced an equally strong desire to be Jewish but, fingers burnt or circumstances changed, have retreated to a less intense position. This state of flux, typical of lost Jews in the west, is captured by Francesca Kaye, an artist and potter from London: 'It's a huge thing and a tiny thing; it's something I don't think about but then I would think about; it's a very big part of me, it's sort of a little part of me as well. It's a combination, it varies, but I definitely feel that my identity is Jewish.'

Chess champion Garry Kasparov, the son of a Jewish father and an Armenian mother, is less ambivalent about his Jewishness. His robust approach is characteristic of part-Jews in the former Communist countries where Jewish self-expression had long been suppressed.

> I was brought up in Baku which had a very strong intellectual Jewish community. My father died when I was seven but I was influenced by my uncle, his brother, to whom I was very close. He was married to an Azeri woman so my cousins are mixed, we're all mixed, but I think they are much less Jewish because their father gave most to me. Through him I became part of a big Jewish extended family.
>
> From what I understand, the Six-Day War of 1967 opened up channels for Jewish self-expression inside the Soviet Union and made Jewish national consciousness stronger. I was 4 at the time, and in the mid-seventies the story of Israel, the whole situation in the Middle-East and the Jewish community in the world, played an important role in my education. As well as my father's relatives, I had many friends in Moscow who belonged to the Russian cultural scene and mostly they were Jewish.

Despite the fact that we were not related directly to anything concrete in Israel, many of us felt it was very important not to lose this last connection, which was the history, and that was why we studied it very carefully and became quite familiar with it. In the late seventies and early eighties things were pretty free and you could have many books. At that time I was building my own identity and my own relationship with the situation as a whole, and I felt if something is wrong I have to speak wildly which in fact I did. Personally I believe and I expressed it publicly that Israel was ostracised just because the Arabs represent the majority and I think there's a lot of hypocrisy involved. This obviously strengthens my support for the cause.

I'm split between my Jewish and Armenian sides. Being Armenian, it's also simple because Armenians have suffered the same, that's why when I feel something is going wrong there I always immediately give as much support as I can. Because of my background and my education I feel I belong to the nations that were oppressed and isolated. I was only once in Armenia and I've never been to Israel. I'm going there and I'm looking forward to it very much. I know quite a lot about it and I really want to see what I learnt from books.

Many officials I encountered in my chess career didn't hide the fact that my Jewish Armenian background, mainly Jewish, was not acceptable for them. It was not only the Jewish background but also the quite dissident view I had because I didn't want to obey the rules they gave me. Before I became world champion, I didn't do anything that could be considered directly against the regime but I was probably a social alien, not only nationally but also socially alien, and this combination created a very bad atmosphere in my relations with the *nomenklatura*.

I learned from childhood that if you want to achieve something you have to fight. It's probably a quality of many Soviets, especially Soviet Jews, that you can't get it automatically, you have to fight for everything and it's probably like a natural selection, only the strongest can survive in this environment. In chess it was also a good combination because it was chess, it was politics, it was life and in every place I had to fight.

I'm quite familiar with the background of all the main religions but I never had a special temptation to join something. For me the only ones possible are Judaism and Christianity. There are plenty of things I could adopt from Christianity but basically I don't feel comfortable within the official church system. As for Judaism, I think it was a very important step forward just to come from polytheism to monotheism. The invention of the invisible God was one of the most valuable contributions to human history. I'm not an atheist at all. I can hardly identify atheism with a strong moral code. People should be controlled by their conscience and this conscience should be related to something higher.

I have one small daughter. I believe that whatever I know and whatever I consider is the hard core of my education should be brought to my children. They have to understand what was my background and what I had to cross in life to accomplish what I eventually accomplished.

Kasparov's story echoes some of the themes that came up in conversations with the lost Jews of all ages who feature in this chapter. As there are more than 30 *dramatis personae* it may be clearer to introduce them in order of appearance. They will then be referred to by their first name:

Gabriel Solomon, young executive, London
Richard Cohen, publisher and editor, London
Laurent Ezekiel, student, London
Ben Cohen, broadcaster, Oxford
Miriam Scott, housing officer, Leeds
Donatella Bernstein, impressario/office designer, London
Penelope Abraham, PA and local councillor, London
Tanya Alfillé, art historian, London
Jessica Greenman, student, London
Julie Clare, actress, London
Esther Halpern*, London
Kajal Naidoo*, London
Monique M-L, UNESCO, Paris
Hannelore Kastly, London
Jana Smidova, journalist, Prague
Jacqui Burke, executive, Hertfordshire
Walter Mosley, crime writer, New York
Kim Kraft, Portland, Oregon
Ben Selwyn, student, London
Philip Epstein*, lecturer, London
Fritz Heegner, psychologist, Essen
John Witt, psychotherapist, London
Valérie L, musician, Paris
David Matthews, Alexander technique teacher, London
Linda Kalvachova, schoolgirl, Prague
Lucy Temperley, art editor, London
Terry Cloper, laboratary technician, Long Island
Carole C, student, Paris
Janet Schuman, dancer, New York

Anna Svobodova, schoolgirl, Prague
Laurence Spicer, religious broadcaster, London
Sandra Kristofova, journalist, Prague

ENTRY POINTS

A Jewish name, the sense of being an outsider, contact with Israel or the Holocaust; any of these factors may evoke an awareness of some Jewish connection among lost Jews. A 'helping hand' extended by a member of the family, some friend or even a stranger, may be an effective introduction to things Jewish or encourage those with a modicum of Jewish experience to pursue their quest further.

Burden or Privilege? – a Jewish Name

A well-known Jewish name may inspire pride or incite prejudice in equal measure. Gabriel endured 2 years of bullying at his north London comprehensive school.

> It was a terrible time. You have no outlet, no one to discuss this with. I guess it's an identity thing but when you're young it's very difficult to come to grips with, especially when you have mixed parents and what the hell, who's going to understand you?

Richard, brought up in the 'peculiar closeness of 1950s and 1960s Catholicism', recalls 'a lot of mental cruelty' at Downside, the well-known Catholic public school. Unlike Gabriel, he confided in his mother who asked if he wanted to take her maiden name. 'I said "No, I'm proud of being Cohen" '.

A schoolboy fencing champion, Richard's results were written up in the *Jewish Chronicle* and he was invited to fence in the Maccabiah games, the 'Jewish Olympics'. Because his mother was an Irish Catholic, he didn't take this up. On visits to New York he has enjoyed mixing in Jewish publishing circles. 'I've been hugely welcomed by them. I'm accepted as one of the fraternity. I say to them, "I was raised as a Catholic, I'd be a fraud." They say, "It doesn't matter. A Cohen is a Cohen." ' In America where he was visiting family, Gabriel was also confronted with his Jewishness. 'It was the first time someone made me realise "Your name's Jewish. You'll always be known as a Jew. Why don't you start thinking about becoming Jewish?" '

Laurent, who attended the French *lycée* in London, has received only positive reactions to his name. 'My friends all know it's Jewish, a Biblical name. I've had no antisemitism at all. On the contrary, people are interested, they want to know more. Maybe I don't know enough about my past history, my name.'

Ben C went to 'fairly ordinary schools' in the south-west of England. 'I was never picked on. I don't think anyone was bright enough to pick up the Jewish bit.' After growing up with transcendental meditation, he became a committed Christian and has been approached by Jews for Jesus. Wary of being packaged as 'Ben Cohen, a Jew who has found Jesus', he has also come across members of the movement keen to purvey Judaism to non-Jews with Jewish origins: 'There are those who see that the Jews can also be a light to the Christians and that it's me that's got to do the learning as well.'

Miriam, American born and brought up in London, was named for her paternal grandmother. This was an asset when her family was lodging with an orthodox Jewish family: 'All the festivals were celebrated in the most wonderful style. I hovered around the edge, the little pet of the family who felt able to include me because I had a Jewish name.' Later, the name in itself was not good enough. 'I felt so awkward having a Jewish name but no Jewish culture. I was going to school with Jewish children and went to my friends' houses and was aware of the Jewish holidays and some of what Jewish culture meant, but I had no part of it.' This was one reason she changed her name to Diana.

A Sense of Displacement

Donatella, who grew up in Italy, was about five when she became conscious 'that Jews were different': 'The neighbours didn't like Jews in general and they blocked our sewage. That wasn't the kind of action they would use against each other. That shocked me.' Her mother was an Italian Catholic and her father an American Jew. Like many of part-Jewish descent, she has often experienced a sense of displacement. 'The problem is if you are discriminated against as a Jew, what is a Jew and where do you fit in? We didn't fit in anywhere culturally or linguistically.'

Penelope only discovered her paternal grandfather was Jewish a short time before our first meeting. Years earlier, she had welcomed taking on the name of her half-Jewish husband. 'I think it was part of my feeling displaced from my own "English" family and my interest in "the other". I was clearly very pleased to take the name Abraham.' Tanya also feels 'on the edge of English society. Yet because I'm not "Jewish Jewish" I'm not totally involved in that. I suppose I don't quite know where my roots are.' Jessica inherits a sense of alienation from her father whom she saw as 'a Jew in exile, an estranged Jew'. Now she feels a sense of belonging when she's with Jews – 'It's some kind of automatic acceptance.'

Others feel less sanguine about being accepted in Jewish circles. Julie, whose adolescence and early adulthood were spent in a predominantly Jewish environment, was very conscious of being 'half in that group and half out'. Esther feels 'sort of stranded. I've always felt different, on the outside of things, which to me is part of being Jewish and part of not being accepted by either place. It's never feeling part of the dominant culture and never feeling you've got a place in a minority culture either.' Her plight is similar to that of many others: 'You're not Jewish but you are Jewish, at least Jewish enough for antisemitism.'

Kajal, the daughter of a German mother and an Indian father, had already suffered from 'not being accepted in the Asian community and not being accepted in the White community'. Developing a consciousness of her Jewish roots – her maternal grandfather was killed in the Holocaust – has made her identity even more complex. Significantly, she does not see 'the Indian connection and the Jewish connection' as 'necessarily in conflict'. Monique has never suffered outwardly from her mixed origins but they remain a problem she has not resolved. Raised as a Catholic, her childhood was marked by being forced by her mother not to say her father was Jewish and she felt unable to mention her own Jewish origins until many years later. It was her father who 'practised nothing but was Jewish in all the fibres of his body and mind' with whom she identified and she internalised his suffering at losing his family in the Holocaust and at having to suppress his Jewishness. Her mother, who hid him during World War II, was so terrified of his being exposed as Jewish that she virtually 'castrated' any expression of his Jewish identity.

Hannelore's father, the *mischling* son of a German Jewish father and a gentile mother, was executed in Austria during World War II. 'His only crime was *rassenschande* – to have Jewish blood and to be involved with an Aryan woman.' Hannelore's life has been stamped by her mixed origins: 'It's not easy to be mixed because you feel you don't belong 100 per cent to one side and definitely not 100 per cent to the Aryan side. I'm very much stronger inclined to the Jewish side, but I couldn't totally agree on everything that is Jewish.'

In Memory of my Father

Haunted by the death of the sensitive young father she had never known, Hannelore has an overwhelming yearning to find his resting place and the roots he sprang from.

> I just love my father more than anything . . . I want to find his grave even if it is a mass grave, I still would want to go to the spot . . . I feel he's with me in my heart. It's like a pilgrimage. I want to find that spot and to know what family he came from . . . If I knew finally where his ancestors came from, if I found the spot where he was buried, I feel at least his soul can be at peace.

A deep identification with a Jewish father who may have died prematurely was shared by other women I spoke to. Jessica acknowledges how bound up her Jewish feelings are with her father and likens his death to his Jewishness. 'When he died it was such a symbolically Jewish thing to do – to die, to go, to be wiped out.' Although Monique's father died an old man, it took her 6 months to recover from the shock. 'I had lost something very important, in effect my roots. With my father gone there was nothing left, nothing of this Jewish side.' Jana lost her father, a prominent figure in the Czech media, when he was 45. Not only has she followed his profession but his left-wing politics and his non-orthodox Jewish stance. Jacqui woke up one morning to find that her father had died of a heart attack, aged 51. By researching his family background she is drawn closer to him.

Donatella speaks of her father's 'Christ-like' qualities.

> My father looked exactly like Jesus Christ and he died at 33 and ever since he's been a sort of Christ figure in our family. He was a kind of scapegoat. He was an interesting person, very intellectual, he painted and he wrote. By the time I could have had something in common with him, he wasn't there. He was sick for a long time. Every illness came his way. He had polio, he had epilepsy, he had cancer. He was a sufferer.

Oppressed Structures

Walter, the son of a Black father and Jewish mother, is very relaxed about his dual identity: 'Politically, America being a very political place, I'm Black, because that's the roots; culturally I'm more aware of the Black side because I spent more time in that world but I think I'm very influenced by my mother and the way people think on her side also.' He attributes this balance more to personal circumstances than to the history of oppression he has inherited from both sides.

> Everybody in my family, regardless of whether or not they had racist feelings, believed you could accept family and because of that I got along with everybody and I felt I belonged. Even relatives who originally didn't like my mother, for instance, that didn't mean they didn't come over and bring a chicken . . .

Similarly his Jewish grandfather's early prejudice gave way to admiration for his son-in-law's practical skills.

> There's much more of a tendency and a possibility for exception between Blacks and Jews because racism isn't built the same way and identity isn't built the same way. Even though the whole structure, the psyches of Jews and Black Americans are very different, they're both oppressed structures.

For this reason, he believes that Jews delude themselves if they see themselves as 'White Christians' even if 'once in a while they're accepted because everyone gets confused and says "They look White".'

Part-Jews, too, may be identified by the majority group as 'non-White'. Walter points out that this happened in Nazi Germany and Francesca got a taste of it at her English boarding school: 'There was a bit of antisemitism. It lay dormant so I just didn't know. I could see that the one Black girl in my class and I were quite similar and singled out.'

Equally, a tendency to feel an affinity with those outside the White Christian camp is common to some lost Jews. Chicago-born Kim with a White, gentile father and a Jewish mother from India grew up in 'a very integrated neighbourhood with a lot of Jews and a lot of Black Americans'. Her early identity was not necessarily Jewish

> but it was definitely not WASP because I grew up in the sixties and 'White' was very unpopular. My question is: how much do I feel Jewish because I grew up round so many Jews and Black people – or did it come from some sense of being Jewish organically? I wonder because the two main groups I'm comfortable with, I feel family with, are Jews and Black Americans.

A variation of this Black–White polarisation can be found in the well-publicised case of Jon Bradley, the natural son of an English Catholic mother and a Kuwaiti Arab father who was adopted by an Ashkenazi couple in Liverpool and brought up as a Jew. Treated as an Arab by Israelis, Bradley felt impelled to seek out his real roots. It is not with the

White Christian mother that he has identified but with the more alien or exotic Arab father.

The Israel Connection

Ben S, with an Israeli mother and English father, had 'no conception of religious or any identity' in his early childhood. 'We had a Christmas tree, we had *Hanukah*, just a lot of festivals but they didn't actually mean anything. I went to Israel when I was ten and after coming back from Israel I felt Jewish only as a means of staying linked to Israel.' Israel also exerted an early influence on Philip, who had a predominantly Catholic upbringing. As a teenager he was involved in a Socialist–Zionist organisation and visited Israel several times. His Zionist identity was particularly strong after he left his Catholic public school and he was thinking at the time of emigrating to Israel.

Many lost Jews who visit Israel later in life experience a special emotional pull. Hannelore 'just loved it so much. I felt so good, I felt so moved. I felt "This is my home, I belong very strongly." ' Jana was also bowled over: 'I was amazed. I liked it very much. I feel it's my country on the cultural level. The people are living fully. They are so strong and so vital.' For Monique, who has travelled a lot, 'Jerusalem was one of the strongest emotional experiences in my life. It's the city where I have felt the greatest emotion.' Fritz, who survived as a *mischling* in Nazi Germany, sees Israel as 'a place where I finally would belong, and a cause, a thing I can be of assistance to. It is the home of the Jews.' He is contemplating living in Israel and accepts that he is not objective on this subject. 'I'm absolutely biased, I have lots of prejudice when there are conversations about Israel. I'm absolutely willing to misinterpret things.'

Israel can also be a source of considerable ambivalence. John, who spent his childhood in Italy, feels very torn emotionally. 'Part of me feels very committed and I'd hate to see Israel disappear. There was a point when I felt very identified with Israel and felt I wanted to contribute to the state.' He has never been to Israel. 'I'm sure at some point I'll go but I've got a feeling of sadness, partly because I don't really know whether Israel will last. I have a fear of getting overconnected or liking the place too much in case I get too affected and want to go and live there.' His ambivalence is shared by Valérie who is afraid of 'throwing herself into' Judaism. 'I'm afraid that this might lead me to want to go to Israel, for example. Then, perhaps unconsciously, I take a step backwards each time I take a step forwards.' David is equally hesitant about getting too involved. 'I have a kind of fear that if I got into it at all, I'd get into it fairly thoroughly, to the extent of stopping doing all the things I'm doing and moving to Israel.'

The Holocaust Effect

Hannelore's life has been seared by her father's fate from the day she was born. Fritz is constantly 'reading and studying and looking into' the period that scarred his childhood: 'It blows my top when I read and hear again about Auschwitz and other camps. I don't know what to do. I'm torn between tears and scorn and rage.' But personal experience of the Nazi period is not necessary for the Holocaust to contribute to the Jewish consciousness of lost Jews, particularly when they are descended from families of Holocaust victims.

Linda attributes her interest in exploring her Jewish heritage to her family's tragic history: 'I spoke a lot with my grandmother and my father about the history of World War II because my grandmother had ten brothers and sisters and only three survived. I started to think about it more and then I decided I would like to study Hebrew and know more.' Jana is also affected by the fact that her father's whole family perished in the Holocaust. Her grandmother was saved when her 'Christian step-grandfather' married her, at a time when many Czechs were divorcing their Jewish spouses. Julie feels that she has 'always known, absolutely always known that one set of my grandparents died in Auschwitz, I can't remember a time when I didn't know that'. John's attitude to the Holocaust colours his ambivalence towards his Jewish identity. 'On the one level I identify with the concentration camps, the death camps, I've read up a lot about them, part of my family have disappeared in there – but I also have that fear that if antisemitism comes up again, part of me wants to put my head under.' More strongly, Kajal speaks of her mother as having 'blocked off what had happened to her father'.

The Holocaust can have a strong impact on Jewish identification without any family connection, as Francesca explains:

> The reason I go to synagogue is out of respect to the victims of the Holocaust. It's obviously mostly because I feel there for the grace of God, if I'd been born forty, fifty years earlier, I might have been in it. That is why if someone asked me what religion I was I'd say 'Jewish'. I feel I need to be a survivor.

Her Jewish identification has also been intensified by reading Primo Levi's books.

Esther was hit when she was flying over Germany on the way to Prague. 'For the first time I felt quite in touch with the Holocaust as something that could have affected me. It was the first time I could see the reality of what had happened.' Lucy, who had one Jewish great-grandparent, grew up in an academic community in Urbana, Illinois, where Jewishness was seen as something very positive. A visit to the Terezin concentration camp in Bohemia with her Jewish husband and his mother added a different dimension:

> It was one of the most horrible days of my life but I was really glad we did it. Of course it was not the most atrocious of the camps but it was a huge shock to me. It really opened my eyes and made me take the whole thing much more seriously.

A Helping Hand

While Lucy had always looked on her Jewish roots as something to be proud of, her awareness of a Jewish connection was reinforced when she met her husband. Family members can help to introduce lost Jews to a sense of Jewishness, as Linda indicated. Jessica and Francesca have been encouraged by their father's families; Esther has a great-aunt who is supportive of her interest in things Jewish and has found an alternative synagogue congregation where she can learn more. David has experienced a taste of orthodox Jewish practice through his sister and her husband.

Terry grew up in 'a very non-Jewish environment' in Denver, Colorado and put up with taunts like 'Jew boy, your father's not going to heaven'. Not long before I spoke to him he had gone with his father to Boston to visit old Jewish relatives. For Terry, aged 37, it was a rather late introduction to the Jewish world his father was raised in. Carole grew up in the bosom of a large Sephardi Jewish family where all the brothers and sisters had married Catholics. The unifying force came from her grandmother: 'The Jewish religion was our grandmother. She was our god, the god after God for us. She lived all the time for her children, so that they stayed together. She gave the family the Jewish imprint.' Tanya also got a taste of Jewishness from a Sephardi grandmother who lived in Paris. Jacqui, whose mother was very ill from her early childhood, was raised by her grandmother, 'very much a practising Jew'. 'From the age of 2 or 3 I spent most of my time with my grandma. She was wonderful. She was grandma.'

A variety of other factors can encourage Jewish awareness. Kim, from a large Sephardi Jewish family on her mother's side, has an early memory of 'feeling more connected watching my grandfather do Friday night prayers' on a visit to England when she was seven. But it was exploring *kabbala* with an older, non-Jewish girlfriend when she was thirteen, that really made her 'go towards Judaism'. Transcendental meditatio years later provided an equally unconventional stimulus. 'I started al feel Jewish when I started meditating. Maharishi is always encouragi people to go to their own religions.' In contrast, she found her Jewish grandmother strangely reticent about her Jewishness. Similarly, Gabriel felt his father and grandfather 'were trying to tell someone else to tell me what the hell to do' and it was left to his relative in America.

> I went to synagogue with him, I went to Sunday chants, people singing very nicely. We shared bagels and lax. He made it fun and enjoyable which it was. It was nothing terribly profound but it gave me a very open, nice introduction to American Jewry. I loved it, I cried, I didn't want to leave.

Julie chose to go to Christian prayers when she first went to her north London school but changed to Jewish prayers about 4 years later. In the meantime, her father had started working on *Last Waltz in Vienna*, the history of his family. 'It must have influenced me without my realising it. I remember being 13 and reading the book.' It was the beginning of a period of intense Jewish identification. John was encouraged to explore his three-quarters Jewish heritage by his non-Jewish second wife. The start of his 'journey of discovery' coincided with the birth of his son. He has also made Jewish friends in a men's group who are helping him in his search.

Janet, whose paternal grandfather was Jewish, found the level of Jewishness of previous Jewish boyfriends superficial. Friday night dinners with the English-born mother of her long-term current boyfriend were very different:

> Diana would have all sorts of people there and it was obviously very important to her and she would lead everybody. She had such passion for the material and such a desire to share with everyone and let anyone be part of the process that it was very inviting for me and very interesting. That was really the first time I said, 'Maybe there's something more here.'

Miriam was helped to go back to her Jewish heritage in an hour of need by Asphodel Long, the Jewish feminist thinker, who was a friend of her widowed father.

Penelope's affinity with Jews and things Jewish was encouraged and supported by her employer, a prominent Jewish philanthropist.

> He's quite nurturing of my interest and has fed it really. He's invited me to come to various synagogues. He didn't put pressure on me, he

> opened the door and I could walk in if I wanted to. It's interesting that I fetched up with a surrogate Jewish father not knowing I had my own Jewish grandfather tucked away.

For Kajal, 'Judaism came about quite strongly' through meeting a *chassidic* Jew with whom she has become friendly and who is the donor of her second child. Her young son has also been greatly influenced by this man and now goes around in a *kipah*. Ben C's awareness of his Jewish roots and their relation to his Christian beliefs has been heightened by encounters with two people he interviewed for his radio programme. One, a Christian woman, prominent in the field of Christian–Jewish relations, gave him a *siddur* and the other was Geza Vermes, author of *Jesus the Jew*.

TAKING IT FURTHER

Religion, culture, history, ethnicity are areas of Jewishness that lost Jews may relate to or identify with. Many people I spoke to were either in the process of exploring some facet of their heritage or were interested in doing so in the future. Others had gone through a phase when they had been eager to find out more but had let the momentum lapse.

The Many Faces of Judaism

Lost Jews who have not been brought up in the Jewish religion sometimes find aspects of Judaism that attract them that 'run of the mill' Jews may ignore. To Ben C, Judaism offers a more down-to-earth faith with a greater focus on human life:

> One of the things in Judaism that maybe is missing from some of Christianity is more of a sense of being a living, breathing person in a human body and that I like, that appeals to me. I think I'm looking for a kind of faith which more and more connects with what I am as a human being so I don't have a separate 'spiritual side'. I have a feeling that at its roots, Judaism has less of this sense of a split.

Janet has a similar impression. 'In Judaism there doesn't seem to be the disconnection between the spiritual and the intellectual. There's something spiritual in a sense of some sort of history and belonging to the earth and to a people before.' The intellectual challenge of a reconstructionist synagogue service she was taken to also appealed to her: 'In other religions you sit and you're told. Here you were talking about things, there was a conversation, a dialogue.'

Ben C believes that Judaism offers a sense of celebration that can challenge New Age teachings: 'I get a sense that there is something in Judaism saying "Hey, let's celebrate that we're human beings and that we're physical beings and let's celebrate that God made the seasons, the stars in the sky."' This vital, life-affirming quality of Judaism also impressed Penelope on her first visit to synagogue.

Some lost Jews look to Judaism as a repository for their strong spiritual beliefs, as Carole explains:

> Why I'm Jewish I think is only because I believe in God. Religion is only a way to keep God. For me I don't care to go to pray in synagogue or church, for me I have only to feel God's presence and I think sometimes when you are in the country you can feel God so I pray in the country – it's a mystical sort of thing.

She admits that she has drifted away from Judaism since her teenage years: 'I wanted to keep more the Jewish religion and speak Hebrew and speak Yiddish to be Jewish, really Jewish. Now I don't care because it is only on my own that I believe in God.' Kim would agree that 'the important thing is to know God in yourself' but relates more strongly to the cultural and ethnic aspects of being Jewish.

For Linda and her friend Anna, the Altneu synagogue in Prague's Jewish quarter, steeped in centuries of history, is closely linked to their search for spirituality. Even passing by the synagogue can induce a meditative state of mind, as Anna, who only learnt of her matrilineal Jewish roots a few years ago, explains:

> I like to go to the synagogue every time I have time. I sometimes can feel something spiritual. Every time I can feel something or I'm trying to feel something but sometimes it's more strong. I think more when I'm there alone or if I pass the synagogue and I start to think about these things myself, I talk to myself.

Other lost Jews are attracted by Judaism's practical approach. To Terry, Jewish beliefs seem 'much more practical and logical', an impression gained from a visit to synagogue with his father.

> The way the prayers were flowing seemed very nice. The English translation in the prayer book was very good. It was like good common sense. It didn't seem they were preaching about a higher being, more about how to live and get on in a community. The words I

was reading in translation were more like the advice a father might give his son.

John feels much the same: 'All I know about Judaism as an ethos, a religion, is that it's really an ethic and there is belief but a lot of it is quite pragmatic.' He has been touched by his early experiences of Jewish practice: 'Some of the ceremonies that I've done together with my friend I've found really moving and a couple of times that I've been to synagogue I found that was really effective.'

Lucy also greatly enjoyed her first visit to synagogue:

> The sort of spirit and atmosphere was so much more relaxed and also more devout than any Christian church I've ever been to. You didn't have to act holy or like you were having an experience. You joined in the service but if you wanted to stop and say 'Hi' to somebody or talk to a little kid, you did. It made it seem much more part of things.

She is also attracted by what she perceives as a 'practice first, faith comes later' approach.

> As I understand it you can be a good Jew without having to prove your faith to anybody. Following the rules you are supposed to follow is very important and doing right is very important but you don't necessarily have to have an epiphany the way my friends who are Christian talk about it. That appeals to me because I do have a vague religious sense but if I want to develop it it's going to take a good long time. I think that has to go on inside me, not be dictated by what somebody else tells me my faith ought to feel.

Miriam, who lost her three month old daughter through a cot death, found great comfort in some Jewish prayers:

> I read the *kaddish* for her. I knew it was a kind of heretical thing to do but it seemed right. It was just a way of signalling the dreadful upside-downness of everything. First of all I was a woman, secondly it's the prayer the son says for the parent and I was a mother saying it for her daughter. Also there is a beautiful Jewish prayer for parents who have lost a child and I can remember saying this prayer in the days and weeks that followed over and over again. It was the only thing that got me out of bed in the morning.

Some lost Jews oppose organised religions but enjoy Jewish rituals or ceremonies on a cultural level. Julie is one: 'The cultural aspect of the religious side appealed to me, the cultural aspect of Passover, *Yom Kippur,* fasting, going to synagogue – all of that appealed to me.' Jessica is drawn by 'the real sense of occasion' at Jewish festivals she has participated in. 'The Jewish thing for me is partly family, you're not necessarily blood related to these people but you break bread with them, you pass things round and you're all organised. There's a real feeling of togetherness without it being a mess.' Francesca relates to Judaism with the perspective of an artist: 'What I feel about the religion, it's something in my past, it's cultural, it's atmospheric. I like the feeling of something medieval, primeval. There's more of a mystery about it, the fact that you can't portray the divinity; it's got to be played down, dark colours and deep reds – that's what appeals to me.' Surprisingly, the *kabbala* and its mysteries not only fascinated Kim, who has strong spiritual beliefs, but appear to appeal to several lost Jews of a secular bent.

An Alien Rite?

Lost Jews may feel distinctly 'lost' when confronted with a Hebrew service and unfamiliar rituals. Fritz is 'lacking in the formation and the knowledge. I do not know the traditions and festivals.' Donatella doesn't go to synagogue 'because I don't know enough about the traditions and I feel out of place'. Unlike participation in a Catholic service where, 'even though I feel hypocritical, I can make the sign of the cross just to please them', she feels that Judaism is not something that can be dabbled in but has to be taken up seriously.

In contrast, Laurence can enjoy a ceremony he is unfamiliar with in a broader religious sense.

> I'm very happy to go to synagogue. I don't understand Hebrew which makes it more difficult but I don't honestly think there's any place of worship where one can't pray and prayer is surely the thing that matters. I go to these places because I like the people. I've got a great friend who is a cantor. I could sit and listen to him singing for a very long time and it would mean an enormous amount to me.

Esther sums up an experience common to many lost Jews: 'I don't understand Hebrew so it feels quite hard to be connected to a lot of what happens.' Similarly, Gabriel was unable to relate to the Friday night ritual at his grandparents. 'The prayers were said in Hebrew. I, being useless, couldn't understand the significance. To me it was just mumbo-jumbo, it didn't have any real sense.' Jessica finds 'things like services' difficult. 'I don't like very formal Jewish things. I don't understand any of that or the language. I'm considerably alienated from that.' Laurent also expressed a strong sense of alienation: 'At a bar mitzvah I felt very out of place because everyone there was Jewish and I couldn't get into it. There was that religious side about it, the rituals, and I just didn't like that, it sort of scared me a bit.' He was also 'sort of scared' by a Passover *seder* at his grandparents: 'It was very strange, maybe because it was new to me. No-one explained anything and I was expected to join in and I didn't really want to.' Richard, in contrast, had a more measured response to the two occasions he has been 'at a Hebrew service': 'They were not alien, just new.'

Something to Learn

Richard sees the task of writing the history of his family as an opportunity to explore further. 'I feel that picking up on my Jewish inheritance is an option I may be able to realise in the near future. I think that understanding a bit more of Judaism is something I will want to do.' Donatella has asked a Jewish friend to instruct her 'in basics like what children learn when they're growing up. After that I would probably feel all right about going to synagogue.' Esther is in the process of learning more about Judaism. She wants it to be a 'gradual process'.

Jacqui is 'trying to piece together' the 'headful of partly muddled stories about the family' which she heard from her grandmother, 'a great one for telling stories of days gone by'. She has joined the Jewish Genealogical Society to investigate her father's background but is reluctant to approach his relatives, an obvious source of information, as all contact ceased because of his second marriage to a Roman Catholic. A few days after we met she wrote to say she was plucking up the courage to make contact.

A visit to America where she investigated 'the very interesting history' of her Jewish family and discovered that her grandmother Miriam had been a successful child therapist and writer led Miriam to take back her name. 'Now I've found out what a splendid person my grandmother was, I feel she can be a little inspiration to me as herself.'

Laurent is also motivated by his name. 'My name's got quite a big history to it and I've always thought one day I should find out and retrace the movements of my family.' He is also thinking of reading the Bible, for cultural rather than religious reasons, and would like to visit Israel 'for cultural exploration'. Significantly, he would like to explore on his own. Similarly, Terry, who is aware his Jewish education 'is so limited', would not want 'anything organised like Hebrew school'. In contrast, Janet who likens her 'genuine interest' in Judaism to her 'genuine interest in dance', is grateful that she has been shown something she can value: 'In Judaism you have a heritage, you have an understanding and connection and that's what life is really about.'

Linda and Anna have made the exploration of their Jewish heritage part of their life style. They attend regular classes in basic Judaism, go to synagogue when they can and participate in young leadership camps with other central European young people of Jewish and part-Jewish descent. John, who sees his journey as 'a process of years rather than months', has also taken a practical step towards identication.

> I've stopped working Friday nights so we have a family meal together and we have a little ceremony we make up ourselves. We light candles, we have the table laid out, we break bread, we pass not wine but some kind of juice together and we reflect on the week. There's a sense of spirituality, of connecting to having a moment of stillness in the week, and we have really quite a feast – not at all kosher in any way – but having the family together feels really precious to us.

John likens the process to 'building up an appetite, getting a bit curious and seeing what happens. I don't know at what point do I say that I'm "in", at what point do I stop my identification, how much will it influence my life and my attitudes – these are questions I don't have answers to.'

Make Me Jewish

From quite a young age, Gabriel observed Yom Kippur with his father. 'I would fast, reflect. It wasn't so much a ritualistic religious thing, it was a time you reflect on your own being, you bring your own judgement on yourself.' He feels it's important 'to be able to talk to someone on a non-commital level, to be able to go to synagogue and talk to the rabbi who's obviously an expert in various fields without being looked down on'. But, he acknowledges, 'ultimately the responsibility must lie with me. If I had the initiative I would go out and say "Make me Jewish". I understand a certain sort of introduction and level of understanding I don't have would be necessary.'

It is not uncommon for lost Jews who are not *halachically* Jewish to toy with the idea of conversion. Jessica had seriously thought about it while her father was alive. 'I asked my grandmother, "What do I do about becoming Jewish? I don't want to do it yet but I'm sure that's where I ought to be." ' Esther has also considered it. 'I was thinking about converting and part of me thought, "Why should I do this, why do I have to do this in order to try to make myself feel accepted?" And there's part of me that thinks that even if I went through a conversion I'd never be fully accepted.' Julie had often thought of converting to reform Judaism, attracted by the strong sense of community and, on a more practical level, to assure the Jewish status of her children. The idea of children has also made Lucy think seriously about converting.

Penelope talked to her employer's wife, herself a convert, the first time she went to synagogue.

> It was very significant and I was very moved by it. She said, 'If you're thinking of converting, I'm the one to talk to.' Some Saturdays later we talked about her experience of converting. We agreed that we had both experienced this feeling of being a bit displaced. At one point I may go and talk to one of the rabbis. There's no kind of pressure to make a move till I feel ready to.

Linda also feels she has time. With three Jewish grandparents but not the vital maternal Jewish grandmother, conversion is something she has to consider. 'I think the conversion is like the last point you can do. I'm thinking about it and I want first to live this life and I'm trying to know more and then I will see.'

SWINGS AND ROUNDABOUTS

Whether people of part-Jewish descent strengthen their Jewish identification or let it slide is often the result of various internal conflicts and pressures as well as external obstacles or encouragement.

Important Enough to Overcome Exclusion?

'I pay lip service to the benefits of Judaism but I do actually nothing. For me to actually get off my arse and do something about becoming Jewish would take – I don't know how to put that, it's something I have trouble understanding within myself.' Gabriel's painfully honest acknowledgement of the ambivalence and inertia which stand in the way of fuller Jewish commitment is characteristic of many lost Jews. Julie is equally honest:

> I used to go to Passover at my friend's house. I loved it. I hated not being able to read the Hebrew but I never actually got down to learning it or asking for lessons. If I really wanted to be Jewish and accepted as part of the Jewish community, I could damn well go and convert to Reform Judaism.

However, because she has no religious belief, she would feel 'fraudulent, a pseudo-Jew'.

Jessica, too, finds her opposition to religion in general an obstacle to converting: 'I consider myself quite fortunate to be irreligious but I still feel I have a Jewish identity. But as I'll never go to the religion, that's why I think I'll never become Jewish.' Esther has similar feelings: 'Even with a conversion I'd still feel like it's forging. It's not going to make me any more anything.'

Jessica's ambivalence is heightened by her identification with her father's sense of alienation: 'In a way being Jewish I'm prevented from being Jewish as well. My Jewish identity has been handed down to me as an alienated Jew.' She is leaving the door open: 'I can see if you really want to become part of the Jewish community, there are things that you're going to have to take on. Maybe it would become more familiar to you.'

Unlike most children of Jewish fathers who grew up in Britain, Francesca was unaware that she was technically not Jewish until a short time before we spoke, possibly because she had lost her mother when she was very young. 'I was so surprised when I heard it, I felt a bit pissed off. I certainly wouldn't start taking exams, I'd never do that. I think actually that if I was pushed that way, I'd feel my Church of England side coming out.'

Most lost Jews who are not *halachically* Jewish are more resigned to their legal exclusion. Gabriel is quite pragmatic: 'I can't be put off by it because that's the way it is: my mother's not Jewish. I feel like I have to feel – I'm not a bona fide Jew.' Jana sees it as 'crazy and old fashioned', while Julie feels 'pretty damn unlucky really'. On the one hand, she can appreciate it from a feminist perspective: 'In some ways I damn well love it that for once the line goes through the woman instead of the man.' Nevertheless, she feels frustrated. 'You do end up thinking it's ridiculous. I want something that so many people have and don't value whereas I at one stage in my life and even now to some extent value it.' Esther is also aware of the irony: 'Maybe that's something that makes you want to have it because of the struggle there.'

Kajal admits to having felt 'almost like an impostor because my mother wasn't Jewish, because my maternal grandmother wasn't Jewish, therefore how could I be?' Suddenly things Jewish seem to be coming at her from all sides. As well as the strong Jewish input from her friend, the *chassid*, which her young son is busily taking in, her mother has started talking about her own father and her Jewish roots. 'So, yes, I'm identifying far more as Jewish and it gets to feel less uncomfortable.' Nevertheless, she is concerned about her son: 'I don't want to see him being hurt or rejected, nor do I want to give him the false impression that because he has a Jewish maternal great-grandfather he can be accepted by everyone because that isn't going to be the case.'

For John who, like Linda, has three Jewish grandparents, the lack of the vital quarter is the key to his ambivalence. 'If my grandmother – my mother's mother – was Jewish, I'd have no problem in identifying, but because she isn't and therefore according to the law as I understand it I'm not, in a sort of way I feel that rejection. It's a sense of being like a chameleon. If I'd just had that quarter, I'd have been "in".' He is unsure of the outcome of his exploration: 'At this point in my life I really don't know which way I'm going to jump. Part of me, I suppose, wants to get away from my history but I can't.'

We're Struggling Too

Lost Jews with the right lineage can identify as culturally Jewish and ignore the religion, something many who lack their credentials may envy. Sandra, a colleague of Jana on the Prague daily *Lidove Noviny*, told me she had felt Jewish from the day she was born. It was an identification her non-Jewish father had encouraged. But hers is a purely cultural identity. More remarkable is the fact that her daughter, who has just one Jewish grandparent, the maternal grandmother, 'feels 100 per cent Jewish'. Again she identifies with Jewish history and Jewish culture. Religion does not enter the picture.

Not all lost Jews with Jewish mothers are satisfied with being legally accepted as Jewish. Both David and Valérie are torn between a deep, underlying longing to embrace Judaism and an equally strong fear of doing so. This is something David experiences on his visits to Israel:

> When I've gone to Israel and my brother-in-law has done these prayer things with me there has felt such a strong connection and sense of familiarity and belonging, that there's almost a fear, it felt physically like a fear, of feeling very attracted to it.

He was first struck by this uncanny familiarity when he witnessed his brother-in-law putting on phylacteries in the very English setting of the family home in Cambridge:

> As soon as he actually put the strapping round his arm, the shawl over his head and was reading this thing I just thought 'This is me'. You have a sense, almost like genetically, of 'I know this stuff, I've done this stuff. This belongs to me in a very "in my bones" kind of way.'

But paralysed by ambivalence and inertia, he is still pursuing 'a completely secular life with no overt spiritual aspect', something he admits to with a certain sadness: 'When I hear myself say it it does sound like something missing and I have a sense that that's a side of me that's neglected.'

Valérie's practical experience of Judaism is more limited.

> I have an ideal, I dream of a Judaism a bit like in the early days of Israel, something very open. It's so strong this notion of Judaism inside me. I'm very interested in Jewish education and finding out more but it's difficult. Maybe I've got a problem inside me, maybe I create my problem because of my ambivalence and it's a big problem in my life.

While David has the strong encouragement of his sister and brother-in-law and has not experienced any rejection from Jews, Valérie's ideal of Judaism is linked to a search for warmth and a welcome, something she has not found in the Jewish community in Paris.

> I think I'm Jewish but even if I try to integrate in the community it's impossible. At the beginning they say, 'Yes, I don't care, you're Jewish because your mother is Jewish', but afterwards, when things get a bit more serious, they always tell me, 'You're fifty-fifty. You're not *cachére*.' It's not something they do openly.

Similar experiences have deterred Carole from her earlier Jewish commitment:

> As we are just fifty-fifty, we've got to do more than the others, to affirm more. It's because of that that I know I'll never be completely Jewish. I really don't want to do *more* than the others to be considered the same as the others.

Kim has also felt excluded in America:

> I had two friends who were Ashkenazi Jews and because both their parents were Jewish they would laugh and have certain Yiddish-type jokes and exclude me even though I got all those Yiddish jokes just as much as anyone who grew up on the same block would.

She recalls the mother of one friend rejecting her because she 'wasn't Jewish enough', an irony seeing that neither friend married a Jew, whereas she herself married a Jewish man in a synagogue.

This feeling of being 'second best' can also persist in a subtle way within the extended family. Kim sensed this:

> I always feel my mother and her sisters are kind of ousted in a lot of ways. I have strong feelings about how they're treated because three of them married non-Jews. Although there's so much love in the family,

> this unconditional love, there is this Jewish thing that I didn't realise was as much of a wedge as it could be.

Laurence, whose mother and grandmother were Jewish but had both converted to Christianity, also felt a slight distinction when visiting his Jewish relatives:

> Not surprisingly one was separate. One wasn't included in *Shabbat* or anything like that. There were lovely meals, jokes etcetera but I wasn't really a full partner from their standpoint. I didn't really question it. I only thought about it a long time afterwards when I realised they liked me and we enjoyed each other's company but I was at an arm's distance because I was not brought up in the faith.

You're not Jewish

The rejection experienced by lost Jews of patrilineal descent, particularly in Britain, can range from the odd pinprick to a sustained battering which is extremely painful. Esther, for example, has held back from activities that interested her or has kept her mixed origins under wraps. 'The reaction I've had all my life is "You're not Jewish, are you." Then you don't want to keep going and coming out rejected.' Her discomfort is exacerbated by the reaction of non-Jewish colleagues, with whom she identifies as Jewish: 'I still have the question, "So who's Jewish? So your mother's Jewish?" It's like an assumption, it's almost like that's the only piece of information they've got about Jews.'

Jacqui was quite unprepared for the reaction of the attendant at a Jewish museum she was visiting as part of her research into her Jewish roots:

> I explained what I was doing and why I was interested and she asked me my background and I explained that my father married out of the Jewish faith and she said, 'That's terrible, that's terrible, that's dreadful. That's how the Jews lose their people.' I came out thinking 'Is this the sort of reaction I'm going to get?' For the first time in my life it made me ashamed to be Jewish.

Penelope was hoping her name might give her an entrée within the Jewish community she was dealing with in her job. Instead she kept hearing that her late husband was not really Jewish. 'I think I had unreasonable expectations that because my name was "Abraham" I'd be accepted as part of the community. Of course I'm not, not at all, in fact I'm considered entirely non-Jewish which was a bit difficult for a few months.' Miriam received a similar reaction when speaking about her discovery of her Jewish roots. 'In Leeds there are so many very conventional people, they make no bones about pointing out, "Of course, that's all very nice, dear, but that doesn't make you Jewish." '

In his late teens Philip was 'a bit hung up about not being fully Jewish'. This concern may have been unnecessary in the open secular Zionist ambience he was mixing in. At Cambridge the identity of the Jews he came into contact with seemed much more 'parochial' and from then onwards the definition of who counts as a Jew has persistently been brought up in his presence. As he admits, 'It does grate.'

Julie has not had to deal with any overt reference to her not being Jewish but the 'Jewish card' has been used against her in a far more destructive way. She once found herself in a rivalrous situation with a Jewish friend who constantly tried to undermine her by implying she was not Jewish. At the time, Julie was seriously thinking of converting. 'This woman didn't put me off but there was a kind of patronising air about the whole thing. "Well, you can convert, but you'll never be really Jewish." ' It was not just this episode:

> The experience I had was an implicit one and in some senses that can be far stronger than an isolated event that you can deal with. When it's actually insidious and subliminal and there is a feeling from every Jew you meet within a particular community that you somehow don't belong, I think that can actually do far more damage.

Within the small Prague Jewish community, Jana can assert her identity in a far more robust manner: 'I feel myself as a Jew, of course, without any problem, but I don't want to be orthodox.' She collaborates with the community 'very closely on a cultural and civic level' and is aware of her value as a journalist writing on problems which affect Czech Jewry. 'I think I'm more useful for this for the Jewish community than if I go to synagogue.'

You're Still One of Us

The majority of lost Jews who are struggling towards some connection to their Jewish heritage respond very positively to encouragement or welcome from Jews. For some, with even a limited sense of Jewish identification, the need or desire to be accepted on some level is particularly strong.

Miriam's recollection of an episode in her schooldays illustrates how deep this need may be:

> I remember a relative of a friend saying, 'She's so blonde, no one would think she was Jewish' and my friend saying, 'Actually, she's not' and how uncomfortable this made me feel. I knew I wasn't but I knew there was some part of me that was. I'd have felt much better if she'd included me and said something like 'She has a Jewish grandmother.'

She has been gratified at the response to her return to being 'Miriam'. 'A number of Jewish feminists in the housing world I work in warmed to me intensely because they thought quite clearly that I must be someone who was acknowledging my Jewish roots. They were very welcoming indeed.' She is also involved with two homes run by the Leeds Jewish Welfare Board for people with learning disabilities: 'It gives me great pleasure to be part of this set-up and to go to meals and take part in festivals, so I feel I've found a niche in something Jewish which satisfies what was lacking before.'

On another level, Tanya, who acknowledges that her interest in learning more about her Jewish heritage has been less intense since her teenage years, believes that 'if there had been more of a welcoming feel, there might have been more response'. Richard agrees that this might encourage people who have left exploring their heritage 'on a back burner' to do something about it.

For Laurence, the desire to be welcomed and accepted within the Jewish community is a throwback to his desire to be fully accepted within his Jewish family:

> I think it would be welcome to a lot of people, not least people like myself, to feel one is encouraged to be part of the Jewish community and to parade one's Jewishness as it were. I'm privileged and lucky as I have been accepted by Jews as I do my job but it would be nice to think that others and indeed myself could come into a slightly warmer place than one goes into at the moment. With my relatives one got wonderful hugs and kisses but still – and I remember it as a child coming over here – still one wasn't quite . . . and I'd love to see a softening of that, that you could come in and they'd say 'You're in the wrong religion but you're still one of us.'

RESONANCES OF THE PAST

Lost Jews may carry with them dreams, expectations and conflicts from previous generations which have some bearing on their feelings about their Jewishness. Resonances of familiarity in alien rituals, as David experienced, provide another link to their past. A similar response to synagogue ritual came from Kajal: 'In some ways the rituals are weird, in other ways they spark off feelings of familiarity rather than something alien or strange.' Coincidences may also be loaded with resonance: Julie 'was born on the birthday of my grandmother, Stella, and my father called me after his grand-mother, Julie, the great matriarch. What have I been landed with?'

Dreams and Conflicts

Valérie senses that her dream of belonging to a strong, open Jewish com-munity is a 'transference' she is making on behalf of her mother, whose Jewish boyfriend jilted her in deference to a whim of his dying father.

> Because of a story like that, she didn't marry him, she married my father. Even if they're a harmonious couple and really love each other my mother always told me from the time I was little, 'If you marry a Jew it will be better.' Somewhere or other I think I've made this trans-ference and I say to myself, 'If I'm going to get married I'd like it to be to a Jew because my mother wasn't able to do that.'

Gabriel also has a dream of a Jewish future: 'In the back of my head I have an idea that if I find a Jewish person I really like and I marry this nice Jewish person and have Jewish kids, my dream is to have a bar mitzvah with the kids.' He was completely unconscious of how closely his words echoed the deepest wishes of his late grandfather. Whether it was an unconscious wish to win over her Jewish family or through sentiment for her grandparents, Kim had 'always wanted a rabbi' to marry her. Her dream came true but her grandparents never lived to see it. Esther also lost her grandparents before she was 'old enough to explore the "Jewish thing". Unfortunately, because I'd have loved my grandfather to have been there.'

Esther has also been affected by intimations of past conflict between her grandparents, who insisted that her mother convert and that the chil-dren be brought up Jewish, and her mother, whose lack of genuine motiva-tion to convert was soon picked up by a supportive rabbi. 'I think that's where a lot of my mother's resentment comes from now and a lot of that got put onto us in terms of not being allowed even to explore our identity.' Even though 'it's all suppressed', she senses that her parents are continu-ing the battle. For Penelope, the suppression of her father's Jewish back-ground is characteristic of suppressed family conflicts both she and her late husband had suffered from. 'A lot is bottled up in my husband's family and there's a strong pattern in my family of witholding information. I think there's a lot of pain around in both families and that generation often managed pain by looking the other way.'

Split Identities

Esther would like to see a mixed marriage where a strong Jewish identity and a strong Christian identity are both supported and nurtured. Philip's father was an orthodox Jew and his mother an orthodox Catholic. 'Our family innovated a combination of Jewish and Catholic domestic liturgy. Although the materials were mostly Jewish, the dominant emphasis was probably on the Catholic side.' *Kiddush*, the Sabbath prayer over wine and bread, was a 'modified *kiddush*', Passover was celebrated by a combination of the *seder* and the Catholic mass composed by Philip's mother. He and his brother had a combined bar mitzvah and Catholic confirmation: 'My mother wrote a combination of the two liturgies. We had a Cohen and an African bishop from Ghana did the Catholic side.'

At home, there was synthesis and unity in diversity. For Philip the split was most evident when he was a boarder at a Catholic public school and at the same time an active member of the Socialist–Zionist organisation, Dror. 'I used to get into trouble. I got into arguments with the priests about the significance of Jewish–Christian relations.' At Cambridge, where he sensed he would not be fully accepted at the Jewish Society and tried to find spiritual expression in Christian worship, he was put off by rigid attitudes towards Jews and Judaism.

Julie, whose inborn knowledge of her paternal grandparents' death in Auschwitz was matched by the knowledge that 'my grandfather on my mother's side was a member of the Nazi party', finds the half-German, half-Jewish split 'a nightmare. It's a huge dichotomy. Why my parents got married in the first place is another huge dichotomy which they don't particularly like to delve into.' She feels it is left to her to find synthesis and unity: 'I feel a tremendous pressure on me to somehow unify these two extremes, it's unconscious and unspoken. I've always felt a pressure to somehow symbolise the rightness of their choices in choosing each other.'

Resolutions

While redressing the balance between the two sides of her heritage by exploring the German side she had 'pushed away for nearly two decades', Julie is in the process of finding who *she* is. Philip, in his turn, feels the synthesis he 'carried' from his parents is something he cannot sustain or pass on in the particular form that he received it.

Both Philip and Julie have been marked by their patrilineal Jewish inheritance. Julie, who for so long had struggled 'to find a place to belong' has come to see the benefits of 'not actually belonging in either camp: I have to find my belonging for myself. In a way it's a tremendous plus.' It was 'this really strong sense of community' which had attracted her to the Jewish faith and which she has now found in her work: 'My sense of community comes very strongly from acting. There're no stronger communities than being in a cast. In that sense that need in my life has been filled.' Philip has had to contend with the identity dilemma common to many: 'When I'm with Christians I feel Jewish, when I'm with Jews I feel non-Jewish.' Through his interest in international relations, which 'resonates with the dialogue between the different cultures of my background', he has found a complex identity which satisfies him:

> There's a long-standing tradition of radical, secular Jewish identity which I identify with and which I've been identified with by other people. Its cosmopolitan character is obviously especially attractive to me given that I don't easily fit within the Jewish community, so that kind of particularism of Jewish identity is not really open to me.

Philip revels in the cosmopolitan Jewish culture which played such a role in 'innovating secular forms of emancipatory thought of various kinds and it's a cliché – Marx, Freud, etc – but there's obviously something there and I love it. For me that's a way of identifying Jewishly with what I live.' His enthusiasm is shared by Ben S, who identifies himself as a 'voluntary Jew':

> The culture of the Jews has so much to offer – it's a waste to throw it away. Maybe if you look at it in a romantic or racist way there's some guiding thread in each Jew. It's not Jewish blood, it's the idea that there's something in that culture that produces these ideas.

Affinities

At nineteen, Hannelore left Germany and came to England as an au pair, fleeing her tragic inheritance and a history of abuse at the hands of her stepfather. Placed with a Jewish family who rejected her because she was German, she then came to another Jewish family. 'They absolutely loved me, I was very, very happy there.' The experience revived fictional memories of the wealthy Jewish grandfather she had created from fragments of information from her mother: 'I knew, I was always told, I came from such a good Jewish home.' Since then, she has always felt a strong affinity with Jewish people: 'I have many Jewish girlfriends, they're like sisters, my best friends have always been Jewish, my former common-law husband was half-Jewish, too, I mainly only socialise with Jewish friends, so I realised that the Jewish blood must be stronger than the Aryan side.' Since our meeting, Hannelore was introduced to a man whose parents had come to Britain from Berlin in 1933. It was a true return to her roots. 'His father Rudi is an artist. I love him to death. I feel God has given me the cultured German Jewish father I never had.'

Monique is immediately recognised as 'Jewish' by Jewish friends. Both her husbands have been half-Jewish, her first husband on his father's side and her second on his mother's. By marrying a girl with a Jewish mother her son, from her first marriage, has continued this pattern.

This sense of affinity, common to many lost Jews, is summed up by Jessica: 'It's just there's this automatic relaxation. It's something I feel very at home with and I think people who are Jewish feel at home with me.'

From Past to Future

Jessica has an uncanny feeling she will marry someone Jewish. Even if she does not, she will 'inspire her children with a sense of Jewishness'. Like many lost Jews, she is concerned to pass something on. Francesca wants her 'kids to be aware they have Jewish blood in them', unlike her cousin's young son who 'is totally not in contact with any Jewishness. I said to my cousin, "I'd like him to be aware that he's fractionally Jewish."' Esther 'would like to give a child the knowledge of Jewish things and then say "You can have it."' Kajal wants her children to have 'a Jewish sense of direction. If they reject it, it's up to them.' Similarly, Anna would tell her children about their Jewishness: 'It would depend on them if they feel it's good or not.' John feels he is 'handing some of my history on to my children and they'll do with it what they want to.' He can conceive of them saying 'we identify' and going into the process. Jacqui 'would hope to continue the stories down the generations that I was told by my grandma and try to keep it as part of the family'.

Carole would give her children 'Yom Kippur and the customs like the food' which she had herself. She can see the advantage, if she married a Catholic, of giving them an upbringing that was both Jewish and Catholic 'with all the troubles that might bring later. If they look for something, it might be easier and maybe they will be less intolerant about religions than I am.' Philip feels he would 'really be faced with a crunch decision about how to pass things on' if he married someone who was not Jewish. 'I feel very much a bearer of things passed on from my parents but in me they assume a different form.' The easiest thing, he feels, would be to find a secular Jewish partner.

David has 'a sense of something tapering'. He is aware that 'by marrying a Jewess I could be passing something on and it would be expanding rather than tapering'. He confronts this dilemma by avoiding relationships.

> I want my children to have the option to be Jewish. That's something I can't leave to chance. So that's the kind of thing that tips the scale towards thinking 'I just can't be bothered to make any kind of choices.' I suppose if I came across someone I liked who was Jewish it would be like killing two birds as I am hesitant to close the door for the next generation.

Linda is quite unambivalent about her role as a bearer of Jewish continuity:

> I think it's a very important part of life to have this spiritual, this religious dimension. I think also that the family connection I have with it is important and since they died in the war I feel I can't stop the connection and I want to support it.

THE CHAFF OR THE WHEAT?

The majority of lost Jews struggling towards some form of Jewish identity or awareness would appreciate a welcome and a helping hand. Given the delicate state of ambivalence and flux that characterises their response to their Jewish heritage, there is fine line to be drawn between acceptance and encouragement, on the one hand, and pressure, on the other, which should of course be avoided. Nevertheless, the present climate of rejection of patrilineals in Britain and the lukewarm reception of children of mixed parentage in France indicates a degree of self-destructiveness and tunnel vision on the Jewish community's part which does not bode well for the future.

6

Finding a Way

A WAY BACK

A remarkable and largely unsung phenomenon of our times is the return of the lost Jew to some form of Jewish life. This is not a mass movement that can be quantified statistically; it is often an internal 'call' that resonates within the individual. For some, particularly those with suitable *halachic* credentials, the process is relatively natural, requiring little more than self-recognition and free choice. Others, faced with obstacles and rejection, need unfailing determination to attain their goal. A variety of journeys have led lost Jews back to their ancestral heritage.

From Priest back to Jew

Can a Jew be a Jew and a Christian at the same time? This question has drawn contradictory responses from *halachists* and secular Jewish legal authorities and played a crucial role in the life of Geza Vermes.

The renowned Dead Sea Scrolls scholar and author of *Jesus the Jew* was born in 1924 in Mako, south-east Hungary, the only child of Jewish parents, 'totally detached from any kind of religious tradition'. Vermes' 'early, very infrequent contact with Judaism' occurred when he was about 5 years old and was taken to synagogue by a visiting relative: 'It stuck in my mind that I was advised, probably by my mother, not to kiss the Torah because that's not hygienic.'

Shortly afterwards Vermes' parents decided the family would become Roman Catholic. 'The idea, obviously a mistaken one, must have been that by formally adopting Christianity, life for me would become easier.' But in an atmosphere of endemic antisemitism which increased once Hungary sided with Hitler, 'being a so-called Catholic' was not much help. 'Legally you were a Jew if you had three Jewish grandparents. You couldn't have certain jobs, you couldn't easily enter university.' And when, after the German takeover of Hungary in 1944, Hungarian Jews were deported and murdered, Vermes' parents were among them.

Vermes progressed almost 'unnoticeably' towards a deeper involvement with Catholicism.

I opted for the lifeline which was open and ended up in theological college. From my class of roughly 30 boys I was the only one to train for the priesthood. The motive was partly pragmatic but accompanied by a corresponding honest acceptance of the implications.

The 'totally primitive' theological college he was sent to was in Satmar, then north-eastern Hungary, a town still full of Jews, many of them ultra-orthodox *chassids*. 'I had inherited my kind of assimilated Jewish reaction to them. They were not civilised, they were *östJuden*.' Unchallenged by the teaching at the college, Vermes spent 2 years 'reading my things, passing the examination, having the top marks – not that that can be considered a great achievement'. By June 1944, he was an ordinand on the run. 'The authorities at the college thought it would be too risky to keep me there. Let's be fair and grateful, those who helped did help very effectively. By Christmas I ended up in Budapest and the Russians were there.'

Vermes remained in Hungary another 2 years in theological colleges in the provinces and one semester at the University of Budapest where he started to learn Hebrew. He had applied for admission to the Society of the Fathers of Sion, whose theological college at Louvain in Belgium was associated with high-grade establishments which offered an opportunity to leave Hungary and extend his horizons.

In Louvain he continued his Hebrew and followed a specialised course in Oriental languages at the university, while researching the Dead Sea Scrolls for his doctorate. Ordained and with his PhD, he left in 1952, spending 3 months in Israel, where he enjoyed the pioneering atmosphere and practising his modern Hebrew, before settling in Paris. Attached to the avant-garde periodical *Cahiers Sioniens*, and researching on ancient Jewish Bible interpretation for the French National Research Centre, his work was entirely outside church activities but did not offer him sufficient challenge; without a teaching post he lacked a forum for expression. In 1954 he attended an international conference in England as an expert on the Dead Sea Scrolls. 'Totally incidentally', by visiting a friend, he met Pamela, the granddaughter of a distinguished former editor of the *Church Times*. It was the start of a companionship cemented by a deep mutuality of interest that ended when Pamela died in 1993, a scholar and lover of Jewish mysticism and author of two works on Martin Buber.

Their 'great friendship' developed over years of comings and goings and in 1957 Vermes took French leave of Paris, the Church and Catholic practice. He and Pamela married the following year. He had taken up a lectureship in the Department of Religious Studies at Newcastle University where he stayed until 1965 when he was appointed Reader in Jewish Studies at Oxford. 'A kind of light entered' after years of hard work that had familiarised him with Jewish history and life in Palestine and he decided to produce *Jesus the Jew,* which came out in 1973.

Spiritually, it was a period of 'floating'; Israel had stirred his Jewish consciousness and in England it was growing.

> I became progressively a Jew by ceasing being a Christian. I became a Christian really without knowing it and I rebecame a Jew without doing much about it. There is a kind of instinctive something that comes through that was not planned or rationally premeditated but which is just part of my make-up.

By the end of the 1960s, he said to himself: 'If that's where I am, why not make it formal?' He joined the liberal synagogue and not long afterwards became editor of the *Journal of Jewish Studies.*

A Would-be *Chassid*

Eighteen-year-old Aslan Devere*, descended through his maternal grandfather from *chassidic* Jews in Poland and the Ukraine, feels an 'ancestral awakening' calling him back to *chassidism*: 'It's a very, very deep feeling. Something within it strikes a chord within me. It just sets me on fire.'

Brought up in the home counties with a sense of Jewish identity but no formal practice of the religion, he was fifteen when he became active in a liberal Jewish community which had just started up. By declaring himself 'Jewish', he exposed himself to antisemitic harassment at school which had not been directed at him when he was merely 'of Jewish ancestry'.

Although the liberals were ready to accept him with only one Jewish grandparent, provided he studied liberal Judaism and learnt Hebrew, Aslan was not satisfied:

> I couldn't reconcile my belief in the Messiah and the divine inspiration of the Torah with liberal Judaism. Although I was trying to return to the faith of my grandfather, I couldn't relate to what I was being told. A lot that had been believed for thousands of years had been stripped away and I found that almost painful.

At seventeen he approached the London *Beth Din* to convert to orthodox Judaism. Told he was too young, he came back the following year and contacted them persistently until he was given an appointment with the *dayanim.* In the meantime he threw himself into Jewish learning, teaching himself the Talmud, Yiddish and Aramaic. His potential as a

Talmudic scholar has already 'amazed' an orthodox rabbi.

After leaving school, Aslan moved to north-west London to seek kosher accommodation and a job, the prerequisites for a candidate for conversion. University had to go by the board.

> I've made everything secondary to becoming Jewish. It's my greatest aim. People ask me: 'Aren't you afraid of *brit mila*?' and I say 'No.' It's just a stepping stone on the route to becoming Jewish. The London *Beth Din* say their conversions are the hardest in the world. I think it will be a good conversion to do. I really want to get cracking. I want to go on and do my own thing and delve into *chassidism*.

The *chassidic* way of life, complete with black garb, a wife who covers her head and numerous children, represents, for Aslan, a means of protecting the Jewish future of his descendants.

> In *chassidism* the attrition rate is very, very low which is my major concern. For me assimilation is such a terrible thing that I want to go completely the other way. Anything I can do to increase the numbers or at least reduce the deficit is my goal. I don't want to risk any of my family ever marrying out like my grandfather did. I don't want my great-great-grandchildren going through what I'm going through.

Aslan intends to become known as 'Mordecai' and take on his grandfather's surname 'Krichevski'. As well as making his grandfather happy, his dedication to Judaism has had a spin-off effect on his family who are now liberal Jews. His younger brother, he believes, will eventually become orthodox. 'I have a dream of becoming a rabbi. I only realised recently I could do this even if I'm a convert. It's a great opportunity for me to start steering people back to Jewish observance.'

Amid the Alien Corn

From the outset, Janet Leighton's* journey back to Judaism has been fraught with rejection, obstacles and suspicion. Her Jewish father, passionately opposed to religion, was 'furious' at the idea of her embracing the faith. Ironically, the warm-hearted Catholics in her mother's family have been more sympathetic.

Quarrels about religion plagued her parents' marriage.

> We were not baptised. We had no religious upbringing. There were ructions in the house from the very beginning. I remember the priest coming in, knocking at the door and my mother would invite him in

> and my father would swear madly. It was quite frightening to have him intruding and creating arguments.

If Catholicism was seen as 'the enemy', any experience of Judaism or Jewishness was non-existent. 'Even when I had no particular religion, I'd always pray, there was always something there. I've always been very spiritual. It was a matter of finding something I could believe in.'

At Leeds University where she studied dentistry Janet met a number of Jewish students.

> I was really interested to go to the *shul* and to some of their meetings but I felt ostracised. They said if you were not Jewish and wanted to go to these things you'd need to convert. I told them my father was Jewish but they were not very welcoming so that took a lot of my confidence away.

In London Janet got in touch with a reform rabbi. Although she didn't find him very encouraging, she attended synagogue whenever she wasn't on hospital call and took Hebrew lessons. 'I really enjoyed it but I didn't go back to the rabbi as I was put off by his manner.'

After working for three years, she went to Cambridge to take a further degree, hoping to pursue her Jewish leanings there and convert through the Reform movement. But the man the reform rabbi put her in touch with never wrote back, further undermining her confidence. She started attending the local orthodox synagogue. 'I went there every *Shabbat* and got to know people and went to Friday night meals and that was probably the watershed period.' By the time she returned to London to study medicine, she was in touch with the London *Beth Din*. A few months later she was given an appointment with the leading *dayan*.

A vivacious, attractive young woman, Janet was visibly distressed in recalling the meeting:

> The first thing he said was: 'So you call yourself doctor, I don't know dentists calling themselves doctor.' He was on the offensive from the very beginning. He made out as if I was insane about what I was wanting to do and the thing he focused on was 'Did I have a boyfriend?'

Janet had been out a few times with a Canadian Jew who was most disparaging about her wish to convert.

> It wasn't something I wanted to introduce because it wasn't relevant to my visit there but this was the crux of the whole conversation; the whole meeting was to do with 'Well, it's a *mitzvah* to marry and have children.' I was approaching thirty and I was very sensitive to the fact that I wasn't getting married or likely to be getting married. That's why I found it so

> traumatic. At the same time he was writing everything in Yiddish, people were coming in and out and it was totally disrespectful. Another thing he said was, if you're a doctor, it wouldn't be possible to be observant. By saying things like that they're destroying people's lives.

The *dayan's* parting shot, *sotto voce*, was somewhat unexpected. 'He said, "God bless, I'm sorry we can't help you, but my suggestion is get married, go through the reform conversion, have your children and then come back." '

Janet went back to the reform rabbi. There, too, she encountered suspicion. Had she not been 'traumatised' by her parents' divorce, he asked? Nevertheless, she was accepted as a candidate for conversion, probably the only one whose conversion was not related to marriage. Meanwhile she had started to lead an orthodox life style, sharing a flat with strictly orthodox flatmates and attending services and *shiurim* at an orthodox synagogue where, ever fearful of rejection, she kept a low profile.

She is frustrated at constantly needing to justify her motives.

> People demand, people feel it's an automatic right to ask. I can't give an answer that satisfies them. It's something deep, it's something spiritual, it's something you can't quantify, it's something I feel in my heart. If they feel people who do this are unbalanced, maybe they are underselling Judaism, maybe they don't appreciate all the things Judaism has to offer.

A few days after speaking to me, Janet went before the reform *Beth Din* and sailed through her conversion with flying colours. Shortly before that she started attending an orthodox Sephardi synagogue and was made very welcome by the rabbi. Still determined to undergo an orthodox conversion, it was only then she started to feel she was on home ground.

The Octaroon

Some unconscious pull has always drawn Anita Fox towards Jews and Judaism. An 'English rose' with a warm, outgoing manner, she believes that her great-grandmother on her mother's side was Jewish. 'There was this thing about "the Jewish aspect of the family" all shoved under the carpet. If anyone mentioned it, it was "Oh well, not really, don't talk about that." ' Her mother's family had a Methodist background but both her parents had been members of the Communist Party since their teens. 'It was a slightly odd background and I found myself wondering "When's this great light going to come on, when am I going to get the message, when am I going to understand it?" '

Christianity only reinforced Anita's basic scepticism. She made friends with an Anglican priest, a celibate, and watched him take a service. 'I was amazed at how theatrical it was and I almost wanted to applaud at one point.' A Catholic mass she attended seemed equally incomprehensible. Her priest friend assured her, 'Anita, it's not a case of "if" for you, it's a case of "when",' but her search had not yielded any answers by the time she married a 'tall, slim blond English ex-public schoolboy' and went to live in the West Indies.

It was when her son was born 7 years later as the marriage was coming amicably to an end that the unconscious forces started to make themselves felt.

> It's no coincidence looking back on it that I called my son Benjamin. And I insisted, in the teeth of opposition from Hugh Jolly, the great paediatrician Hugh Jolly, on having him circumcised. I couldn't have told you logically why I had it done. I just knew here down in my gut it was something I really needed to do.

Back in England after the marriage broke up, Anita settled with her son in a small cottage and took in lodgers to make ends meet. One prospective lodger had also returned to England after a marriage break-up.

> We were sitting in the kitchen discussing whether he should rent the room and after twenty minutes of chat he said 'Tell me, are you Jewish?' and I said 'So many people ask me. I don't think so. If you graded me as the West Indians used to grade their slaves I'm probably a Jewish octaroon!'

The lodger, himself Jewish, became Anita's second husband and they had a baby daughter. They moved to London, took part in Jewish cultural activities and spent time with Jewish friends.

> There was such harmony between us and I suddenly appreciated that however fond I was of my first husband, it didn't have that deeply satisfying core because there was something missing in him that existed in me and now I'd actually found another person to share it with. Suddenly I realised how all my life I'd been out of my true place living in a very gentile community in south-west London where to find a Jew is like finding an oasis in the desert.

Some years later Anita's husband decided he would like to pick up his lost Jewish past and they considered joining the nearest reform synagogue. Ben, then in his early teens, was a choirboy at the local church with some cousins and was due to become head choirboy. They decided to let him lead the choir at the Christmas service and then join the synagogue. But in November Anita's husband died unexpectedly after an operation. She had to get hold of a rabbi for a Jewish funeral.

Impressed with the rabbi's sensitivity and compassion, Anita decided to go ahead with what she and her husband had planned. She started attending synagogue and took lessons in basic Judaism with a view to conversion. Six months later she hesitated, unsure whether she was doing this for her late husband or for herself. Meanwhile Ben had joined the synagogue youth club and attended services regularly and Zoe, aged five, was happy at the *cheder*.

Anita came to the conclusion that it really was 'her thing'. She continued studying until it came to the point of applying to the reform *Beth Din*. 'I suddenly got scared and said to the rabbi: "What am I going to do? If they ask me if I believe in God I'll have to say I don't." ' The rabbi reassured her. 'Where you are in your relationship with the deity is of no interest to any other Jew. What you are as a Jew, how you behave, your commitment to your community and your willingness to bring up your children in that way is all they're interested in.'

Anita and the children duly appeared before some of the most prominent figures in the Reform movement and, after quite a challenging encounter, were accepted as converts to Judaism. She regrets she wasn't asked *why* she wanted to convert. 'I could have told them that all my life I'd been deeply attracted to noble thoughts and high ideals and really fine gut stuff and I find this in Judaism. It actually has it all.'

Back home that evening she phoned her friends: 'I said I'd be kosher by Christmas.' Suddenly it seemed she was not alone. 'I had this very strange feeling that there were spirits of ancestors somewhere out in the ether saying "Thank goodness, someone has returned." '

The Samech Tet

Jean Pato* was born in France during World War II. When the French army surrendered, his father got away with a few officers and joined the British, leaving his wife literally 'holding the baby'. It took Madame Pato eighteen months to escape slowly across France; eventually she came out through Spain and Portugal with a British convoy.

Pato grew up in England a nominal Christian, attending public school with chapel twice a day. His father, a non-practising Catholic, put in an occasional appearance in church. 'I can't say I was a great believer. When I left school, like most people I didn't go back to church. There was nothing very Christian about me.'

His identity as a non-religious Englishman of French origin remained unchanged until he was in his forties. His parents were both dead when he was contacted by a cousin on his father's side who was compiling a history of the family. 'I found out that we had come from Portugal, that we had originally been Jews.'

Pato discovered a colony of Marranos or Portuguès in Bayonne, on France's Atlantic coast, where his ancestors had arrived in 1560 as 'new Christians'. Most of the family had long been settled in Portugal, but some had also come from Spain. With the granting of freedom of religious practice at the beginning of the nineteenth century, some of the 'new Christians' reverted to Judaism, some, like Pato's family, remained Catholic and some became Protestant. Until Pato's father's generation, the family had married among themselves.

He now sought to find his mother's roots. This wasn't easy as she was an only child, her parents were dead and he didn't know any of her relations. On holiday in France with someone who volunteered to help him, he struck lucky.

Both sides of his mother's family were Sephardi Jews. 'You can't say in retrospect that you had a specific reaction, a revelation or a flash of light, but it was very interesting because my relatives regarded me as Jewish.' His mother's mother's side had come to France in 1795 from Morocco and before that to Morocco from Spain; his mother's father's ancestors had arrived in France in the 1830s from Gibraltar. 'I'm actually what they call a "samech tet", the Hebrew initials for a "pure Sephardi".'

Pato was warmly welcomed by both sides of his family.

> It made me more of a family person. As a result of that – these things evolve – you gradually get more involved. Like a lot of Sephardim, my mother's family have a much better synthesis of religious, cultural and secular life, for example they go to synagogue in a very natural way, there's no big deal about it, there isn't such a thing as being religious or *frum*. For myself I didn't rush out to go to a synagogue. I'd never been in a synagogue before and I didn't go for a year or so. I now go to Bevis Marks for the High Holydays. I think it's nice to be in a community and to be part of a family but in religious terms I feel absolutely nothing.

Although Pato accepts that assuming a Jewish identity has affected the balance of his relationships, with a few of his acquaintances less eager to know him and other, well-meaning people amazed that 'anyone would voluntarily want to take this burden on', he feels his has been 'a very relaxed, easy call'. 'There aren't any brownie points for this. We live in a very easy-going age. I'm absolutely unable to tell you what would have happened if I'd found myself in the mid-1930s.' He is well aware that with a Catholic father and a Jewish mother he has 'the best of both worlds'. 'I have spoken to cousins who have dropped out of Jewish life because their mother wasn't Jewish and their father was and they weren't accepted at university or wherever, openly, totally and warmly accepted, and they felt "What do I need this for?" '

He regrets that he discovered his identity so late.

> I wish I'd known before I got married and had children because that would have given me a sense of continuity. It's very sad when you come back by accident to something that is lost but in practice will be lost. On the other hand you never know the twists of fate. I can have a grandson who marries a Jewish girl and whose children are therefore Jewish and the whole thing continues.

COMING OUT

A Friday evening with a congregation in west London. After the Sabbath eve service and a communal supper, preparations are taking place for a panel discussion. The subject: 'One of my parents is Jewish'. The name of the congregation: Beit Klal Yisrael, the House of All Israel.

I introduce myself to the rabbi in a peach-coloured tracksuit and to the three women panellists. A young man is chatting up one or two young women. When we sit down, I see that the male members of the audience are greatly outnumbered. Rather than taking place in a forum within mainstream Anglo-Jewry, this discussion on a subject so relevant to Jewish life has a primarily feminist audience, several of whom are lesbian.

Beit Klal offers a haven for people on the margins of Jewish life who wish to explore their Jewish identity, as I discovered when I spoke later to the panellists and some members of the audience. The congregation is officially affiliated to the Reform Synagogues of Great Britain which takes the *halachic* line on Jewish status but welcomes members without *halachic* credentials.

A Place Where I Would Have Been Normal

Berta Freistadt looks warmly, comfortingly Jewish, at ease in the social environment Beit Klal provides. It was different when she was a child in a predominantly gentile environment.

> There was this thing about me being unattractive. When I look at photos of myself I was just Jewish looking, a really nice-looking young Jewish girl, but I looked so foreign, so out of place in south London in the 1950s, I practically got beaten up because everybody said I looked so weird. I'm really sorry my father didn't pursue being Jewish and take me with him to the synagogue so that I could have found a place where I would have been normal.

Her father never wanted her to be Jewish. A refugee from Czechoslovakia, who 'embraced Britishness with the sense of a life-raft', he was always afraid that the horrors of the Nazi era might happen again. Berta remembers him saying *kaddish* for his parents and taking her to synagogue once or twice when she was tiny. Nothing more. Except for the connection with the Holocaust which dominated the early part of her life and made her feel different.

It was left to her half-Scots, half-Irish mother to give her a sense of Jewishness. 'Special' in some ways, she was also the butt of stereotypical comments like 'You're good with money because of your Scots relatives and your Jewish relatives.' Not having encountered rejection because of her non-*halachic* status – she still has Jewish friends from a young people's drama club where she was the only 'out-Jew' – she accepted that her Jewish blood made her 'special': 'I took what I had. It never occurred to me until recently that I could become "more Jewish".'

Beit Klal has given Berta, educated in church schools and 'absolutely revolted' as a teenager by the 'barbarism' of the Eucharist, the opportunity she never had to experience Judaism as a religion. 'What I like about the services is the feeling "Okay, so you don't believe, come anyway." In Christianity if you don't have faith, you're in trouble. Judaism feels very pragmatic, very down to earth; it feels like you can touch the holiness in Judaism.' She is gratified to find 'a lot of women-orientated things within Judaism. There's the moon calendar, very matriarchal, very pagan, I like that. And the *shechina*, the Jewish "holy spirit".'

A Mature Commitment to Roots

Beit Klal for Kathryn Fuller, with her 'WASP' name and 'non-Jewish' appearance, is a community she can be Jewish in. 'They try to welcome everybody and I was comfortable identifying myself as someone who was half-Jewish and hadn't been raised Jewishly.'

Her childhood in Indiana was anything but Jewish. The family had a secular Christmas and Easter; religion was never discussed: 'It was too important to talk about, we avoid all such matters in my family.' Her father, an agnostic, was a member of the dominant culture; her mother, the daughter of Jewish immigrants from Odessa, had an unsettled childhood and seemed happy to blend in. Kathryn today is disturbed by the pictures of her parents outside the church where they got married: 'It really bothers me to see this evidence of my mother's heritage being denied.'

Early intimations that she was forging a different path for herself included an obsessive interest in the Holocaust and close friendships at high school with Jews who shared her social values and concern for civil rights. Like her own family which had no roots in the mid-west, Kathryn was aware that her friends' families were deracinated. Nevertheless, they had something she envied. 'My friends, when they had their *Shabbat* evenings, seemed to get in touch with their roots, although their roots might have been all over the place. In my home there was nothing like that, no rituals or anything that looked back and put us in touch with our past.'

Kathryn distanced herself from her mid-western upbringing through her involvement in the civil rights movement and in feminism, in 'coming out' as a lesbian and in leaving the United States. She did not explore her roots for many years. Nevertheless, the only country she felt impelled to visit was Israel. But the time she spent there did not result in any 'great awakening'.

Years later she settled in England, bought a flat, got a suitable job and finally found the space to seek her identity. At Yakar, an alternative orthodox educational and cultural establishment, she was welcomed by the teacher and her fellow students but was conscious of being an outsider. The other students had been raised Jewishly and were familiar with 'the in-jokes, the lingo and the jargon, even if they just picked it up by osmosis'.

At Beit Klal where 'there's a lot of space for learning and for asking questions' Kathryn has found a commitment and rootedness she had not experienced before.

> It's given me things to consider, things to go home and think about. I'd never read the Bible and now I am and I'm thinking about what is real and what is metaphorical so it's been an education as well. It's given me a link, maybe a very tenuous one, with the past and with my mother's side of the family. Claiming that heritage has been an important aspect of establishing a Jewish identity for myself.

Blowing the Ram's Horn

For musician Rebekka Wedell, with only one Jewish grandfather, blowing the *shofar* at the *Yom Kippur* services at Beit Klal was the vindication of a lifelong struggle to preserve her Jewish identity.

> I felt this is just right, the fulfilment of something, a real arriving and yet I had the feeling 'If only they knew who's standing here blowing the *shofar* for them.' This encapsulates the tension I live out between feeling totally part of it and 'Who am I? Am I?'; it's crystallised in that ancient ritual I am doing on behalf of the community.

From the age of six, Rebekka, named after an aunt of her Jewish grandfather, was conscious that her name was a continuity of her Jewish background, a continuity she felt deeply within herself and clung to amidst the strong sense of displacement that came with her complex heritage. Her great-grandfather, a Polish rabbi, had emigrated to Germany and married the daughter of a German rabbi. Her grandfather married out. Her father, raised a Christian and a refugee in England with his family, married a German woman who was also living in England. Rebekka's German relations had an exemplary war record: her mother's father was imprisoned for his anti-Nazi stance and members of her father's mother's family were executed for their involvement in the plot to assassinate Hitler.

> I've tried to understand what it was I felt so strongly as a child. I felt my grandfather made a choice to marry out and my father also did and yet that wasn't necessarily a choice I had to make. It was made for me in previous generations but it was also very important for me to make the choice my own way.

Maintaining her choice in the face of her family's denial of their Jewishness, on the one hand, and the ostracism of the Jewish establishment, on the other, has been so painful that Rebekka broke down more than once during our conversation.

> You could say perhaps the denial provoked an overreaction. Maybe it made me think 'Something's being shut off here and that doesn't make sense and it's the only thing I've got to hold on to right now.' I felt very early on that there was something enormously positive to connect to, and a kernel of my Jewish identity is the continuity of a spirit of survival.

Her mother would pronounce dogmatically 'You're not Jewish. Jewish law says this' and make comments like 'the exclusivity of Jews' and 'Why do they have to make such a fuss about what they eat?' Her father, piecing together his German and Jewish roots, gave her information about her Jewish heritage 'in little drips. But it was always about things in the past, not anything in the present.' During her childhood her Jewishness was something she kept 'very private, very hidden' except from a few friends who were also 'outsider Jews'. Later, at university, she made more Jewish friends and began to feel more accepted. Ironically, it was in the Jewish feminist movement where establishment attitudes were 'vocalised' that she had her first experience of rejection.

Further close relationships with Jewish women have led to Rebekka's Jewishness becoming very much part of her life. 'I've been able to come out of hiding. I started observing a few festivals through friends and partners. It always meant a lot to me going to *Yom Kippur* services although there was always this fear of "I'm going to be thrown out." ' In recent years she has discovered and become close to some Jewish relatives and taken part in a family bat mitzvah.

Beit Klal was a big step. 'Within a very short space of time I've become very involved, very accepted and part of it. I remember the miracle one *Yom Kippur* when I was in a service and I felt "I can go and talk to the rabbi." This is an incredible thing for me to feel.'

ABOUT AS FAR AS THEY CAN GO

Kinsman and Friend – the Perfect Patrilineal

Stewart Steven, the genial editor of the London *Evening Standard*, often feels 'a bit of an impostor'.

> Because I look Jewish and have represented Israel's interests and written a book about Israel, I tend to mix with a lot of Jewish people and talk to Jewish groups and there is a natural assumption among a large number of people that I am Jewish. I can't go around in my life denying things so I've sometimes allowed that assumption to run, then I suddenly find myself in a position whereby I have to deny it because I know nothing about Judaism whatsoever, at least the religious practice of Judaism, and I feel a bit awkward.

He was born Stephen Gustav Cohen in Hamburg in 1935 to a prominent Jewish businessman and his Aryan Christian wife, a film actress. In 1938 the family came to England where Mr Cohen had already set up a business named 'Walter Steven' after his father and his son. The family name was changed to Steven and 3-year-old Stephen was deprived of what would have been 'a wonderful journalistic byline' – Stephen Steven – and given the name Stewart instead. After his father's death in 1941, Steven's mother, formerly Lutheran, became a devout Catholic and he was educated at Catholic schools: 'I was a good Catholic boy, I believed and went to confession and at the normal age when Catholic boys want to be priests I wanted to be a priest – and at the age of 18 I was no longer a Roman Catholic, I ceased being religious.'

Because of his appearance, he encountered a lot of antisemitism at school and 'had to fight for my life in the school playground'. It was a training he was almost grateful for. 'It gave me an inner toughness and strength to deal with what is a very tough world.' Puzzled at being called 'Jewboy' at school, he suspected it 'wasn't such a good thing to be Jewish', but had 'no idea, interest or knowledge of' the subject.

When he was in his twenties someone insisted he must be Jewish because all his male friends were – as opposed to his invariably blonde girlfriends. 'I suddenly realised that there was something afoot, that this Jewishness within me gave me an affinity to Jewish people.' He began to take a slight interest – nothing major – in things Jewish, but was quite indifferent to Israel and opposed British involvement in the Suez escapade. A short spell in Israel on behalf of the *Daily Express* at the time of the Six Day War was the start of an attachment which again he didn't make much of as Israel was then flavour of the month.

It was different after the *Yom Kippur* War in 1973.

> I took the view which I take today that Israel is certainly not always right in what it does but that the issue for Israel is always one of survival and 'Do I wish Israel to survive? Yes, I jolly well do.' I feel very, very strongly about that. It's a purely emotional attachment – a blood thing, no question about it – and an understanding that the Jewishness within me is an important part of my character and personality, of what I am and what I've achieved and where I come from. All these things clearly are very important and therefore Israel is important.

Well known for his robust support for Israel as a journalist and editor, he asserts that 'you have to go back to the principle' in all political issues and keep that principle 'pure and clear'.

While professing ignorance of and indifference to Jewish religious practices – he gets no 'emotional charge' from Passover, for example, but enjoys Christmas and Easter because he was brought up with them – Steven has no doubt that the survival of the Jews as an identifiable people, something which fills him with awe, is largely due to an extremely powerful central religious force. We've got this cranky, difficult, totally illogical religion with its extraordinary rules which are difficult and time-consuming and nothing to do with the real world and that has kept the Jewish people going and that is the wonder of the religion.

In the same vein he accepts as 'perfectly proper' the ruling which denies him Jewish status.

What he can claim is a remarkable 'genetic inheritance'.

Anybody who's got a bit of Jewish blood in them can trace their way right back in time. 3000 years ago they were in Jerusalem, before that they were in the desert. If, like me, somewhere in the family you have the name 'Cohen', you know you were a big noise 2000 years ago. You look at a Jew – he was once a slave in Egypt, he was once taken into captivity in Babylon, he was once fighting the Romans at Massada, he was kicked out, he somehow survived, he went to Spain. You can tell that person has a story, that family has this incredible story that you can actually tell, you can begin to chant . . . That makes the Jewish people really quite extraordinary and distinctive and gives them something very special to hang onto.

Steven concedes that he 'feels Jewish rather than anything else. I'm attracted to Jewish people, Jewish subjects. If I go anywhere in eastern Europe I'd always go and look at the Jewish cemetery, at the synagogue.' In memory of members of his family who 'disappeared' during the Holocaust he has visited Auschwitz, Dachau and other camps. His Polish-born wife, one of whose relatives was honoured in Yad Vashem for hiding Jews during the war, is sometimes irritated by his obsessive Jewish search. 'I'm drawn to anything that is sort of Jewish. Jewish writers like Saul Bellow, Roth and so on I find myself very much attuned to. That is something which is part of me. I can't really explain why that should be the case because I was never brought up with it.'

Accepting the Birthright

Like several children of mixed marriages, Cambridge undergraduate Suzie Pool was brought up 'in both religions but really in neither. I've been to a Passover *seder* every year, we always light *Hanukah* candles, we always have a Christmas tree and we usually go to church at Christmas and Easter.' Invariably the *seder* was more a social than a religious occasion and *Hanukah* was just the Jewish Christmas.

At state primary school there was no religious instruction but she had a Catholic friend with whom she used to play 'Jesus, Mary and Joseph'. Secondary school was a Church of England foundation with compulsory church attendance and religious education had a strongly Christian slant. Twenty-five per cent of her class was Jewish, however, and there were a number of girls from other minority faiths.

Constantly told by her Jewish friends that she was Jewish because her mother was Jewish, Suzie used to counter this by saying, ' "Yes, but I've got a Christian father and that makes me Christian." I used to say "I'm both" and I think my Jewish friends didn't quite understand that.'

At 16 or 17 she had enough of learning about Christianity and began exploring Buddhism and Hinduism. Israel came into the picture after a very secular relative of her American mother urged her to go. 'I thought "Seeing that I have connections to Christianity and Judaism, and Israel is connected to both, maybe I should go." '

Israel was a vital ingredient in building her Jewish identity. She went on tour just after finishing school and went back for part of her year off, against her parents' wishes but with the encouragement of the interviewers at her Cambridge college. This time she learnt about the Jewish religion, learnt Hebrew and got to know Israel much better. She also visited Christian sites in Jerusalem and at the end of her stay toured the country with her parents and got to see many more Christian landmarks.

> This was really interesting but it didn't change my views at all. My views by then were that I was Jewish. I had gained my Jewish identity on the first programme I went on but the second visit really made it stronger. I feel it's more a cultural identity than a religious identity. I don't necessarily keep anything like *Kashrut* or *Shabbat*. When I remember it's Friday night I light *Shabbes* candles at home. I still go to church with my father because I feel I should.

Suzie is aware of the significance of accepting her birthright. 'I'll probably marry someone Jewish and bring up my children as Jews and in that way continue the line.'

A MULTI-FACETED HERITAGE

While all the stories in this chapter focus on finding a way to some form of Jewish experience or Jewish life, each is very much a personal journey.

The absence of a common thread, the difficulty in defining the pull that Judaism or Jewishness exerts, testify to the richness and complexity of the Jewish heritage that offers such a diversity of aspects to the individuals who seek to explore it.

7

Mixed Blessings

REBIRTH IN PRAGUE

Sabbath eve in Prague. The Altneu synagogue, the oldest in Europe, is packed to overflowing. Jewish tourists rub shoulders with Czech Jews of all ages, among them many 'lost Jews'. Friday night dinner in the neighbouring kosher restaurant with spontaneous outbursts of *zmirot* and *benching* is one of those rare occasions when Jewishness to me is a joy.

With twentieth-century Central European Jewry decimated by assimilation, virtual extermination and suppression, the tiny remnants of once vibrant communities are in the vanguard of Jewish experience. In these communities, where mixed marriages are virtually inevitable, survival and continuity are today's battles, not tomorrow's. The role played by lost Jews in the struggle to maintain Jewish life is particularly evident in Prague. Jiri Danicek, the president of the Jewish community, tall, very slavic-looking and wearing the skullcap which marks the orthodox Jew, is generally spoken of as a gentile convert to Judaism; he told me he had a Jewish grandmother. 'All the reasons that led me towards my way are utterly personal,' he says, preferring not to divulge his story. An even more significant 'lost Jew' who has returned is Karel Sidon, Chief Rabbi of the Czech Republic.

The Search for Father

In 1968 Karel Sidon, the dissident writer and intellectual, published *Dream of my Father,* foreshadowing a return to his Jewish origins. Sidon was two when his father was executed at the Terezin concentration camp. His 'second father' – 'a very simple man, a tradesman' – whom his gentile mother married after the war, was also a Jew and suffered greatly during the Nazi era. 'I grew up in an environment like a Jewish one. I thought we were Jews.' There was no Jewish practice in the home, however, just 'a belief that God was one and that's all. For me for many years Judaism was just the Jewish destiny, that's to say something terrible happened, and I had no idea that it was also a religion.'

Sidon received a communist education in an agnostic school. Like many adolescents he experienced a thirst for spirituality and 'had to think a lot about belief and what that was'. Marxism and Stalinism were the first belief systems he was faced with. To compensate for the lack of religious education at school, he read books on different faiths. 'I went through Christianity, Buddhism, Zen Buddhism, Hinduism, all that culture.' Western philosophy, including existentialism, was another set of ideas he took on board. 'When the Russians arrived here in 1968, suddenly I saw that all these belief systems were, on the whole, stupid and I felt that the truth was that there is another force above man and his beliefs, who does what he wants.'

It was time to 'think about Judaism and whether it was at all possible to be a practising Jew'. Sidon read the Bible in Czech and started to learn Hebrew. Ten years later he reached a decision, impelled by events and a new spiritual reckoning.

> In the meantime there was Charter 77 and problems with the police. I also had family problems. Finally, I got to the state when I saw, on the one hand, that I really haven't the strength to say I am so independent and don't need something and, on the other hand, with the secret police, I saw I had some power that didn't come from myself to stand up to someone stronger. After that I decided to be a Jew.

Sidon had already come to the Prague Jewish community where his welcome was lukewarm. 'At the beginning it was difficult. They believed that it was the end of the world and they did not know how to relate to someone relatively young. Afterwards it was okay.' After studying for some time and making the necessary arrangements, he converted to Judaism in 1978. 'There wasn't a rabbi at that time but there was a relatively large group of orthodox Jews who prayed at the Altneu synagogue and they formed a *Beth Din* and I went through a conversion according to the *halacha.*'

Sidon's 'second father' said 'You're *meshuggah*. Here any Jew with brains leaves Judaism.' Certainly everyone who came regularly to the synagogue and the kosher restaurant had problems with the police. As a dissident who had signed Charter 77 and resisted the Russian occupation in 1968, Sidon was definitely *persona non grata*. In 1982 he left for Germany – 'It was easier to be a Jew there than in Prague' – and enrolled at a high-level institution of Jewish studies in Heidelberg: 'I used the opportunity to learn basic things not about Judaism but within Judaism.' He remained there until the 1989 'Velvet Revolution'.

Shortly before that, Sidon received the offer that determined his future: to study at a *yeshiva* in Jerusalem to become Chief Rabbi of Bohemia and

Moravia. He found an institute which trains students to serve as rabbis in the diaspora.

> I didn't know I would find a place that was so good for me. I found a spiritual mentor there. He helped me a lot in my studies and also with personal problems. Afterwards he helped me in Prague when I was already rabbi of the community. Till he died he was my guide. He was like a third father to me.

Bringing Father Back: Daniel Kumermann's Story

> I grew up in a small town outside Prague and was basically brought up a Catholic. I knew Jews existed but it didn't mean anything. My father hid his Jewishness. All his friends were Jewish but I didn't realise it. They were assimilated, they didn't *davven* or eat kosher, nothing outward. I also had a classmate who was Jewish but again this didn't mean much.
>
> I was trying to believe in Christianity. The communists were suppressing it very much and I was probably more into it than many young people in my generation. Then when I was seventeen or eighteen the Catholic church suddenly became comparable in my mind to the great communist system. I had this big crisis of belief and didn't know what I was looking for.
>
> Then a friend who knew I had some Jewish background took me to the Jewish community. It was somehow love at first sight, I knew I belonged. By that time I knew my father's Jewish past, although he couldn't pass anything on to me because he was totally assimilated. But he had lived in it and everybody was Jewish round him when he was growing up so somehow I just connected to that.
>
> I learnt about Jewish things from books and asked around and actually my father knew quite a lot. When it came up he was very much against it. He said, 'As you are half, why not choose the easier, safer half?' But on the other hand the fact that he was 100 per cent Jewish was the major influence in his life – his family was killed for it, he was a Jew in the British army in Palestine in the war – so he had a lot to tell. Although he still said he wasn't happy, it all came out of him like a big stream, he couldn't help it. He could suddenly talk to me about a major part of his life which he was hiding.
>
> I took him to the community for *Pesach* and he enjoyed it even though he didn't know how to behave, so suddenly even for him it was

a bit of a return. The community was relatively strong, there were lectures organised for Jewish youth and quite a lot of people to communicate with. It was probably more a cultural interest then, I didn't go to *shul* much. I had also toyed with Buddhism but somehow it wasn't part of my world so I couldn't accept it.

Then in 1975 my father died. I was 24. For 11 months I went very regularly to synagogue to say *kaddish*. Even though I can't understand Hebrew much, somehow this participation became part of my life and began to mean more than just repeating words.

When I first came to the community in the early 1970s and said 'My father's registered here', immediately they registered me as well. There were no questions, it was very liberal then. After that I went to have the operation [circumcision]. I realised that this is one of the first conditions and if I could not provide much more I could at least do that.

So now I was going regularly to *shul* and I was faced with a problem. I was a registered member of the community but they couldn't use me for a *minyan*. This went on for some time. By 1977 my situation had changed politically with Charter 77 and I got into all kinds of trouble with the authorities and it makes you get more involved in a smaller community because they cut you away from the larger group. Even after the *kaddish* period ended I was all the time getting deeper and deeper into Judaism and still went regularly to synagogue and the *minyan* matter came up again.

They made conversion very easy for me. After all I had been a regular member of the community all these years. As I'd had the operation already, all I needed was *mikveh* in one day and to be called to the Torah.

THE PROMISED LAND

A Panacea for Lost Jews?

Lost Jews who wish to immigrate to the Jewish state can take advantage of the 'Law of Return' which entitles anyone with a Jewish grandparent to Israeli citizenship. Among hundreds of thousands of former Soviet citizens who have flocked to Israel in recent years there are many lost Jews; a survey in 1995 indicated that 8.3 per cent of these immigrants are in fact gentiles connected to Jews or lost Jews. Similarly the large ingathering from Ethiopia has included a number of former Christians. Mass immigration inevitably brings in its wake a proportion of 'Jews of convenience', some of whom avail themselves of Israel's modern facilities and immigrant benefits before moving to another Western country. The unprecedented challenge to the demographic character of the Jewish state is viewed with anxiety by orthodox rabbis.

How easy is it for lost Jews without *halachic* credentials to be absorbed in Israel? Again marriage is the crux of the matter. With no civil marriage and with religious affairs in the hands of an orthodox establishment, conversion to Judaism offers the only solution for a lost Jew who wishes to marry a Jew.

Centres for conversion abound throughout Israel, as do a variety of institutions offering newcomers with no formal knowledge of Judaism some grounding in Jewish religion and culture. But attitudes to Jewish status vary. Take the Ethiopian immigrants. Because of marriage and divorce customs which have diverged from the Jewish norm, even Jewish Ethiopians are considered problematic from the orthodox standpoint and are required to undergo token immersion in the *mikveh* as if to renew their Jewish status. This requirement is viewed with horror by the very vocal secular Israeli majority. The result, of course, is confusion.

A special breed of lost Jew found in Israel in small numbers are presumed descendants of the lost ten tribes who are congregated in various corners of Asia and whose links to the Jewish people have been discovered by organisations such as 'Amishav', under the guidance of Rabbi Eliahu Avihail of Jerusalem. At his home I met a young boy from the tribe of Menashe on the India–Burma border, wearing the *kipah* and *tsitsit* of the orthodox Jew. He spoke glowingly of Rabbi Avihail as a Messiah and saviour. Such organisations are also involved in finding descendants of Marranos in parts of Spain and Portugal, Mexico and Latin America. Selected members of these communities are instructed in mainstream Jewish practice and undergo conversion. Some come to Israel, while others remain in their communities as teachers.

But Israel is not always a panacea for lost Jews. A number of Russian immigrants take the conversion option, as do gentiles, for example volunteers on *kibbutzim* who wish to marry Israelis. Again standards required for conversions, all ostensibly orthodox, vary enormously. Rural centres, while presenting a rigorously orthodox instruction programme, often turn a blind eye to the practice adopted by prospective converts once they return to their secular habitat. The Jerusalem *Beth Din,* in contrast, is notoriously strict, turning down some 50 per cent of applicants and reputed to give lost Jews a difficult time, even those who observe an orthodox life style.

This discrepancy is partly due to the fact that the religious establishment is trapped between the ultra-orthodox and the secularists, generating an ambivalence which was manifest in a rabbi I met who works in a conversion centre. He produced the file of a prospective convert from Holland living on a kibbutz. 'He's a fine young man', he declared, 'but the London *Beth Din* wouldn't accept him.' He forbade me to switch on my tape-recorder, protesting that the standards demanded in Israeli centres were equally rigorous but retracting this the next moment. I asked him about the young Dutchman. 'Are you glad that he has decided to become a member of the Jewish people?' He had no answer.

Mixed Marriages

A variety of mixed marriage in Israel involves Israeli Jewish women and Muslim Arab men. In these cases the women are almost always absorbed into the Muslim cultural and religious environment and while the children are Jewish according to *halacha* they are Muslim under Islamic law and raised as Muslims.

Marriages between Jews and Christians in Israel are another story. Where else would one find a Christian priest who has a Jewish wife and children and is a member of two synagogues?

Bringing Daniela to the Land

From his 'first steps in life', Michael Krupp felt connected to the Holy Land. A child in wartime Germany, he was eight when he finished reading the Bible for the first time. 'My real existence was the life of the Bible and I was very strongly identifying with biblical figures like Abraham, Isaac and Jacob. In 1948 I was ten years old and I heard that there was a state of Israel. From that date on I was interested to see this.'

It was not so simple. 'As a German you couldn't come, you had to have an invitation. But how do you get an invitation from a land where you don't know anybody?' Several years later, in 1959, he succeeded and spent 9 months working in *kibbutzim.* 'I came a bit into contact with Israelis and life in Israel, so it was normal that I should come back to finish my studies at the Hebrew University in Jerusalem.'

In the meantime he had met Daniela, a young Jewess who had come to France from Algeria and was working in Bonn doing French programmes for German radio. Michael, a young ordinand, and two fellow students were playing host to the younger members of the Jewish community, including Daniela. 'The youngsters had problems with the older members of the community. They met only in our house. They celebrated *Shabbat* and so on and we taught them several Jewish customs. They had good intentions but not such deep knowledge.' Daniela and Michael's romance, even in its early stages, was frowned upon by the young Jews. 'They were not shocked exactly but they thought it's not okay for us to go out together.'

Not long after they met, Michael left for Jerusalem to do his doctorate. It was a good opportunity for Daniela to visit Israel for the first time. 'I liked it very much. Before that I was not so interested in Israel. If I hadn't met Michael and he wanted me to know Israel, maybe I would never have come. My family kept the festivals like other French Jews but I was very assimilated.'

The fact that Michael was a student in Israel and had written a book about Zionism helped Daniela's family accept the relationship. They were married in France in 1966 and went back to Israel for 6 months. On their return to Germany, Michael's church was not so understanding. 'They chucked me out because I had married a Jewess.' He was welcomed into another church, however, and some years later was sent by that church to Israel.

The Krupps settled in the Jerusalem suburb of Ein Karem. Their four children are well integrated into Israeli Jewish society. Michael tries to give his children an understanding of Christianity and of the importance of living together but is quite happy that under the *halacha* they are Jewish. The family belongs to the local Yemenite orthodox synagogue but when their daughter wanted to read the Torah in synagogue at her Bat mitzvah, they joined a reform congregation as well. 'Even here the Jews are much more open than the Christians,' Michael explains. 'I, too, am a member of the two synagogues but I and only me am a member of the Lutheran church.'

Is it only in Israel that Jewish continuity can emerge from a mixed marriage? 'It can be much easier in Israel,' says Michael. 'You are anyway in a Jewish society, in a Jewish community. But I know many families of mixed couples in Germany, for instance, and they are all good Jews. So it can work elsewhere too.'

The Israel Factor

Individual 'lost Jews' who settle in Israel are drawn there for a variety of reasons. For many, it is the ultimate affirmation of their Jewish identity.

The Last Jew

Lindsey Taylor-Guthartz had 'the great illusion that every Jew in the world desperately wanted to live in Israel. The only people who didn't were either living in repressive countries which wouldn't let them out or had sick parents they couldn't leave.' From her early teens she devoured every book about Israel she could get hold of and was amazed some years later to hear people talking about going on holiday there – 'You mean just go for a while and then go back?' She, however, went on *aliyah* immediately after university.

She was born in Australia. Not long afterwards her parents split up and she and her mother returned to England. Her father is a gentile and her mother the product of an extremely assimilated Jewish background.

> My grandparents were both completely non-practising. They married in a registry office in 1919. The last synagogue marriage in the family was that of my grandmother's mother in the West London Reform Synagogue in the 1880s. My grandmother's grandmother was married in 1848 by the then Chief Rabbi of England. That was the last 'kosher' marriage. My mother married in church. All my cousins, without exception, married out – the marrying out goes back two or three generations. I'm the last Jew in my family apart from my children.

Although Lindsey's grandparents lived in a Jewish area and had Jewish friends, they

> were so traumatised by being Jewish, they couldn't bring themselves to say the word, they would talk about people being 'J'. They would have flipped if my mother or uncle had married anyone Jewish. The only Jewish artefact, my family's entire Jewish heritage, consists of a small early twentieth-century cookbook called *Dainty Dishes for Jewish Families* which is wrapped in brown paper, presumably so that you can't see the title.

Lindsey's mother was fourteen or fifteen when she learnt she was Jewish from a schoolmate whose brother was at school with her brother. Lindsey assumes her uncle was circumcised and this gave the game away. 'She and my uncle grew up with the most incredible complex about being Jewish. If she could wave a magic wand and not be Jewish, she would.'

Not surprisingly, Lindsey was given no information about her Jewish roots. Her mother had remarried and they were living in Cornwall.

> I remember saying to my mother in the kitchen one day, 'I wonder if our family came over with William the Conqueror?' and she said rather bad-temperedly, 'No, we didn't. We're Jewish.' It was a slight shock at the time because even at that age – seven or eight – I had absorbed some vague stereotypes like 'Jews are mean', 'Jews have big noses.'

Lindsey couldn't keep the knowledge to herself. At Christmas at the grandparents she spilt the beans to her cousin, much to the family's horror.

In the meantime she was participating in 'Christian this and Christian that' and at ten was sent to a Church of England boarding school. While church on Sunday was generally considered tedious, confirmation classes were popular. 'I remember being fairly enthusiastic. I wanted to be confirmed. Oh, Jesus was there, everyone else believed in Jesus. It was a sort of given.' She was duly confirmed in Truro cathedral by the Bishop of Truro.

Then the worm turned.

> After that, in a *davkaish* sort of way, I started getting interested in things Jewish. The more I read about it the more I liked it. I can remember walking along at school one day and thinking, 'I believe in Jesus, I wouldn't want to really give that up,' and thinking, 'Don't be stupid, of course you're going to be Jewish.'

It was the beginning of a marrano-like existence. Lindsey read whatever she could, taught herself the Hebrew alphabet and got hold of a booklet of Israeli songs which she learned by heart. Chaim Raphael's *A Feast of History* and Leo Rosten's *The Joys of Yiddish* were especially exciting finds. Surreptitiously, she observed the festivals, not eating on *Yom Kippur*, reading the book of Esther at *Purim*, making herself 'a remarkably inflammable and dangerous *hanukiah* out of a large cork and wire covered with gold foil'. At *Pesach* she managed to buy a box of stale *matzas*, used a glass of water for the four glasses of wine and some chocolate for the meal and read through the *hagadah*, part of which she had painstakingly copied out of the Raphael tome. In the meantime her mother would be making hot-cross buns for Easter.

After a nervous beginning, Cambridge was the start of the wonderful new Jewish life she had dreamed of. Lindsey threw herself into the Jewish Society where she received a warm welcome, got a more rounded picture of Judaism and adopted an orthodox life-style. Her mother was anything but happy about her overt Jewishness but on occasion 'aided and abetted' her, out of her stepfather's view.

And then to Israel, fresh from Cambridge. Inevitably, there have been shattered illusions:

> In some ways I've been disappointed because I had this ideal of everyone going around building the country, this very naïve view that it was full of people nobly striving for a perfect aim and since then, of course, reality has impinged. I dislike intolerance very much and it's all around you in Israeli society. Sometimes I think I want to leave, I hate living in the Middle East but I don't have any desire to stop being Jewish.

The attitudes of the Israeli rabbinate have not helped. 'The official establishment is horrible, they are inconsiderate, you have people completely divorced from the world around telling other people what to do.' Not surprisingly, she was reluctant to confront the *Beth Din* to validate her Jewish status but when she met her future husband, she could no longer put it off. With the help of a relative in England who is interested in genealogy, she collected the birth and marriage certificates of her direct female ancestresses back to 1848.

Lindsey's process with the *Beth Din* dragged on for 2 months through bureaucratic delays and sheer bloody-mindedness on the part of the *dayanim*.

> I showed them all the documents, they sniffed, they fussed, they weren't very happy but they wouldn't put their finger on anything. They wouldn't say 'No, you're not Jewish,' they wouldn't say 'Yes, you are Jewish.' Eventually they hummed and they haaed and, said 'Okay, you are Jewish but you have to go and do *tvila*.'

After a farcical procedure during which she was treated like a convert, Lindsey was duly 'dunked' in the *mikveh*.

> I emerged seething with fury. I was given a piece of paper which said 'Leah Hannah, otherwise known as Lindsey Taylor, is a Jewess born of a Jewish mother and she can't marry a Cohen.' So Norm, my husband, had to prove he wasn't a Cohen.

Over the Sea from Skye

For psychologist Rowena Macdonald, 'Jewish with a funny name, Scottish with a funny religion', Israel is a place where she belongs. Exempted from Sunday church attendance at her high school, she felt 'I didn't belong there, I didn't belong anywhere really.' As an undergraduate she became very involved in Jewish student activities but the feeling persisted: 'I didn't fit in on the Isle of Skye, I didn't fit in in London.' So after her degree, it was off to Israel to stay: 'I felt pretty much at home when I came here. It's nice that my name isn't considered strange here. People hear a foreign name and they don't classify Jewish or not Jewish. They never even ask me if I'm Jewish, they just assume I am.'

Throughout her peripatetic childhood when the family celebrated *Hanukah*, Christmas, Easter, 'almost anything there was to celebrate', Rowena knew she was Jewish. Her parents met at university in America, spent a year as exchange students in Scotland where she was born, returned to the States and then travelled from country to country until they separated in Turkey when Rowena was six. The wandering continued: Greece, back to Turkey, France, then England where her mother remarried. Eventually, when Rowena was twelve, the family settled in Scotland. 'They wanted somewhere that was very far away and remote so they moved up to the Isle of Skye.'

Rowena's father's family, originally from Scotland, had gone to Canada several generations back and then moved down to the States. Her mother had come to America from Germany at the age of four. 'She went to *cheder*, she celebrated the main *hagim* but the house was very much an assimilated house. The whole emphasis was very much on being an American citizen and the need to fit in.' Nevertheless her mother's family were 'very, very upset' when she married Rowena's gentile father, even though he went through a reform conversion. This Rowena derides: 'It was nothing. He met the rabbi three times and the third time he had a token circumcision. It was highly ritual and he fainted.'

While her brothers and sister are indifferent to their Jewish background, Rowena has inherited her mother's 'very strong Jewish identity'. There were books by Jewish authors at home and books on teaching yourself Hebrew, so at the age of fifteen or sixteen, Rowena taught herself the Hebrew alphabet. Her mother, who had learnt to read Hebrew at *cheder*, was very sympathetic.

Rowena's first taste of Judaism as a religion was in Edinburgh where she spent a year before university. At the synagogue she met a couple who invited her to live with them. She became observant which, at first, her mother found hard to accept.

> I'd come home and I wouldn't eat and things like that and she'd get very upset but some years later when I was in my early twenties she said it was very important for her because she kind of gave up the heritage and she was very happy that one of her children at least was going to maintain it.

Family ties are an integral part of Rowena's Judaism.

> I think you have to have a lot of respect. When I was becoming religious, a rabbi in Glasgow told me I should keep *Shabbat* and keep kosher and not eat in my parents' home. I said 'Isn't that like not respecting my mother who cooks me something special?' Anyway, they were vegetarian. Your real roots are your family ties in you and these universal values of respect and love and caring and giving each other space. It's not a Jewish thing, it transcends all religions. So I guess as a

good Jew I didn't keep kosher or *Shabbat* 100 per cent when I was at home but I felt I was being a good Jewish daughter.

She does not regret coming from a mixed family:

> I had a very, very good childhood. I had a complicated childhood with a lot of conflicts, a lot of identity problems – I still have it – but I don't think we're born into this world to have easy lives. Complexes and conflicts are part of life and I can't see why my life would have been any better if my father had been Jewish too.

Is the Law an Ass?

Israel is where James Moses* was finally accepted as an orthodox Jew. The descendant of a distinguished Anglo-Jewish family, he was born 'a half-patrilineal. My mother was a liberal convert which meant I had to go through conversion again.' Strung along by the London *Beth Din* for several years, he was eventually packed off to Israel by the *dayanim*.

Moses and his sisters 'were brought up thinking of ourselves as Jewish. I was only vaguely aware that it made a difference having a mother who was a liberal convert.' The family attended synagogue about twice a year, fasted on *Yom Kippur* and had a *seder* night. Moses' grandfather, though not especially observant, was president of the orthodox United Synagogue for many years.

> Paradoxically, I imagine if my father had married a Jewish woman from the same background we'd probably have been brought up with an assimilated English background, hardly aware that we were Jewish, and might never have become more aware. The fact of his marrying a convert and having to go through education made him more committed to the liberal synagogue than he would have been to the United Synagogue.

The advent of student rabbi Julia Neuberger at the synagogue religion school which Moses joined to prepare for 'confirmation' at sixteen was something of an inspiration. 'About the time of the confirmation my sisters and I started getting more interested and more committed and persuaded our parents step by step to make the home more kosher. We began by not having pork and shellfish and moved on to not mixing milk and meat.' By the time he went up to Oxford to read Hebrew, Moses was living the life of an orthodox Jew.

> It was then that I discovered the full implications of the situation that they wouldn't count me in the *minyan*. Up to then when I'd been to

> orthodox services I'd occasionally been tenth man and been called up to the Torah without realising that anything was wrong with it. One day I was talking to someone there about my family and said my mother was a liberal convert and he said, 'Wait a minute, don't you realise that you shouldn't be counted in a *minyan*?'

This was evidently a very painful memory for Moses: 'I felt terrible.' He applied straightaway to the London *Beth Din*.

> I imagined it would be a fairly straightforward procedure. I was observing *kashrut* and *Shabbat*. They gave me a very, very long runaround. I had several interviews. The *dayanim* were quite avuncular. I was about 18 or 19 and they wanted to be sure I was completely committed. I was still living at home and they were very worried about the *kashrut* at home. What also bothered them was that I was studying Hebrew and they thought I must be getting all sorts of horrible heretical opinions from my professors.
>
> There was a point when I decided to let them go to hell. For about a year, I gave up the whole thing, stopped eating kosher. After my first visit to the *Beth Din* they sent me to an excellent rabbi, Rabbi Wiesenberg. I used to go and study with him and he invited me on *Shabbatot*. We used to talk a lot about the *Beth Din*. There was this marvellous phrase he used: 'There are people who say the Law is an ass. The Law is not an ass but those who administer the Law are frequently asinine.' I didn't stop seeing Wiesenberg, I didn't stop going to synagogue. I travelled on *Shabbat*. I was at that stage a progressive Jew, I certainly wasn't a secular Jew. Wiesenberg was understanding. It was really he who brought me back out of the non-kosher phase. I think that ultimately the whole progressive Jewish bit doesn't satisfy me – I have no intention of delegitimising it – but as soon as I spent more time studying I wanted to be more orthodox. It was more authentic for me.

Nearly three years had passed after Moses' first visit to the *Beth Din*. He returned after hearing nothing from them for a year. They obviously knew of his lapses.

> They were much more difficult. Now they wanted me to move in with an orthodox family in Golders Green. I didn't. The following year I went to Jews' College. I spoke to the principal and he accepted me in the Rabbinics programme. He said the best method to deal with the *Beth Din* was *chutzpah* but I'm not like that. The *Beth Din* didn't like me studying at Jews' College. At that stage the then Chief Rabbi came into

it. This, I think, was at my grandfather's prompting. I saw him once. What he said, in essence, was that he would love to help or be seen to be helpful but he didn't dare stick his neck out against the *Beth Din*.

By then Moses had made overtures to the Sephardi *Beth Din* and was attending Bevis Marks. The Sephardi rabbi suggested he should do his conversion in Israel.

Eventually I finished here in Israel. I think the *Beth Din*'s nerve finally failed them and they sent me off there. They said, 'Go to Israel and you'll be better off where the Jews are in a majority.' What they didn't add was 'Away from bad influences like your parents and progressive Judaism.'

I went to the Jerusalem *Beth Din*. It all went rather quickly. Everything must have finished about 6 weeks or 2 months after I'd applied to them. The whole style is totally different. The London *Beth Din* is gentlemanly, slow-moving and pompous, anything you want from them you send them a letter. Here it's standard Israeli bureaucracy, you're in this reception room full of people and you fill in these complicated forms. Eventually you got a time for an interview. At the second interview they already gave me a time for the *mikveh*. Painful memories. If you've been circumcised you have to do what's called *hatazat dam brit* – drawing a drop of blood. The *dam brit* and the *mikveh* were the same day. I got a good feeling from the *mikveh*, I'm all for it.

Years of struggle had finally ended.

I did feel relieved after the conversion. I was then 23. I think *halacha* is a sort of rule of thumb that isn't going to apply in all cases. It always upset me that what I was doing was called conversion. I felt in myself that what I was doing was rectification of status.

The Hand of Providence

Helen Matthews, now Ruth Weinberger, was forced to go to Israel.

My father and my sister took me to the plane with tears streaming down my face. I felt they were doing what was right for me, I knew they cared and loved me, but I felt rejected by my family. My father and my sister were pushing me out on my own into something quite unknown, something I didn't even want to do.

Now an ultra-orthodox Jewess in Jerusalem, Ruth sees the steps that led her to Israel and Judaism as *hashgacha pratit,* the hand of providence.

Ruth's mother's family were refugees from Nazi Vienna. Everyone except her mother's father managed to escape, some to England and some to America. Miraculously Ruth's grandfather was saved by a gentile lady in England who responded to a magazine advertisement and sent the fare for him to be evacuated to Boston. This lady was to be Ruth's great-aunt.

Ruth's father, a conscientious objector, worked in China during the war. On his return to England he was looking for a wife.

> He remembered this sweet Jewish woman he'd met at his aunt's. He wrote to her, obviously they'd kept a connection. My mother had Jewish suitors at the time but when my father wrote there was no doubt in her mind. She just got up and left very quickly and went to England to marry him. I have a feeling that her parents' gratitude for the fact that they were saved by this family meant they could give their daughter.

It was a stable, middle-class Engish family. Ruth's father, the son of a missionary, was agnostic, and the children were raised basically non-religious. For a short time Ruth was taken to Sunday school and church by her grandmother. 'It made a strong impression on me and I did enjoy in a way going to the church. It felt something secure there, but at the same time I felt it wasn't right.'

Ruth's mother had always impressed on her that she was a full Jew. 'She told me if Hitler should come again I would be killed along with the other Jews. I also knew the expression "a miserly Jew". So I was brought up with "A Jew is persecuted, a Jew is a miser".' Visits to her mother's parents in Boston hardly improved the image. 'My reaction as a child was that they were very odd and strange. I was much more familiar with my English grandmother's tea tray, scones and watching Blue Peter on TV.'

However, there was an underlying sense of displacement. 'I always felt alienated with the *goyim* and I never knew it was because they were *goyim* but when I was with Jews I didn't feel great either and still to some extent struggle with that. I think people coming from an intermarriage do struggle with it. We don't fit.' Nevertheless she and the only other Jewish girl in her class at school 'gravitated together and formed a close friendship'.

At York University she studied education with biology. After graduating she had no wish to start teaching immediately, but spent a couple more years in York working in a garden centre and then went to Manchester. Three years after graduation it was too late to get a job as a biology teacher. About the same time she broke up with the university crowd.

Now Ruth had to think 'What do I really want?' She applied throughout England and Wales to do nursing with a view to taking up community midwifery but was not accepted – something she sees again as *hashgacha pratit.*

Her mother's Jewishness was expressed very rarely. She may have put a stop to churchgoing and took Ruth – though not her brothers or sister – out of scripture class at high school. Instead of writing a note, she made a tiny Torah scroll and sent Ruth to school with this to give to her teacher. 'That's how my mother was struggling and fighting to make her conscience clear,' Ruth recollects. Now her mother stepped in. 'Go to Israel. It will offer you community life. You'll get a new start,' she said. Ruth refused point blank. Her mother bought a ticket but after a family disagreement the night Ruth was supposed to fly, she ran off with the ticket and Ruth missed the plane. A year later Ruth had still not settled and again her mother said 'Israel'. This time there was no turning back.

At a non-religious kibbutz, Ruth started working in the kitchen and attended the *ulpan* to learn Hebrew. 'It was a joke, I fell right behind, I'd never seen an *aleph*, let alone a *bet* or a *gimel*, the whole alphabet was hieroglyphics to me.'

On a free weekend she found herself at the *kotel* in Jerusalem. 'It was Friday night, I was in my denim jeans and T-shirt and a rabbi asked me "Are you a Jew?" ' He invited her to have a *Shabbat* dinner.

> It was in a beautiful modern building in the old city, very atmospheric. There was no electric light, just the candlelit table with about thirty people and for the first time in my life they made a *bracha*, I washed my hands, I made a blessing on *challa*. It probably tasted like dew from heaven.

Ruth was deeply impressed. 'It was strange but somehow all too familiar. It felt right. Like walking at last in a really comfortable pair of shoes.' Two days later she met the rabbi again by chance and told him she didn't want to return to the kibbutz. 'Maybe you'll be happy in a *yeshiva*,' he suggested. Ruth didn't know what that was but thought it worth a try. 'I just had this sense of discovery, journey, I have to find my niche.'

Her niche was clearly in the orthodox world. It was then she took her new name, keeping Hebrew versions of 'Helen Charlotte', names she had been given for aunts killed in the Holocaust. After a year at *yeshiva* in Jerusalem, she spent 2 years at the Lubavitch seminary in Safed. Then, with a *bracha* from the Lubavitcher Rebbe, she came back to Jerusalem to find a husband. Through a recommended *shadchan* in the Mea Shearim, she met her husband, an American *ba'al teshuva*.

Her parents were thrilled.

> I feel I gave them *naches*. They loved my husband, my first child was the first grandchild and my mother was so happy and my father also. My mother koshered her kitchen, put a *mezzuzah* up on the door and

started to light *Shabbes* candles. My father kept the kitchen kosher. I feel he was a potential *ger.*

Tragically Ruth's father was killed in a road accident and her mother died of cancer 2 years later, with Ruth and her sister holding her hands.

Even though they died in very different ways I feel my mother and father passed away almost together. Despite my mother's probable deep loneliness living as an assimilated Jew, my father adored her. Some people think that there can be no love between a Jew and a non-Jew but my mother and father loved each other very, very much.

MIXED BLESSINGS

My grandmother was engaged to a Jewish boy but she broke the engagement to marry my Catholic grandfather. There was a big scandal. She didn't tell her parents she was married for a very long time. She went home every night and finally told her mother. Her mother said, 'We can't tell your father' so they made up some story about her living with a friend. When they finally told him, he completely ostracised her. He didn't speak to her for three years until they had a child, my mother.

My grandmother kept kosher but she would prepare non-kosher food for my grandfather. Before they got married they agreed the children would be raised Jewish. They had both Jewish and Christian holidays in the house. My grandfather was a practising Catholic, we used to dye Easter eggs with him and celebrate Christmas. I knew he definitely never understood our customs.

My grandmother is very strongly Jewish. It was very important to her to talk about being Jewish. She, who married a Catholic, only wants me to marry somebody who's Jewish.

Rebecca Kravitz, New York

Not Damaged Goods

The hostility that confronts many mixed couples is, itself, a test of devotion. Daniel* and Sophie's* relationship provides a telling example. It also shows how the non-Jewish partner can contribute to the couple's Jewish commitment.

When they got together at university, Sophie had little knowledge of Jews and was hardly aware that her handsome, Italian-looking boyfriend was Jewish. Now, she observes things Jewish with an insider's practised eye. But on her first visit to the family's north London home, she was surprised to hear his mother say, 'Not as a girlfriend, Daniel.'

Daniel's family, four generations in England, were not very observant. Rejection of any non-Jewish partner remained the last bastion of their Jewish identification. They were a close extended family, characterised by 'extensive quantities of food and extensive pressure to eat'. While Daniel and his siblings reacted by assuming 'a forced cool', Sophie, the illegitimate offspring of a three-month liaison, craved these warm family ties.

'That's why it was so hard when they rejected me in the beginning,' she recalls. Having suffered for some time from bouts of depression, she found this was exacerbated by being banned from Daniel's home. All the while, his continuing attachment was causing ructions in the family.

A turning point came when Daniel could afford to move out and gave his parents an ultimatum: 'I just said, "You want me, you get the whole package." ' Sophie, still feeling unwell, was promptly invited round to tea. She was received politely, but any warmth was lacking.

From then on Sophie came 'every so often', still feeling completely unwelcome. The 'minutest change' in Daniel's parents' behaviour seemed 'months apart'. Her depression worsened and she had to go into hospital for a while. 'I felt I was completely damaged goods. I was not only not Jewish, I was totally and utterly useless to them. I was making their son's life a complete misery by being such a drain. Daniel stuck by me through all of this.'

Luckily, Sophie found a psychiatrist who diagnosed her as manic depressive and prescribed lithium. Miraculously she improved and got a good job. Soon after that the couple took a flat together. Daniel's parents were certainly impressed by the change and in due course Sophie was completely accepted as one of the family. She has shown her own devotion by being strong for Daniel and offering his parents support and advice. On occasion, Daniel's mother has turned to her more readily than to her own daughter.

Although Daniel was turned off by Jewish ceremonies his parents observed in their lukewarm fashion, he is now 'retasting things' through Sophie, who appreciates customs scorned by 'cool' young Jews like lighting Sabbath candles. He has also become fascinated by aspects of Jewish culture and ritual. An actor by profession, he has won acclaim in Yiddish theatre, taking his family's original name as a stage name. While Sophie does not intend to convert to Judaism, she might decide, if they eventually marry, to take the course of study the Reform Synagogues now offer non-Jewish wives which entitles their children to be raised as Jews.

Still Jewish

Not all mixed couples encounter opposition. Ivan Ezekiel, the son of Sephardi Jews from India, recalls that his parents were 'fantastic' about his marriage to Ginette, a gentile Frenchwoman, even though 'marrying out' had been extremely rare in the small, highly cohesive Calcutta community. 'I'm sure the fact they liked Ginette was the overriding factor.' There is, he feels, greater tolerance of intermarriage among the immigrant Sephardi community his parents belong to than among the London Ashkenazi community which, as a young man, he found as hard to penetrate as English society.

The Ezekiels' two nearly adult children were brought up with no religion, as Ginette explains: 'I didn't want to force them to be Catholic and they couldn't be Jewish because I'm not. It's not fair for Ivan because they have to be my religion if we wanted to give them a religion.' She has felt very comfortable at religious ceremonies with her parents-in-law or family friends and, Ivan believes, knows 'quite a bit' about the Jewish faith. 'My impression is that when she talks to other people about it she speaks about it quite proudly.'

Jewishness, for Ivan, is more than a religion. 'It says more about you. I'm not English, not British, not Indian, not any of those things. When someone says "What are you?", at least the one thing I can say is "I'm Jewish". That's very important to me and I use that almost in place of a national identity.'

He is conscious that he has not communicated much about the religion to his children but feels their Jewish ties might strengthen later. 'What I have communicated I've communicated quite strongly. It may be something for them to hang onto.'

Air Commodore Antony Wober was also born in India but his father was Ashkenazi. He believes that since his childhood, when he sometimes got taunted with 'dirty Jew', Jewishness has become acceptable and even fashionable.

> I think my children have grown up in a time when it's something to be proud of to have Jewish blood and Jewish connections. There's a certain cachet about it, so I think it has been more comfortable for them than my Christian wife who was a child in the prejudiced-against-Jews era.

Although no family members died in World War II, the Holocaust has exerted a profound influence over him ever since, as a young boy, he sat in his north London home with a magazine of pictures of the gas chambers in his lap. A particularly apt way of balancing his 'diluted Jewish life-style' and reaffirming his Jewish identity was to visit several Nazi concentration camps with his family. Standing on Hitler's bunker in Berlin he experienced complete catharsis, at the site of the Warsaw Ghetto, a moment of triumph, in Jerusalem relief that the victims had a final resting place.

Conscious that he and his wife have each suppressed a side of themselves in order to preserve a *modus vivendi* and raise their children without a particular religion, he has felt increasing nostalgia for 'singing those familiar hymns or doing some familiar rituals which are in themselves a comfort', for experiencing 'the joys in religion as a family'. However, he has come to realise that his pilgrimage on behalf of the Jewish dead has been a uniquely personal and valid way of expressing his Jewishness. 'Each time I stopped to pray at one of these sites, I created my own shrine and I wanted it to really count.'

Family solidarity inspired by her mother enabled Madame C and her brothers and sisters, immigrants to Paris from Tunisia, to preserve a Jewish family life although each of them had married a non-Jew. 'As we took the good things of the Jewish religion, we took some of the customs, for example the meals, because that united the family. We only went to synagogue for the Day of Atonement. We had Passover at my mother's. We were all together.' Since her mother died, the family bond has continued, but is threatened, not by defections from the Jewish fold but by the intolerance of some of the younger generation who have formally converted to Judaism. 'Because they weren't really born Jewish they have become very strict. I find they exaggerate.'

NOT THE END

As the stories in this chapter indicate, Jewishness can emerge from a mixed marriage, even without any Jewish upbringing. For the majority of Jewish partners in mixed marriages, the return of a child to the ancestral faith provides intense gratification and even a sense of 'repair'. While in mixed marriages nowadays the Jewish partner is not renouncing a Jewish identity, a greater acceptance of such couples and their families within some Jewish framework is likely both to bolster the identity of the individual and increase the likelihood of continuity.

8

The Promise Spurned

THE PROMISE SPURNED

The 'Israel experience' is increasingly recommended as a means of re-inforcing the Jewish identity of diaspora youth. Many secular Israelis, however, are extremely ambivalent about their Jewishness. The dichotomy between a state officially functioning according to Jewish law and the Jewish calendar and the large number of flagrantly secular inhabitants comes as a surprise to many first-time visitors to Israel. Abroad, too, the majority of secular Israeli ex-pats have no absolutely no connection to any Jewish institutions.

Israelis or Jews?

Shai Ofir* and his wife Ronit* share a hostility to Judaism characteristic of many secular Israelis in their thirties or younger who grew up with a political establishment dominated by blatantly unsavoury horse-trading by the various religious parties. They came to England 'to have a different experience' from a neighbourhood in Israel where there was no synagogue and have no desire to mix with Israelis or Jews. The predominantly Jewish neighbourhood where they happened to rent their first home was, for Shai, 'like waving a red rag at a bull'.

Muli Kellner has lived in Canada, England, Hong Kong and the United States for some twenty years. About 50 per cent of the population in his Manhattan neighbourhood are Jewish. This does not appear to bother Kellner. He feels very comfortable in New York 'where everybody is a foreigner and nobody is a foreigner'. His circle of friends includes 'Israelis and non-Israelis, Jews and non-Jews'.

Both Kellner and the Ofirs come from extremely secular backgrounds where none of the Jewish festivals was observed in a religious fashion. Instead, Passover and *Rosh Hashana* and other festivals are celebrated with get-togethers of family and friends.

Yom Kippur is not observed. Kellner recalls his youth in Israel when, like many secular Israelis, he used to go to the beach on the most sacred day in the Jewish calendar. In New York, he and his Israeli wife 'tried to go to *shul* on *Yom Kippur* for the kid and all three of us felt we were in the wrong place. We do not enjoy the congregation or the procedures so we've given it up.'

The Ofirs' approach to *Yom Kippur* is more aggressive. 'I'm really quite annoyed by *Yom Kippur*,' says Shai, who made a point of spending this day doing reserve duty in the army during his university years. 'It's pure hypocrisy, pure rubbish to fast on *Yom Kippur*.' Instead, the Ofirs 'do our own thing at home with a lot of food and a lot of friends'. As a youngster, Ronit once wanted to fast on *Yom Kippur* 'as a sport. My parents told me, "You will fast between meals."'

This spirit of dissension is fuelled by the non-separation between religion and state in Israel. 'We hate so much the Jewish faith because it controls all the areas of life,' Ronit explains. 'There can't be something in the middle. It's all or nothing.' 'I would respect people who were religious if they behaved as they behaved at home, if they didn't influence my way of living or prevent me from driving on *Yom Kippur*,' Shai adds, referring to whole neighbourhoods in Israel where traffic stops on that one day. 'I would respect them but I would like them to respect me at exactly the same level – they can't.' Hence, his suspicion and resentment of religious Jews across the board who, he feels, are intent on making Israel an absolute theocracy. 'If people like myself will not be a watchdog that liberty will be preserved and that one will be entitled to lead a liberal life in Israel, very soon, sooner than we think, we will not be entitled to this.'

Not surprisingly, this resentment influences the Ofirs' sense of identity. 'In Israel I'm defined as a Jew on my identity card – unfortunately,' says Shai. 'In England, I will not identify myself as a Jew.' Ronit agrees. 'I'm Israeli, I'm not a Jew.' Kellner, in contrast, has a more mellow view of his identity:

> Am I a Jew or an Israeli? Living abroad for very many years the distinction gets blurred. But I'm both. Being Jewish is the religion you carry and Israeli is a nationality and citizenship and I happen to have one of each. I was born Jewish, I am Jewish, I'm not a practising Jew but this is who I am.

His young daughter, who was heard asking 'Daddy, are we Jewish?' is 'American for all intents and purposes. There's no question that that's what she identifies with.' But she speaks Hebrew fluently and likes to know about Israel and not be considered a foreigner when she goes there.

It is the American Jewish establishment that Kellner and his family find particularly unpalatable. 'It's a very materialistic, show-off type of society. They use *shul* and bar mitzvahs and other things to compete. We simply don't like it, we don't like the people so we are having a rough time adjusting to being with them.' His daughter's hostility became apparent when she refused to go to Sunday School like many of her friends to learn to read and write Hebrew. 'She hates the *shul* and that's part of the *shul* and she reacts against this environment.'

Kellner believes it would be the same to him whoever his daughter were to marry. 'It's easier said than done but I think so.' The Ofirs would be very upset if any of their children married traditional Jews. Shai is sensitive to the 'cultural gap that will develop between my children and myself' if they were to marry a foreigner. 'But I couldn't care less if they married an Israeli Catholic if there was such a thing.'

Lost Illusions

> I belong to the *aliyah* of the seventies. We were idealistic, we were Zionistic, we wanted to belong to the Jewish people, to work for the Jewish country, to be part of the brotherhood because we were tired of being second-class citizens. When I came here I went on *Shabbat* to the synagogue, I said the *brachot* and all these things but not now because I don't feel anything.
>
> Religion supplies morality and ethics and this could be instilled in people through education without all this dependence on the rabbi and all these funny things. All these rituals, they're just paganism, because what is pure religion, just belief in the contact between the individual and God, you don't need church or synagogue for this. People waste all their life sitting and studying and fulfilling *613 mitzvot* and being terrified to start washing their hands not from the left but from the right and so on. That's why I think being religious is a waste of time, both for them and for society.
>
> Most of the immigrants of my generation came to understand that our idealism, like any idealism, was a wrong idea and slowly moved away from being part of the nation. From my point of view supporting and emphasising and developing ideals of nationhood works against the positive development of mankind. All this leads to quarrels, to complications, to wars, so to support national belonging, to support being Jewish as opposed to being human, I think historically and generally it is wrong.
>
> Russian immigrant Boris Rubinstein, sculptor, Tel-Aviv

DISSENT OR SOMETHING ELSE?

Increasing numbers of Jews from a variety of backgrounds see the faith of their ancestors as something alien. Where Jews in the past abandoned both faith and identity to further their social and professional ambitions, Jews today may seek some alternative to Judaism but retain some form of Jewish identity.

Where Do They Come From?

> I grew up in a strictly orthodox household which I took for granted till I came to my senses. I was then about thirteen. I had a huge bar mitzvah. I rather revolted before then but it took shape after that. I didn't go to synagogue unless I had to take the old man [His father Moses Gaster, the former Haham, who was then blind]. I got into the very wicked habit of taking the old man, seeing he was safely installed in his seat and then vamoose and come back in time to pick him up.
>
> Jack Gaster, former member of the Communist Party of Great Britain and retired lawyer, London

> I lived in an orthodox Jewish home until I was sixteen. Actually, I existed, that's more like it. I did take part, I went to *shul* every *Shabbes* and did whatever was required of me. I was very restricted and I left when I was sixteen and since then I haven't been observant.
>
> Asphodel Long, feminist writer and lecturer, Brighton.

> My family is orthodox. I went through the rituals of bar mitzvah, Sunday school, Friday night, all at the orthodox level, and experienced a complete lack of spirit. My bar mitzvah should have been some type of threshold into manhood but was an actual denial of any type of manhood. At seventeen, I was sitting by the Wailing Wall in Jerusalem feeling this immense sorrow that Jerusalem had been destroyed so many times in the name of religion when a rabbi representing one of the schools in the area picked me up. 'What is it about Jerusalem that all this fighting and destruction symbolises for us today?' I asked. He answered that I needed to come to a *shiur* and spend many years in religious practice and maybe I'd like to give them some money. I looked at this man and thought: 'If this is where

our religion is, I have real difficulty in being with my Jewishness in the form he wanted to present it.'

Robert Wallis, businessman, London

I was brought up 'mock-orthodox'. The vast majority of the community were only orthodox when they were in the synagogue. As far as I could determine at a fairly early age they were also agnostic. What held them together and gave them a sense of belonging and satisfaction was strongly based on ritual. I thought it was really a sort of spiritual masturbation and decided when I was 16 that I would walk away from it.

Mike Goldmark, bookseller, Rutland

Where early experience of orthodoxy may result in alienation, less intense or virtually negligible levels of Jewish religious experience often leave a void. Although Helen Shapiro, the British singer, grew up in a very traditional Jewish environment she 'didn't know much about what Jewish beliefs were'. Unlike her brother who went to *cheder* and had a bar mitzvah, she had no formal Jewish education.

At school the Jewish kids only took Old Testament so I knew all the 'hit' stories, Moses and David and all that. I also knew about this person or this something called the Messiah who was going to come one day. I must have absorbed it by osmosis.

Tamar Witkin, a musician who grew up in Vermont and now lives in Connecticut, also found that Bible stories were not enough.

We were told what they mean and what their moral implication was. All this was intellectually stimulating but it didn't grab me. My mother did what she could but everything was kind of haphazard because of the culture being so Christian-dominated. We did celebrate *Hanukah* and *Rosh Hashana* and sometimes we'd observe the Sabbath but not consistently, not on a regular basis.

Allen Ginsberg, the American poet, did not have a bar mitzvah although he lived across the street from a synagogue and was sent to Hebrew school by his left-wing Bohemian Jewish intellectual parents to have some experience of Jewish culture. 'I didn't last there very long. There was a very intemperate rabbi who kicked me out for asking questions. I must have been about 8 or 9 and began enquiring about what was going on, trying to figure it out.' Not surprisingly, the young Ginsberg sought answers to the mysteries of the universe elsewhere. Daniel Cohen, a retired lecturer whose parents were agnostic, attended Jewish prayers at Manchester Grammar School but found the services meaningless. 'I never learnt Hebrew. My parents asked me if I wanted a bar mitzvah, expecting the answer "no".' He remained an agnostic until he was about forty.

Secular agnosticism serves some as a kick-off point for further exploration. For others it remains their philosophy of life. Stephen Bloom, named 'the most prolific scientist in Europe' by *The Daily Telegraph* in 1991, also had agnostic parents. His mother had converted to Judaism 'to appease the family'. 'My father was the person who took the active step to reject religion. I've drifted into non-belief, following my father.' Not wishing to disappoint his grandparents, Bloom had a bar mitzvah in a progressive synagogue in London. 'I was quite interested in the process, how a service worked, who was involved, what religion was about. It was part of my education really. I didn't positively disbelieve at that stage.'

Bruce Bart, whose parents were part of the hip Bohemian Communist scene of the 1930s, was brought up in a very Jewish town in Long Island by his atheist Jewish mother after her separation from his Italian atheist father. Now living near Woodstock in up-state New York, Bart, who remains a fervent non-believer, is a hippy lookalike of Chief Rabbi Jonathan Sacks, bearded, but with a pigtail and a tattooed leg. He was never sent to Hebrew school and feels he missed something. 'I felt kind of left out when other kids had bar mitzvahs and I didn't. Maybe it was just the party and the presents but whatever it was I didn't get it. I knew all the *haftorahs* because I memorised every other kid's.'

Voices of Dissent

Jewish separateness and the superiority it is perceived to imply often provoke dissent. Allen Ginsberg, for example, likens a particularist Jewish identity with claims to salvation made by the other monotheistic traditions and contrasts these with eastern religions – Buddhism, Confucianism, Taoism – which are concerned with aspects of nature rather than a divine centre. For Ginsberg, 'the Judaeo-Christian tradition of the monotheistic dominant hierarchy seems hallucinatory – hallucinating at God'. A differing perspective is put forward by René Reims, a psychic and mystic living in Paris, who had a Jewish father but was raised a Catholic. Where Reims sees Christianity with it's notion of sin and pretensions to salvation as out of touch with current trends of thought and doomed to extinction if it doesn't adapt itself very seriously, he believes Judaism and Islam, like Buddhism, are religions that will last because they accept other religions and make of the religion 'an art of living'.

Mike Goldmark feels very strongly 'that if one was to be worthwhile on this planet then one ought to sever one's ties with any group'. His rejection of Jewish separateness led him to brush off his ex-wife's sincere conversion to Judaism and eventually 'kill' her desire to be Jewish. Bruce Bart sees conversion as 'witchcraft, the same crap as every other moronic religion'. His Italian father, who had always admired certain Jewish attributes, converted to Judaism some years ago. 'Why would anyone ever want to do something like that unless you totally had an identity crisis and needed to identify with some group. It's like people being in a complete state of *anomie* if they don't attach themselves to whatever's happening.' Boris Rubinstein is equally dismissive of Russian immigrants to Israel who conform: 'There's a kind of mimicry – like when insects try to look like the background – because they feel, like most people, a necessity to be like other people.'

Bart's first wife also converted – in order to have a Jewish wedding. Her conversion, under the auspices of a prestigious Manhattan reform synagogue, was accomplished in two 3 hour sessions with a young 'hipster flipster' rabbi where 'instruction' was interspersed with bagels and lax and 'a big brisket dinner'. The absurdity of the process reinforced Bart's anti-religious sentiments.

> The whole thing was nonsensical but I think all religions are. I don't think because I like some of the teachings of Buddha I'd call myself a Buddhist and just because there might be something interesting of some great Jew, Moses or someone, that I become a Jew.

To have no use for religion may be a luxury. Stephen Bloom sees it this way:

> I was lucky I never underwent any particular emotional trauma like a parent or brother or sister who died which might have increased the emphasis on religion or the need for religion as a support. Also under other circumstances, if we'd been persecuted as a people in Rumania or something, I'd probably have been far more religious because there would have been perhaps more need and more example. When one sees members of one's community sacrificing themselves for their religion, you can't help feeling it should be taken more seriously. In our rather comfortable plenty of food no problem society, the need for religion is less obvious.

An excessive emphasis in Judaism on rules and ritual as opposed to spirituality is another factor which generates dissent. Goldmark sees this in many Jews: 'There's so much noise and clatter in terms of what they do that I don't actually hear them leading a spiritual life. They may lead a very rigid life in terms of rules but I never really got a sense of what their God was.' Helen Shapiro senses that the Jewish concept of 'good works' has been transmuted into a code of behaviour:

> So much is like you scratch your ear with your left little finger and not your right little finger and that's where I say 'Come on, do you think God really minds if you do it with your left finger or your right finger?' I know I'm taking it to silly extremes but I believe that God sees into the heart and that's what He wants to know.

A Spiritual Menu

> You Jews are so spiritual. Look at Buddhists, Hindus, Sufis – so many of them are Jews.
>
> The Dalai Lama to Ram Dass, Jew and Hindu;
> anecdote recounted by Daniel Cohen

The alternative spiritual direction taken by many Jews is not a new phenomenon. Lost Jews of mixed parentage spoke of parents or grandparents who had experimented with a variety of spiritual cocktails. Robert Beecham's grandmother, a Jewess from India, was educated in a convent school.

> The nuns would beat her for being Jewish or having Jewish ideas. Her mother would beat her for whatever the nuns taught her. So she turned away from all formal religion and delved into everything from Buddhism to Subud to Rosicrucianism to Spiritism and Christian Science, she went through the gamut really.

Erica Ferszt, a student in New York, grew up in a Christian–Jewish hotch-potch:

> My mother in her childhood was strictly Roman Catholic. She wanted to convert to Judaism but they wouldn't let her unless she denounced the New Testament. Now she works for *Hadassah*. She goes to church every Sunday, she's a born-again Christian but she has a soft spot for Jewish people. My father was born Jewish, he became a Christian about 3 weeks before he married my mother. He's now remarried a fanatic Jew but he's still Christian. He goes to synagogue on Friday nights and goes to church on Sunday morning. In America today, you have people converting all the time if they care about what religion they are.

Ben Cohen's background is steeped in alternative spirituality. His grandmother was from a liberal Jewish family while his grandfather – 'Mr Cohen of the *Dictionary of Modern Quotations'* – was 'secularly and culturally Jewish'.

> My grandparents got into a thing called 'The Work' and the Theosophical movement. I think my dad picked that up. My mother and father met as Quakers. From the Theosophical Society my grandparents followed the Maharishi Mahesh Yogi, as did my parents – they followed Quakerism and Maharishi at the same time, Maharishi taking a front seat. As the movement gained apace and became multinational, my grandfather became a bit disillusioned. He and my grandmother then found a Tibetan Buddhist pen-pal and later converted to Tibetan Buddhism. My grandmother, who feels very Jewish by race, feels herself to be a Jewish Tibetan Buddhist.

The Search

To find a spiritual home may involve a lengthy search, with alternatives taken up and rejected. For some, like Robert Wallis, the search, itself, becomes a kind of home.

> At eighteen I started to get pains in my heart and develop what I see now as actual stress. I went to doctors and had tests over a period of years and they told me there was nothing wrong with me. I was experiencing huge amounts of pain and getting very depressed and withdrawing from the world. It was definitely the searching. I felt lost.
>
> My experience was of feeling separate from the actual being I am. The separate feeling with religion and Jewishness is that God is outside, separate from the human. In my particular instance the idea of God outside my being presented me with huge problems, because what it means is as a human one can never really achieve godhead.
>
> I eventually ended up seeing an ayurvedic, Indian-based holistic doctor and he was the first person to say he actually knew what I was experiencing. What I have experienced in fact is that there is an inner life of every single being and that inner life leads one to the experience of being a seed rather than only being a tree. This doctor sent me to a psycho-synthesis therapist – I'm now one myself. One of the main contributions of psycho-synthesis is recognising the spirit or self or higher self which actually is our essential being. Over a period of time I have come to understand something of my own being. From that

paradox of living, that paradox of my seed, I experience more of who I am as a tree.

I meditate in a number of different ways. My main practice is silence and to just be with myself. I have explored Vipassana meditation, more Buddhist, following the breath, also transcendental meditation and mantra meditation. For me spirituality is beyond any definition of form. The expression could be anything – eating an apple, looking at a tree – it could be sitting there absolutely doing nothing. I'm a member of a men's group which is mytho-poetic in nature. We are interested in the symbolism that is contained in stories and myths and applying that through into our daily existence. I enjoy self-expression through movement, I've done all sorts of dance classes and been to a Shamanic lady. I'd like to get to grips with this idea of New Age . . .

Through this whole cycle, this whole journey, I'm coming back to searching for where this spirit that I've certainly experienced is in my own Jewishness. I had an answer the other day sitting in synagogue – I go as and when I feel I want to. I was sitting quietly with my eyes closed listening to the prayer that was going on. That wasn't where my spirituality was felt. It was with all the Jews whispering underneath the prayer. That was where the soul was – in the whisper underneath the prayer.

Wallis has attained an eclectic synthesis of alternative spirituality and traditional Jewish observance. While Mike Goldmark's rejection of his Jewish background was more absolute, his life has also taken the form of a spiritual quest.

I was drawn to the spiritual life quite strongly in my late teens. For ten or twelve years it was basically a slow conscious working out of my own philosophy without any understanding of whether it was near any other religion. By thirty I found I was drawn more to the ideas of Buddhism. All I did was to go through the induction of TM and then promptly walked away from that. By forty I had already spent a little time in a Buddhist group or monastery – more Zen. It was not to align myself with them but to feel what they were about. Now I try to lead as spiritual a life as I can, what the Buddhists call 'right livelihood', holding an internal set of values which, I suppose, are common to most religions and practising a form of meditation, not TM. I have little interest in ritual or indeed in words. I don't think they have much to do with truth.

Helen Shapiro found the traditional Judaism she grew up with more a way of life, a code of behaviour than a source of spirituality. To pursue her 'vague idea that there was God in some form or another', she explored the periphery of the paranormal.

> I knew there was something more but I didn't know whether that was the way. I would read books on the subject and I read books on Buddhist beliefs as well. All that stuff is very attractive, the general thing of not religion but the idea, in some cases, of reincarnation, that there is a life beyond this life. It was a general sort of package, a little bit of this, a little bit of that. I suppose nowadays you'd call it 'New Age'.

With her singing career at a low in the late 1960s and early 1970s, the feeling that 'at least I know there is something more' gave Shapiro something to hold onto.

> It tended to give me a Micawber-like attitude. I had this very passive belief of 'there's something beyond this earthly life' and my belief in God had grown to what I saw as a more sophisticated idea of a supreme force rather than a personal God. Jewishly there wasn't much going on.

Asphodel Long left the narrow world of orthodox Judaism for communist universalism.

> I was in this world of communism in which there was a large number of atheist Jews who had a messianic drive and who were fighting for a better world. I joined the Communist Party and I was going to save the world and I was going to save women. I was going to be a strong, independent woman and I wasn't going to give into patriarchal and capitalist society.

Determined not to be a 'bourgeois wife', she had two sons with different partners. Nineteen fifty-six was a turning point, however. 'There was the Twentieth Congress and Hungary. I tore up my Communist Party card.'

THE ALTERNATIVES

Communism

Jack Gaster gave up his membership of the Communist Party of Great Britain when he was over eighty. 'The Communist party changed. It became a social-democratic mess.' His life long commitment to left-wing politics and ultimately communism began when he joined the Independent Labour Party (ILP) in 1926, aged nineteen. In 1946 he was elected member for Stepney, one of the only two communists elected as communists in the history of the London County Council. He also served as chairman of the National Jewish Committee of the Communist Party and was leader of the anti-Zionist section.

Gaster's involvement with the ILP gave his life a meaning 'in a better sense'. His allegiance, strange for a young man articled to become a lawyer, intrigued his father, the former *Haham*. 'The old man used to tease me about my ILP badge,' Gaster recalls. Years later paternal endorsement was more overt. 'I remember talking to him in the 1930s when Mosley was active and his line to me was "If you believe in something, fight for it."'

In 1932 Gaster became chairman of the Revolutionary Policy Committee of the ILP which stood for uniting all communists in a common party. In 1935 he joined the Communist Party, disenchanted with the ILP and impressed by the Seventh Congress of the Communist International. 'It came out for a bold united front of a broad character. That was the decisive turn for me.'

With the increase in antisemitism in the 1930s after the Blackshirt movement came to the fore, there was a natural alliance between Gaster's left-wing sympathies and his Jewishness. 'All of us, all socialists, opposed antisemitism, we opposed any sort of racialism. There was no left-wing antisemitism at that time.' Although non-religious, he remained on close terms with his family. The rift with his father came with his marriage to Moira Lynd, whom he met in 1934 when engaged in united action with the Marylebone Communist Party of which she was a member. The family liked her very much and she was later to become very close to Gaster's mother. But she was not Jewish and unwilling, as an atheist, to convert. 'The old man was very cut up about it. I was of course not able to visit the house after I married, not while the old man was alive.'

Buddhism

> I began veering towards Buddhism when I began asking how big the universe was, at the age of twelve. The basic questions, natural questions of any religion but also natural psychological questions any kid encounters as soon as he begins to look up at the sky, are Buddhist questions: What is the meaning of the unborn? How can the universe be born from nothing? How can you trace the birth or the end or the extent of the universe? What is basically natural to Buddhist thinking is the notion of the universe being beginningless that in Buddhism is translated into the metaphor of the unborn – something that you can't trace back to its womb.

By the time I was eighteen I became interested in the texture of my own consciousness, working with Burroughs and Kerouac because we were all concerned with those very basic things – what's the nature of consciousness, what's the nature of the material universe and what's the origin. I think I got the Buddhist formulations and terminology and the conceptual handling of that from Kerouac when I was about twenty-four. Already at Columbia University I'd had some experience of Buddhist art and culture.

I'm a non-theist, I don't think there is a divine in the sense of *deus ex machina*. The word 'spiritual' actually comes from the Latin '*spiritus*' which means breathing or breath. In poetry, perhaps, it relates to a very specific thing but it has no relation to a divine image. I'm interested in spiritual as far as it relates to breath.

I used to know Gershon Scholem, a major scholar of *chassidism* and *kabbala* and I did meet Martin Buber in Jerusalem. I was interested in his attitude towards LSD. I had asked him about some experiences I had which seemed to me non-human levels of consciousness. He said he thought our business was with the human, which was a very humane answer but wasn't quite satisfactory. I've done some Sabbath ceremonies with Rabbi Zalman Schachter, an ex-Lubavitcher, hip rabbi. He's also mixed it with Buddhist meditation and we've had some meetings at weekends with Tibetan lamas comparing Buddhist and Jewish ritual and ideology.

I identify myself as a poet, I identify myself as a Jew, I identify myself as a Buddhist and I identify myself as gay. I identify myself as of a family of Ginsberg, I identify myself as an American, I identify myself as a photographer. They are all aspects but I don't think there is any inherent, essential, permanent identity to any thing or person because the very nature of existence is transitory.

Allen Ginsberg

Ginsberg practises a form of Zen Buddhism and sees Nichiren Shoshu Buddhism, a popular and expanding version with many Jewish adherents which revolves round the chant *Nam-myoho-renge-kyo,* as a degraded form of Buddhism: 'Their interest seems to be in abandoning any effort to widen consciousness and like the Hare Krishna people cling to a sound as a channel to the divine which is then undefined and leads also to God knows what kind of spiritual materialism.'

Tamar Witkin, whom I met with her friend Lenny Wulkan at the community centre of Nichiren Shoshu Buddhists in New York's Union Square, acknowledged that when Nichiren Shoshu was relatively new to the West in the 1960s people would chant for totally materialistic reasons.

> Chant for a new car, chant for this or that. So many people who were inducted into this practice lost touch with what it was about fundamentally. It was about bringing one's sense of desire and one's tremendous frustrations in life and chanting about them and then transforming them into enlightenment.

Lenny, who has suffered eight strokes and twice had open-heart surgery, had only recently begun to chant. Tamar helped induct him into the practice and had since observed a remarkable improvement in the mobility of his right hand.

> He's been able to exert mind over matter and conquer those self-defeating beliefs he had that he couldn't ever regain mobility. The chant's not magic but what it's doing is helping him to summon forth courage from within himself and really make the efforts himself.

For Tamar,

> the Buddhist practice is a spiritual discipline that I totally lacked in my life. Being a musician I have this extremely great need for discipline and a daily ritual. In chanting your body is still like a column of energy so that you have to focus on your mind, your thoughts. It's called observing the mind.

Central to Nichiren Shoshu Buddhism is the *Gohanzon*, a scroll inscribed with Chinese and Sanskrit characters, which Tamar's mother likened to idol worship when she first saw it. 'Think of it like the Torah,' Tamar told her. 'It's got the mystical law and symbolises enlightenment.' Like many adherents of eastern religions, she finds the way of life prescribed in the Torah very external and restrictive. 'It cramps my sense of freedom and my belief that the human being is unlimited.' Neither can she accept what she perceives as Judaism's hierarchical approach. 'It's like God is really right there on top and we have to thank God for everything we've got and have this humble attitude. In Buddhism I see that God is in every one of us.'

Tamar has, nonetheless, found common ground between the two religions in various rituals and prayers and met a Lubavitch rabbi who took an interest in her chanting and likened it to *davvening*, the orthodox Jewish way of praying. Like some orthodox Jews, she touches the *mezzuzah* on the doorpost of her mother's house. 'I believe it brings good luck. It's got a scroll. To me the *mezzuzah* represents the Jewish kind of *mandala* – object of respect or good luck.' Similarly the Jewish custom of burning a *yartzeit* candle on the anniversary of a loved one's death is echoed in her Buddhist practice: 'In the fifth prayer we do every morning and every night we pray for our deceased relatives and all those who have passed away. You sound the bell and each bell ring is the thought of another relative and you have a candle burning during the prayer.' For Lenny, the recitation of the fifth prayer is particularly significant as it reminds him of his 64 relatives who perished in the Holocaust.

Like other Nichiren Shoshu Buddhists who have invited me to meetings and urged me to chant, Tamar and Lenny were eager to share their practice with me. Before I left the community centre, they took me to the chanting room. Facing the *Gohanzon* which looked to me like a tiny ark of the Torah, hundreds of people were chanting *Nam-myoho-renge-kyo.* They asked me to chant three times. 'Think Jewish,' I felt instinctively as I repeated the alien sounds. *Adonai, Hu haElohim*, the Lord he is God – I was filled with this affirmation, chanted at the end of the *Yom Kippur* services seven times. This time the chant was infinite.

New Age Spirituality

The women's movement which started up in 1970 attracted many Jews and provided a base for alternative forms of spirituality often classified as 'pagan' or 'New Age'. Asphodel Long, a one-time communist, became involved in the women's movement for political reasons.

> Along comes another universalist movement that I'm happy to join. I became a founder member of the matriarchy study group. To start with this was a women's political group that wanted to counter accusations that women had always been the subordinate sex and that God had always been worshipped in the masculine gender. We worked very hard to share our discoveries concerning older forms of religion in which there were goddesses and female divinities, female aspects of God, priestesses. I was coming up to retirement from work and I decided to explore the formal evidence for this. So I took a theology degree at Kings College, London.
>
> But in the 1970s we had antisemitism in the women's movement and I was held responsible for whatever the Israeli government did. So suddenly the universalism in the women's movement breaks up. I had to renew my *yiddishkeit*, my Jewishness, to renew roots in the Jewish world. I met lots of Jewish feminists. I particularly had to fight a new form of antisemitism that crept in. Goddess women began to say that the Jews killed the goddess.
>
> If you look at the Bible you'll see how the Jewish leaders tried to put down goddess worship in the Jewish religion. On the whole they didn't

succeed, even in their own very small community. And how did they kill the goddess everywhere else? I was faced with a new challenge to explore the Jewish area, to find the goddesses, if there were any, in my own roots.

I found at Kings that as I studied the New Testament, particularly the Fourth Gospel, I was faced with the core, the centre of antisemitism. So I'm forced back to being the protesting Jew about Christianity but at the same time I'm given the opportunity to learn how to study and the means of finding the material I am looking for. I was able to continue studying after the degree and concentrated on *hochma* (the Hebrew word for wisdom) and on the goddesses of the near-east – *Ashteroth* who you find in the Bible, *Ashera* and *Tiamat*, the goddess of the depths.

Since 1983 I've researched[1] and taught in women's workshops, in adult education, in day schools. This is my task, to communicate, particularly with women, that they've been brought up on a lie that only the male can be divine, and that we as women can identify with the divine and this can have an enormous effect on our individual lives.

When you start talking about goddeses it's natural to think of paganism but I don't identify as a pagan. Maybe this is my Jewish psyche although I am still very angry with the male supremacy in Judaism. I'm still not really religious but in doing the work and going to the places, to the goddesses, I've felt spiritual channels open in me that I didn't know were there. I do feel a spirituality about female aspects of deity which I don't really feel about the old fashioned God. I've reached a kind of spirituality by chance although the aim was political.

Daniel Cohen, who does identify as a pagan, was also influenced by the feminist movement.

My attitude to spirituality changed in the 1970s. It was partly some of the aspects of feminism and feminist spirituality which tied together my attitudes to nature and related to politics, generally leftist politics. One of my objections to spirituality as it is commonly conceived is that it doesn't relate to the world and I found feminist spirituality did and this is also one of the positive features of Judaism, the spirit is acting in this world.

I very strongly object to talk of a Judaeo-Christian tradition. I think there is a Christian tradition and a Judaic one and without knowing it they're putting down the Jewish tradition when they try to assimilate it to a Judaeo-Christian one. I believe this is the world we're meant to live in, not just a preparatory stage. Although Judaism as such has never spoken to me it's clear to me that my approach to the spiritual world is very much coming from Judaism.

When I was in a workshop with Rabbi Zalman Schachter, they were blessing the bread. It was very moving, but I found I needed to take some of the bread and physically cast it on the earth as an offering – an offering to the divine and the divine in nature, possibly the divine outside nature. The blessing was not complete for me, I had to do something further.

There is also the area of wanting to bring aspects of Judaism into other celebrations. I was in a workshop with Ram Dass, you might call him a 'lost Jew', he's now Hindu. They were singing hymns to Hannuman and Krishna and they meant nothing to me. I could see the point of a mantra but instead of having people saying '*HareKrishna, HareRam*', I just found myself wanting to say '*Baruch atah*' because it's like a mantra and it was establishing my Judaism and I would never do that under normal circumstances.

I would describe myself as part of a pagan movement. I've got my spirituality and again I can bring my Judaism into it because typically the Christian attitude to the divine is 'God bless this food' while the Jewish attitude is 'Blessed art thou who created the food' and that is much closer to a pagan attitude. What I practice is basically a celebration of the seasonal festivals, celebrating, noticing, observing the changes in the year, that's a good part of it and again I recognise that as part of Judaism.

Who are the people who almost automatically plant trees in celebration of some special event? Jews. I was rather pleased and anxious to do that and do it via the Jewish National Fund because a friend of Jewish origin in my circle gave birth to a daughter and I became not godfather but goddessfather. It felt absolutely appropriate to give some money for tree-planting in her name and it was also appropriate for me to comment to other pagans and people in the green movement: 'Look, this is a good thing to do and look, we Jews have been doing it for many years.'

CHRISTIAN OR JEW?

Messianic Jews, like Jews for Jesus, believe that Jesus – or Yeshua – is the Messiah. Messianic Jews also observe a form of Jewish practice. Their gentile counterparts may be 'Messianic Gentiles' who share the same forms of worship and participate with their fellows of Jewish origin in celebrating

Jewish festivals. Or they may be Christians who identify with the early followers of Jesus and see themselves as 'Jewish Christians'. All reject the path followed by the Church after it was taken over by the Roman empire.

A Messianic Jew

Helen Shapiro's discovery of Messianic Judaism was the culmination of her long spiritual search.

> I had this mish-mash of beliefs in the 1970s and 1980s until 1987. Things were going well in my life but something was missing. One morning I woke up and I didn't believe any of that mish-mash any more. Looking back I realise now that was God getting rid of that stuff to be ready to put the right stuff in.
>
> During this time of soul searching, I was round at my musical director's. He's a committed Christian. Occasionally he mentioned Jesus but I never thought about it as anything to do with me. This time he said he was giving up the music business because he felt God wanted him to be a preacher. I envied him because he seemed so sure, so solid in his faith. I started to think about this Jesus he believed in because I'd always had the confusion about him in my mind which maybe many Jewish people do.
>
> One night I couldn't sleep and I said 'All right, Jesus, if you're the Messiah, show me.' I felt quite peaceful after that and went to sleep. In the following weeks, everywhere I went I seemed to bump into things pertaining to this Jesus, there was just so much of it, and some weeks later we were coming back from a show in Germany and at the airport my musical director put a book in my hand.
>
> It was called *Betrayed* and it was by a Jewish believer, basically the story of how he came to be a believer that Jesus was the Messiah. I went home and devoured this book. It was very moving but what was really mind-blowing were the Messianic prophecies he quoted from the Hebrew Bible.
>
> So I'm reading these things and I think, 'Blimey, I must go and get a Bible.' It was a semi old-fashioned version, and I read up on these prophecies and yes, they all seemed to be pointing to Jesus so I thought 'I've got to read this other book (the New Testament)', so I opened it up and read it and it reached out from the page and grabbed hold of me. The first thing that grabbed me was the genealogy of Jesus. There were all these familiar names going back to Abraham, obviously via David. So I'm reading this stuff and I'm realising 'This is a Jewish book.'

I came to the conclusion in my head and a large part of my heart that what I read in the gospels must be true. Not long after that I was just dwelling on it and praying and I was filled with – I can't explain it – it was like God pouring his spirit on me and into me and it was like I'd always known Him, I'd just asked Him to enter my life. I actually prayed a prayer saying 'Be my Messiah' to Jesus who was God, God the son. I believe in a plural God. The holy spirit is there in the *Tenach*, like when they say 'The spirit of God – *ruach hakodesh* – came upon David and upon Moses.' I believe God is a compound, God is a godhead and within that godhead is the Father, the Son and the Holy spirit. I don't call it the trinity, triunity is better because there is only one God, a personal God.

I prayed on 26 August 1987 at 10.30 pm – I remember it because it changed my life, it turned my life upside down. I'm totally committed, I'm a Messianic Jew, I believe in messianic congregations where Jews and gentiles worship together in a Hebraic expression of their faith. Messianic Jews are changed in that we are fulfilled, we believe, in our Jewishness by the Messiah, just as Yeshua fulfils the prophecies of the suffering servant and will fulfil all the Kingly prophecies when he comes again.

We are Hebraic rather than Greek. We tend not to celebrate Christmas or Easter because they were based on pagan things. We keep all the Jewish festivals, we traditionally observe them but we see their fulfilment in the Messiah. On *Yom Kippur*, for instance, we fast, but not in fear and trembling because we believe Yeshua was the once and for all sacrifice and atonement for sin, that's the whole point of him. We fast in identification with the Jewish people because we are Jews and we do what we're commanded to do, but not for salvation but to draw close to God and give thanks that he has sent the once and for all atonement and to pray for our people that their eyes should be opened.

We believe that the Messiah was promised to the Jewish people and to the world and that over the last two thousand years the Messianic faith has lost its Jewish roots. When it became the official religion of the Romans under Constantine he threw out *Shabbat* and the Passover and anything Jewish and brought in a lot of pagan stuff which has heavily influenced a large part of the Church. We believe as Messianic Jews we have turned back to God, the God of Abraham, Isaac and Jacob. We believe with total and utter faith that the Bible is the word of God, that's why I cannot tolerate spiritualism and New Ageism. Many Jews don't seem to have a problem with the New Age stuff but it's totally unbiblical, totally ungodly and yet people like me they have a go at.

Godfearers

Erica Ferszt speaks of her parents as 'avid Christians' although they are members of Jews for Jesus. 'I think it's interesting, I think it's probably the best combination of the two religions but I wouldn't go into that because there are too many problems there. Nobody accepts you. The Christians don't believe you and neither do the Jews.' If she were to become more religious, she would stick to the Episcopalianism of her upbringing.

Others are prepared to take a more individualistic stance. Robert Beecham, teased for being Jewish at his select preparatary school because of his large nose inherited from his gentile paternal grandmother, had already developed an anti-Jewish feeling when his mother told him she was Jewish. 'My reaction at the time – I was eleven – was shock-horror really to discover I was the very thing I'd been developing a hate for.' A 'rebirth in Christian terminology' when he was eighteen changed his attitude radically.

> I began to rethink everything. Obviously, if you take anything Christian or in the Bible seriously you can in no way be ashamed of being Jewish – contrary to what the Church has taught, I have to say. I learned Hebrew to study the Old Testament and that just led to an increased interest in things Jewish and you increasingly find the more you know of a Jewish background and of Hebrew the better you can understand what happened in New Testament times and in the end you have to break totally through Church tradition to get to the truth.

Beecham and his family do not celebrate Christmas. He also condemns the paganism and anti-Jewishness introduced into the Church in Roman times:

> The true Christian faith is a spiritual growth on the foundation of the Old Testament whereas the Church world seems to me a pagan perversion of the truth. What I believe seems to be a total building on the original Jewish revelation. My foundation really is the Jewish world. We named our first child Judith – Yehudit – which means Jewess or possibly praise, partly to undo what I did in denying I was Jewish earlier on.

Beecham is embarassed, however, to find his Jewish connection considered 'a feather in your cap' in some Christian circles. Ben Cohen has had similar experiences. 'I think people have funny ideas about what being Jewish and Christian means. They think it's special.' Even within a Christian context he can see the value of learning more about Judaism.

> There's so much Judaism at the heart of Christianity that I realise there's probably quite a goldmine there to be discovered in terms of learning more about Jewish spirituality. I've not investigated far enough to see how easy it is to discover more. I think there's a lot to be said for trying to find out.

John Greenhalgh, a gentile Christian married to a Jewish wife, has always felt some Jewish link:

> All along I felt something, having read about early Christians, gentiles like me, who became Jews first or people who had a Jewish father and a gentile mother or the other way round and were already circumcised, and I suppose having been circumcised in a non-ritualistic way at birth, I somehow identify with that.

Although Greenhalgh's wife was baptised when they married, he has helped her come to terms with her Jewish heritage in her own way. One thing he insisted on was that their son should be circumcised.

> My mother-in-law was delighted that I wanted him to become a Jew. So it was done absolutely properly with a *mohel* and a naming ceremony and my father-in-law was there. My children think of themselves as being Jewish, and Christian if they want to be. They have no choice about being Jewish. The choice was made for them.

Despite the 'agony and misery' that accompanied her son's circumcision, Greenhalgh's wife recognised the atavistic instincts that enabled her to go through with it. ' "I don't think," she said at the time, "unless there was something in my blood going back thousands of years I'd be able to do this." And I said, "I'm so pleased because I think you'd regret it enormously if you hadn't." '

Greenhalgh feels he and his wife have attained a spirituality based on the moral concepts of Judaism.

> Two thousand years ago when the Jesus movement began, the spiritual and moral heart of the Roman empire was Judaism. It wasn't only the one God that was preached, it was the very high moral standards and the distinctiveness of keeping the Torah. There were people who were called 'godfearers'. They used to attach themselves to synagogues and worship. Some of them would convert and become proper Jews but others were just happy to be godfearers and when this particular Jewish movement arose, attached to Jesus of Nazareth, they found it quite easy to assimilate into that. The basis of it was this religion with such an important moral tone and I feel really that's where we are now.

STILL JEWISH?

> The whole Jewish world that I meet that identifies itself in some sort of synagogal terms always thinks that other people who are not in a synagogue are not Jewish. On the other hand all of us, hundreds, thousands, maybe hundreds of thousands, certainly tens of thousands born Jews who are not interested in that synagogal Jewish life, we consider we're just as Jewish as anybody else.
>
> Asphodel Long

Jews today might reject Judaism or seek an alternative direction but the majority hold onto their Jewish identity. Only Robert Wallis has incorporated synagogue into his range of spiritual options. But both Tamar Witkin and Lenny Wulkan would bring up children, if they have them, within some synagogue framework while continuing their Buddhist practice. Daniel Cohen and Asphodel Long are aware of the services held at Beit Klal Yisrael, the alternative feminist congregation run by Rabbi Sheila Shulman. While both admire what Shulman is doing, neither feel it's right for them. For Asphodel, 'it's too much of a synagogue'; for Cohen, 'it's not far enough from traditional Judaism'. Yet Asphodel has lectured at a reform synagogue and Cohen subscribes to the Socialist Zionist organisation, Mapam, which has always been sensitive to Palestinian rights.

Jack Gaster is no Zionist, has 'no part in the Jewish community and I'm not a member of any synagogue but I'm still Jewish'. Judaism, he feels, 'is not a national question. It's ridiculous to pretend that all the Jews of the diaspora are one nation. Under any conceivable definition of a nation they're not.' Bruce Bart would agree. 'A Sephardic Jew has as much in common with a German Jew as a Finn and a Pole. A Syrian has more in common with a Syrian Jew than a Jew from Paris has with a Jew from Russia.' He, himself, is happy to assume an ethnic Jewish identity: 'I certainly don't feel religious Jewish but I feel Jewish, especially when they say Jews are not considered White males. I feel really good about that.'

Jewish ethnicity is more prevalent in America than in Britain. For Stephen Bloom, with his non-religious stance, Jewish identification is more complex.

> I'm keen, I suppose, not to be thought of as a deeply religious Jew and I'm not, so if people say you're Jewish I deny it, not in the sense that my ancestors were Jewish, in the sense that I don't go to synagogue and

> I can never remember the dates of the Jewish festivals. In my lab people I've employed who are Jewish come along and tell me they're off on such and such a day and they think I should know and that it's rather affected that I don't but I genuinely don't. I suppose my basic emotion about Jewishness is being proud of it, so it's positive rather than negative but I don't feel part of it very much.

Allen Ginsberg considers himself 'definitely Jewish'. He is particularly attached to Jewish cosmopolitanism, 'what Stalin called "rootless cosmopolitanism", the entire European intellectual tradition wiped out by Hitler, from Kurt Weill to everyone else involved, any number of circumcised geniuses'. With his Central European background, Ginsberg has always felt

> This affinity with that old Hungarian, Ruthenian, Polish intelligentsia. When I first met Burroughs we used to play charades. He always took the role of the WASP governess, Kerouac took the role of an American country bumpkin and I took the role of a well-groomed Hungarian art dealer – Jewish of course.

9

What is Left?

Because of the persecution and the anti-racial laws in Mussolini's Italy my parents did a religious wedding and my father was baptised. Before my arrival my mother wanted to separate but she changed completely and wanted to help when she saw my father was in danger. He couldn't bear the humiliation, like when a woman spat at him in the lift and said 'I don't go in the lift with a Jew.' He escaped to Switzerland at the right moment so I didn't see him till the end of the war. Only some time after the war I realised it was because he was a Jew.

The Anne Frank book was my first shock – I was about eleven or twelve. I identified with this Anne because she was a girl, because she was young, because she died. I started to know more about the concentration camps and felt an enormous guilt because I was a survivor and a lot had died. I was also wondering why my dad, whom I always felt was a bit primitive, a *commerçant*, survived and not better people and I felt we were the two who survived who didn't deserve to.

I couldn't stand Jews because of their dark skin. Perhaps I had the racial type of milk of the Aryan. People in Milan wondered if I came from the south because they were much whiter than I was. I didn't resent that because it was like I was the Jew that deserved to be punished – not so much as a Jew but the one who survived. Olivetti is a Jewish name. I didn't experience antisemitism but often people were saying 'It's nice but it's a Jew.' These things made me laugh but I didn't want to be differentiated as a Jew.

I had a boyfriend, a half-Jew, who was like the child I had to protect because he suffered so much. When I left him and was with somebody else – a beautiful, handsome man that the Aryans like, my ideal in fact – I felt he needed me and the non-Jewish one could survive without me so I went back to him.

I worked as a psychologist at a school run by the Jewish community and was welcome because of my name. I was quite taken by the bright pupils and the very bright young teachers and fascinated because a lot of Jews came from Persia and Africa where they were persecuted. You can see how often the Jewish community has to absorb people from many different cultures. When I came to England I felt I could do useful work in a Jewish organisation but I was told no, here they don't have any kind of apartheid.

As a child I had a Catholic education and was very devout. I did part of my secondary education in Switzerland because my father was mad about me learning a lot of languages – this I think was in the Jewish tradition. I stopped going to church but I always felt quite mystic, I felt something could be *au-delà*, but no more than that. Then I became an agnostic.

I would like to integrate a kind of identity of the Jewish culture that is not religion. It's very difficult for me to identify what it is. It's a kind of distance because Jews were never integrated to the society, an ability to observe more than others, a respect for language – they are so able to speak with words. Also a kind of honesty, a search for the truth.

Then there is the kind of bitter, critical mother who picks up all the time the negative without holding the positive. When I read about the Jews, then I understand in a more tolerant way that these women really never had a secure place and had to push children to be the best intellectually, that because they had such a tough life this underlined more the negative. And the bitter mother that I can see around in Golders Green or inside a lot of my friends, yes I can see it in myself and it comes from my father who was incredibly critical and all the time wanted to prepare you for the worst.

My father never had a property in his name. In contrast, I feel the need a little bit like a peasant to have the bricks. Bricks don't betray you.

Sandra Olivetti*, psychologist, London and Milan

Olivetti's Jewishness is only residual. Other lost Jews whose connection is similar or even more tenuous are as follows:

Baroness Tessa Blackstone, Master of Birkbeck College, London
Isabelle Reims, student, Paris
Michael Palmer, solicitor, London
Claire Calman, editor, London
Laila F, linguist, London
David Casper, musician, Pacific north-west
Glenn Casper, Seattle
Rahel K, Surrey
Martin Daltrop, London
Sidney Tuck, retired businessman, Hertfordshire

Sonia Ezekiel, student, London
Hannah Abraham, student, London
Leah Friedlander, office-worker, London
Lindsay Rothschild, student, Michigan

IMPRINTS OF JEWISHNESS

Olivetti, who comes across as the quintessential ex-pat Italian, is under no pressure in England to confront her Jewish origins. In this respect she is like many lost Jews who do little more than acknowledge their part-Jewishness. Where she goes further is in attributing several characteristics of her psychological make-up to her Jewish past and attaching considerable significance to these traits. Others, too, may single out certain traits within themselves or stemming from their Jewish forebears, without feeling that these shape their identity.

Lost Jews who have featured in previous chapters, many of whom display a more dynamic relationship with their Jewishness, are also conscious of certain 'Jewish' traits or imprints of Jewishness which tend to be constant and are unaffected by the fluctuations of their Jewish sensibilities. As Julie Clare puts it: 'I'm very definitely racially Jewish, I'm very definitely influenced by Jewish culture in a major way. Heritage, culture, past history, all of that has had an influence and effect on my life and in how I see the world.' Similarly, Jacqui Burke believes that Jewishness is something that cannot go away.

> I don't think you become a non-Jew or an ex-Jew because you've decided on something else. Being Jewish has less to do with what you think and what you believe than what you are. Whatever happens I always feel I'm partly a Jewish person because that is my racial origins, that's something that won't change. It's quite fundamental, certainly to me.

A Sense of Family

To say families play a key role in Jewish life is almost a cliché. Janet Schuman, who once lived in a *chassidic* Jewish neighbourhood where large families are frequently seen out walking together, believes many New Yorkers identify Judaism with '47th Street Brothers', the large electrical goods store run by *chassidic* Jews. For lost Jews, too, an awareness of family or more remote ancestry can provide some Jewish link or, equally, offer an explanation for the dilution of Jewish identity.

Laurence Spicer, for example, is 'immensely proud' of his family. He was named after his great-grandfather, Laurence Bowman, the headmaster of the Jews' Free School and a parliamentary candidate for the Liberal Party and derived his political principles from him. 'He instilled into me quite remarkably things like social justice, education, the classless society.' Bowman's wife, Fanny, 'a wonderful Russian Jewess', was a playwright. Spicer's grandfather, Sir Sidney Abrahams, was an older brother of the Olympic champion, Harold. Sir Sidney, the first Jewish Colonial Chief Justice who ended up as a member of the Judicial Committee of the Privy Council, was himself an Olympic athlete, as was another brother, Sir Adolph, the dean of Westminster Medical School.

Baroness Tessa Blackstone was very attached to her maternal grandmother, who 'didn't in any way identify with her Jewishness but was Jewish in terms of some of her personal traits which were derived from her upbringing'. Some of these traits, Blackstone acknowledges, are 'slightly stereotypical'. There was, for example, her slight hypochondria – 'She used to be terribly constipated and to have senna pods soaking in a little bowl by her bed every evening' – and her regular poker-playing at the Curzon club. 'She was a tremendous player. She always used to at least break even and sometimes actually make a little out of it. I think that's very much part of the Jewish culture of her social class and generation, playing cards and doing it well with a gambling element to it.' She was also a very good linguist and very careful about her finances. 'I think this is typically middle-class Jewish. At one level she was generous with her children and grandchildren but at another level she would write down every phone call she made. She would keep meticulous accounts rather like a small Jewish businessman might.'

Miriam Scott's discovery of her grandmother's family who arrived in the United States from rural Lithuania in 1890 led her to the Ellis Island Museum: 'Having learned something about the reasons behind the Jewish immigration and early immigrant culture in New York I think "Well, this is part of me" and I feel more myself because I know about that.' Lucy Temperley had a sense, albeit dormant, of some Jewish connection after hearing her father speak about his Jewish ancestors. Isabelle Reims is very curious about her Russian Jewish grandfather. 'I'd like very much to know his origins, his story. I'd like to know why he said "I don't want to have this religion any more." Now I know that my name before was Stalevich. He changed it when he arrived in France.'

Kim Kraft feels a sentimental attachment towards 'the Judaism of where my mother sprang from, from India which allowed all my Jewish ancestors to live there in a Jewish community, so some of the Indian spices and flavours set in.' On another level her mother's demonstrativeness – 'she will grab a stranger in the street and hug them' – has led her to associate 'Jewish' with 'a social and emotional behaviour and reaction to people' and to feel most comfortable with 'people that touched'. Similarly, Tanya Alfillé has fond recollections of 'Memé', her 'cuddly and touchy' Jewish grandmother. Jacqui Burke was reminded of her grandmother by some Jewish girls at her exercise class who were talking about lighting candles on Friday night: 'When people mention things like that I feel, "Yes, I know what that's about." It's like a nice childhood memory, something I think of with nostalgia.'

For Michael Palmer, Jewishness is inextricably linked to a powerful extended Jewish family.

> When you're with the family you certainly get a feeling much more readily of feeling Jewish. The family's an awfully nice bunch so you feel very much at home with them and I suppose that does instil a slight sense of history into it. When you get together with them it's difficult not to feel that you're part of this river, it's terribly easy to want to be part of it.

However, Palmer admits, 'you get to be an awful chameleon. When you go home you forget all that.' Laurent Ezekiel observes the same closeness in his grandparents' circle but doesn't 'really like that sort of thing': 'What's important for them is the family first of all, their children and grandchildren. They like a lot of unity in the family and they have many friends and cousins and they all seem to know each other and it's like a big community.'

Closeness, of course, is a double-edged sword. Ezekiel has noticed that the parents of some of his Jewish friends fit the interfering parent stereotype. Claire Calman, daughter of the late Mel Calman, has also seen Jewish parents exerting unwarranted pressure and has found some of her Jewish friends reluctant to cut the umbilical cord. 'They kind of live in family flats. It's very much a half-way house, like they're sort of living at home but living physically in a separate place.' She feels she, too, fits that mould: 'The very Jewish thing is that the house we bought was my mother's house and she then moved which is, I have to say, a fairly classic Jewish set-up.' One reason Claire invested in property was her 'real horror' of poverty, influenced by 'some strange kind of race memory that there was some degree of poverty on both sides of my family in the past'. Family closeness is something she appreciates, provided it is based on choice rather than obligation. Tanya Alfillé also likes 'the feeling that you have a close family and that people are concerned about you and you have that support'. And it was these qualities which she had observed in her father that led Jana Smidova to pronounce that 'Jewish husbands are the best in the world!'

Mixed Heritage

> I'm of such a mixed background. It's almost as if you're being defiant in the face of the rest of the world saying 'Look at me, it doesn't matter, I'm a bit Jewish, a bit Muslim, a bit Christian, all the people who've been fighting with each other.' The really important point is the mix because you feel all these different cultures and religions converging within you.
>
> Laila F

Few lost Jews can boast a heritage as complex at Laila's. Yet a similar internalisation of mixed heritage was evoked by David Casper. 'I believe that my mother's experience as a Jew who grew up in a Catholic boarding school in a Hindu country, that that upbringing did something to her inside and that that being half of what formed the parental influence on me has something to do with who I am inside.' His brother, Glenn, sees it from a different perspective: 'I think it's a matter of process versus content and I might have picked up some of my mother's process. Her experience teaches me a certain way of looking at the world and interpreting it perhaps.' The Caspers, who recognise that they have absorbed something of their mother's experience, are cousins of Michael Palmer, who speaks of his own mother's experience with typical British detachment.

> Mother came from a very orthodox family but disappeared up to a Catholic convent in the hills for nine months at a time and inevitably they were forced to go to mass twice a day and everybody around them was Catholic. The length of time they could be properly influenced back at home in Calcutta was such that they inevitably lost touch.

While the Catholic schooling may have led to the loss of his mother's religious and cultural heritage, Palmer emphasises that her sense of Jewishness was actually hardened by the discrimination and exclusion she confronted.

While a mixed heritage is often experienced as something to glory in, it has its down sides. Laila's mother, of Jewish–Muslim parentage and with a Hindu grandparent, tended to 'play with the different facets of her cultural background'. She would give her daughter, raised in India, little

Jewish objects as presents – 'we were constantly reminded of this connection in little ways' – and send her sister's daughter, raised as a Jew in America, Indian skirts and pyjamas to remind her of the Indian side. Yet, as Laila observes, both she and her mother often miss having something they can claim as their own, something about which they can say, 'This is how we do it in my family.' David Casper also recalls the pros and cons of being mixed. While 'it was nice to feel you could be part of whatever group you're hanging around with', since with his Jewish mother and gentile father he was accepted by both groups, he resented his parents for depriving him of a particular religious identity, although he now has more empathy with their eclectic approach.

Sometimes a complex heritage is something to claim when the tension between losing and retaining a Jewish identity becomes too painful or fraught. Rahel K, Laila's cousin, had a Jewish father and is, in many ways, a 'marginal Jew'. She now lives with her non-Jewish husband in England, where, 'overwhelmed by the sameyness of society', she feels 'a woman of colour'. Her Jewish practice lapsed after festivals which she had experienced as 'very family and friend orientated' became lonely experiences when she was away from home. 'That then became an experience I didn't repeat. I don't go to synagogue and there's part of me that experiences a kind of loss because I very much associate my Judaism with childhood because there were rituals I have very fond memories of.' She acknowledges that her husband, who refers to himself as her '*goy* boy', would be less than happy if she did something positive about being Jewish. 'He's not really thrilled about the *menorah* on the window-sill. He puts pretty pictures in front of it. I have a little prayer book and my husband keeps putting pictures in front of it.' In America, Rahel feels, it would be easier to express the Jewish side. In England, where 'you have to make a deliberate statement about being Jewish', she is more inclined to emphasise her Asian background.

The process of getting rid of Jewishness is something Robert Beecham can trace retrospectively in his mother's family, also originally Jews from India.

> My mother said she cried all day when her mother changed her name from Cohen to Cairn. Later I think my mother and aunt were aiming to pass themselves off as English – I don't know with how much success. My father and uncle had no English blue-blood in them whatsoever. Their father's grandfather started life as a shepherd and then joined the *nouveaux riches* by making Beecham's pills. To the young girls from India the pedigree would have seemed quite impressive. They wanted to

> forget any Jewish background basically and be country ladies in Warwickshire. None of my generation is happy that our parents covered up being Jewish.

A Persecuted Race

> I think about the things that have happened to the Jewish people like the Holocaust and basically discrimination against the Jewish people because of their faith. It makes me mad. I feel sorry for these people throughout history who had to go through this. Christians complain about what the Romans did to the Christians. It seems nothing in comparison with what has happened to Jews and continued to happen.
>
> Terry Cloper

> I identified with the persecution factor, the loss, grief factor which is not the backbone of the Jewish identity but merely the backbone of what I conceived of was the Jewish identity.
>
> Jessica Greenman

The image of Jews as a persecuted race persists, not least among people whose experience of Jewish life is limited. Indeed David Matthews speaks of 'a big kind of schizophrenia' in his teens between his concept of Jews and the reality of Israel: 'I'd always thought of not seeing Jews in terms of militarism or colonialism or oppression. They were the oppressed, they were the unarmed and I guess there was quite an adjustment in terms of Israel becoming quite a warlike and quite a potent nation.' Taking this further, Matthews sees a confusion between his 'perhaps idealised notion of what's instrinsically a Jewish way of running things or behaving – a compassion and a caring and a kind of looking after a whole community rather than everybody scrambling' and the less attractive features of the political actuality. The more idealised perspective is also held by Janet Schuman who feels that Judaism represents the antithesis of hate, separatism and violence.

Jews, like other minorities, can sometimes make a career out of their persecution according to Julie Clare:

> You think that just because you can turn round and say 'Well, you can't know what it's like . ..' That can be an extremely dangerous argument. That doesn't mean to deny anybody's experience. But a nice middle-class Jewish girl or even half-Jewish girl is not likely to have experienced that much persecution in Britain.

Penelope Abraham, in contrast, believes Jews in Britain do carry the weight of the past. 'I think there's a tremendous weight of misery that sits on the shoulders of my generation.' Her own readiness to identify with a persecuted race is viewed with scepticism by her teenage daughter, Hannah.

Julie Clare's view is shared by Carole C and Isabelle Reims in Paris who feel too many Jews focus excessively on antisemitism and persecution. Isabelle sees this as more typical of the Sephardis from north Africa: 'They are the ones who suffered the least from persecution and they are the ones who are talking the most of that.' Nevertheless, like many lost Jews, she makes a link between persecution and feelings of Jewishness when she speaks of her grandfather: 'I'm sure he was like Jewish inside because when the Germans came to France he had to go and hide in the countryside and the Germans took everything, he had a castle and they took it and he never had it again so I think he should have felt Jewish – you can't hide it.'

Animosity towards Jews may be made too much of but it remains a reality. Walter Mosley sees this as one reason Jews have retained more identification with their culture than other immigrant groups in America: 'There's so much dislike that they're continually reminded "Oh you are a Jew". It's not the same if people say "You're Italian." ' Bruce Bart sees his own identity shaped by this hatred and the way he internalises it: 'If you've grown up knowing that Jews have been hated round the world for lots of reasons, some warranted and some not warranted, you see yourself as part of the things you hate in Jews and part of the things you love.' Persecution and animosity have contributed, historically, to the Jew's inability to settle too long in any one country. This movement is seen by John Witt as an integral part of his identity: 'The history of my family is generations moving from one country to the other, my personal history is moving from one country to the other. So it's that sense of movement rather than having roots in one country and belonging to it.' This rootlessness, he feels, is 'exacerbated', by being 'so near' to being a Jew 'yet not quite'.

For many lost Jews with only a remote connection to Jewishness, persecution – often in terms of the Holocaust – remains a key link. Erica Ferszt would like to have learnt more from her grandfather, a Holocaust survivor: 'I wish he had lived longer so that I could have discussed it with him. I remember the one time I did bring it up – he had the numbers on his arm – and I asked him what they were and he just got very angry. I was about five. I think it's a massive piece of history he had to live through.' Reading books by Elie Wiesel and Primo Levi has furthered her knowledge. Martin

Daltrop admits to being 'obsessed' with the Holocaust. 'I think it's something people not from my background wouldn't share. That was the bit of Jewishness I've felt. My father, my grandparents and other relatives have been through this thing so I think that's the connection.' Daltrop concedes that his reaction to people who claim that a catastrophe like ethnic cleansing in Bosnia is as horrific as the Holocaust – 'I'd say it wasn't, I'd say it wasn't' – is 'quite a Jewish reaction' and that he may have an affinity for Jewish issues. However, he does not feel or think of himself as Jewish. Had he had a Jewish mother he would have been quite happy to say he was Jewish, although it would only have meant accepting 'other people's labels' and would have made no difference to him or his life.

Stephen Bloom is 'very emotionally moved' by films about the Holocaust. 'It was obviously a disaster and a major social crime. I've known about it all my life and I've known family who've lost members and of course in the scientific community there are a number of Jewish refugees who have made good.' He sees the Holocaust as 'a form of madness of one particular person based on the fact that an immigrant population worked harder than the indigenous population and therefore became very unpopular' and likens Hitler's behaviour to that of other autocratic rulers in history. Similarly, he believes that Jews, like the Armenians and the Kurds, have had more than their fair share of persecution. 'It's partly being a minority, partly geography. I think if the Jews had formed a nation living in an island like Britain, they wouldn't have had any problems. It's always much worse if you're part of a main continent and you don't have an obvious boundary. People are always invading and grabbing you.'

Philip Epstein finds that his complex, composite identity is bound up with the fate of the Jews in twentieth-century Europe.

> Doing research on the general crisis of European development in the first half of this century, which is also the time of the Jewish catastrophe, I saw how much the fate of the Jewish people was caught up with the wider historical development of Europe and I just had a very strong sense that the part of me which is the Jewish identity and the other parts, the socialist, the intellectual and the cosmopolitan, were all part of the same thing not just in me but in the real history I was trying to reconstruct.

The Power of Survival

If persecution is one side of the coin, survival is the other. To have survived is one of the great feats of the Jewish people; not surprisingly, an instinct for survival is perceived as 'Jewish'. As Isabelle Reims put it, again with her grandfather in mind: 'One of the advantages of being Jewish is being able to survive.' For her father, René Reims, too, the capacity to 'start all over again' is peculiarly Jewish:

> Among the Jews I've met I've seen these qualities like in the well-known case of the man who lost his wife and family and each time he built a new family. His last wife was French and she was burnt in a fire in the Pine forests in the Midi, and he went to the United States, he married again, he pulled himself up with his own hands. It's the power of survival.

Ben Selwyn sees the survival instinct as intrinsic to Judaism.

> I think Judaism over the last two thousand years has become more a reaction to what is around the Jewish community. It is a survival instinct to push yourself harder. The population of Jews in the world is tiny and yet you still have a great many minds. Persecution, paranoia, a lot of the negative things have produced the idea of striving, making sure you can never be defeated in yourself.

He places the Jewish mother who pushes her children 'to do better' in this context: 'Jewish circumstances have meant that they have to do it slightly more.'

While the emphasis on education is one factor he sees as influencing Jewish survival, the crucial ingredient in Stephen Bloom's opinion is 'the ability to work in groups and be loyal and decent to the group. The emphasis on pulling together as a group must have been helpful so that the Jews as a whole knew what they were doing and understood what was going on in the world about them.' Since he believes that 'most of the current Jews are descended from converts and not the original Israelite population', he identifies the key to holding the group together as ideology rather than kinship.

Closely linked to survival is an instinct to better yourself. Jacqui Burke inherited this from her father: 'One of the big messages I got from him was that everybody should do the best they can to better themselves and that if you were prepared to work hard, there were no limits to what you could have.' This drive, which Donatella Bernstein saw in her Jewish grandfather, is also something she recognises as 'Jewish': 'You can say Jews are quite direct about going about getting where they want to go.' On a wider level, she feels that the whole 'chosen people' concept obligates Jews to be better. 'In a way it's like representing God, you're supposed to be better, you're not allowed to make the same mistakes as others.'

WHAT IS LEFT?

Intelligence, culture, humour, volubility, a love of food, hypersensitivity, anxiety, a tendency to excel at individual rather than team sports – Richard Cohen points out that fencing has a very strong Jewish intake: 'It's a rather anti-team game, bloody-minded sport'; whether these qualities are personal to an individual or seen as representative of the group, they are associated with Jewishness by lost Jews as well as others.

A Superior Race?

> I make assumptions that Jewish people are cultured. I have a sense of them being an important race, maybe a superior race, cleverer, better, more dramatic-looking, more highly coloured, warmer . . .
>
> Jessica Greenman

> Well, what is Jewishness? It's a general tendency to high seriousness, a range of interests in all the arts, it's a certain, probably not bloody-minded individualism; it's a strength of family, a tremendous both physical and general warmth. In all those things and the importance of being hospitable, I'm not saying these are the main things about Jewishness but they all play an important part and I greatly respond to them.
>
> Richard Cohen

> I sometimes get the impression that the whole world is Jewish because every single book and every single modern philosopher, whether French, German, Russian or Italian, they're all Jewish.
>
> Donatella Bernstein

> The greatest sociological minds are Jewish, like Marx and Lévi-Strauss and Durkheim, Freud as well, and they all had something to contribute. That's what I see as positive chosen people. They're contributing to understanding of the world.
>
> Ben Selwyn

> There is something particular about Jews in the sense that they are the ideological forerunner of the current dominant civilisation and a lot of Western ideals are based on Jewish principles. Jews have made a

> disproportionate contribution in the past. Individual Jews like Einstein have made individual contributions of some magnitude. In his day it was a traditional Jewish thing to spend a lot of time having free thoughts about the way things worked.
>
> Stephen Bloom

These accolades are fairly characteristic, although Bloom differs from the others in his belief that the major Jewish contributions to civilisation were in the past. Indeed it is sometimes possible to speak of 'positive racism' in favour of Jews. Glenn Casper, for example, has picked this up in his adult life while Baroness Blackstone recalls her father saying the Jewish side was where the intelligence in the family came from. More idiosyncratically, David Matthews associates with his Jewishness 'certain qualities of a more balanced male and femaleness in either men or women'.

But behind the attributes perceived as 'Jewish' are certain inner qualities also perceived as such which suggest that the feats of Jewish cultural genius may not have been achieved without a measure of angst. Greenman sees Jews as 'earnest, thinking and not laid back. I haven't met a laid back Jew'. She senses in them, too, an ability to be disgusted by atrocity and a lack of complacency. Rather than a race, Bernstein defines a Jew as 'someone who is uncomfortable with established reality and makes other people uncomfortable'. She, herself, is 'always uncomfortable when I'm too comfortable' and tends always to find 'the hardest way out. For me every day is like New Year and *Yom Kippur* all the time. I have to count up how far I get.' For Monique M-L, hypersensitivity is a very Jewish trait. This was the sole characteristic in her second husband, *un écorché vif* (a man flayed alive), she recognised as 'Jewish', having encountered it in her father, her first husband, her son and, not least, herself.

Humour

> Woody Allen is still making a contribution. He stands for a certain neurotic Jewish approach whereby you constantly self-examine, not in a very admirable way but in a way everyone can relate to. In other words one of the things that is distinctly Jewish is a certain sort of cynical outlook on city life. That's a kind of Jewishness that's making a contribution at the moment.
>
> Stephen Bloom

> I love Woody Allen and it's that type of Jewishness I can really relate to. He knows so much about the human condition, anxieties, insecurities, neuroses. I think if you don't like Woody Allen it's a kind of marker. Whatever he is, he's about that sort of soul that I think Jewish people do have.
>
> Francesca Kaye

To many, Woody Allen's brand of humour is synonymous with Jewishness. Kaye, who recognises a 'Jewish' sense of humour as an important part of being Jewish, detects the Woody Allen persona in 'the little old Jewish man' she observes in elderly couples, but fears such people are in danger of extinction: 'They're getting on a bit and they've got that sort of wisdom and that humour. I don't see those types of people re-emerge in our society and it's they who give Jewishness that special quality.'

There is also the tradition of Yiddish humour which Bruce Bart missed out on because none of 'his Jews' spoke Yiddish: 'I hated that, that I didn't have that Yiddish thing, Yiddish humour.' Nigel Harris, who regards himself as 'an assimilated, rapidly fading Jew' is 'glad to be able to appreciate Jewish jokes and to tell them'. Similarly, 'the Jewish humour and the mannerisms' were the last vestiges of Jewishness Ben Cohen observed in his father and uncles. Cohen also liked the 'self-deprecating humour' in members of Jews for Jesus he met and found this reflected in some of the tracts they were handing out. Julie Clare, who admits 'being formed by Golders Green', is suitably self-deprecating in describing how she looked sitting in the office of an Arab in Paris: 'I was two stone heavier, Jewish as they come, I looked like Miss Golders Green.'

Claire Calman differentiates between 'English Jewish jokes' and 'Jewish Jewish jokes'. She enjoys 'that dry, quite black sense of humour' that characterises the latter but finds the other kind 'terrible' and offensive. Her father, Mel Calman, recalled his friend, the late American Jewish writer S. J. Perelman, 'sprinkling his conversation with occasional bits of Yiddish and old Jewish jokes' which were 'an unmistakeable part of his identity'.

Calman expressed his own inimitable brand of humour that could also be regarded as 'Jewish', not least in his book of jokes about God.

> It's very hard to be clear in one's mind how one feels about God. I did the book because there's a tradition in Jewish humour of talking to God. Rationally I feel there isn't but having been as it were

brainwashed by my upbringing I couldn't convincingly say it's been erased from me.

Food

Jackie Mason had this joke: 'In the interval at a normal English theatre you can always spot the Jews and the non-Jews. The non-Jews are going, "Let's go and have drinks, where shall we have a drink?" and the Jews are going, "Where shall we eat?" '. Afterwards Dad and I came out and said, 'Where shall we eat?' and laughed.

Claire Calman

The other night we went to *Angels in America* which was three and a half hours long and I said to my friend Debby, 'I must make a sandwich before we go.' 'Oh I didn't know you were going to make such a fuss,' she said. I said, 'I only want it for the interval.' In the interval of course she saw it and she said, 'Can I have a piece?'

Mel Calman

That Jews eat and gentiles drink is another virtual cliché. But enjoyment of and preoccupation with food and nostalgia for certain 'Jewish' foods are seen as typically 'Jewish' traits, shared by lost Jews and Jews very remote from their heritage. Jessica Greenman's picture of Jewishness includes 'smoked salmon sandwiches, tables groaning with food'. Tanya Alfillé reminisces about her grandmother's culinary traditions passed down through her non-Jewish mother to herself and the 'huge family cous-cous' they used to cook once a year. Martin Daltrop recalls the 'matzah dumplings' he 'may have eaten' with his grandmother as 'about the limit of my Jewish experience'. Michael Palmer speaks nostalgically of his grandfather's food: 'There was a certain amount of Indian feel to his cooking and every so often I can smell something somewhere else completely and that's grandpa's cooking, particularly the way of doing roast potatoes and a chicken soup he used to make which had a lovely smell to it.'

Often food represents more than something to eat. Rahel K mentions her husband's addiction to bagels as an example of cultural compatability. Laurence Spicer speaks of his 'love of food, the thing that's come down through the family. Whenever there's something wrong one does something about it by getting some food.' Hannelore Kastly, too, finds consolation in

Jewish food: 'Nothing helps me more when I'm ill than the chicken soup my friend makes for me. I love Jewish food.' Food is also perceived as an element of comfort and security by Julie Clare: 'If my house is stocked, if there's food in my house, if I know people can come to my house and be fed and warmed and taken care of, it makes me happy.' Needless to say, there was a scrumptious cake just out of the oven when I went to see her. An extension of the desire to feed people is the wish to create a home. Julie Clare contrasts her need for four-walled stability with her father's approach: 'He has that ancestral thing, "Always have money in your pocket wherever you go." To me that's a real kind of flight syndrome, a refugee thing.'

A Voluble People

> Either I'm being too vehement or I'm being too demonstrative or I'm being too emotional in an argument with somebody and I suddenly feel – which may be a projection – that they're thinking 'Oh, he's like that because he's Jewish.'
>
> Mel Calman

'Jewish' behaviour and mannerisms may be hard to detect in Mediterranean countries but tend to stand out where the 'norm' is more restrained. These traits are often genetic rather than cultural and are characteristic of many lost Jews. Julie Clare, for example, describes herself as 'a very overwhelming person at the best of times' with a loud and forceful personality. Laurence Spicer has the 'ability to talk a hind leg off a donkey', while Hannelore Kastly is aware that her German mother might dislike her 'Jewish behaviour', her emotions and the way she speaks with her hands.

Sidney Tuck, a retired businessman with remote Jewish ancestry, is often taken to be Jewish by his friends: 'It could be my roots. I have the mannerisms and so forth. It's all a question of genes, I suppose.' He spent a great deal of time in business with Jews, has Jewish friends and is 'always very comfortable with Jews'. Jessica Greenman, too, who comes over as very 'Jewish', speaks of 'a weird kind of elemental bonding between Jews' which she shares. Such bonding could also be cultural. Bruce Bart felt more comfortable with Jews when he went to college, a feeling shared by the Christians who grew up in his town. 'It was such a Jewish town that the few Christians in our school, most of them when they went to college joined Jewish fraternities because they felt very comfortable with Jews. They couldn't be part of a Christian group that were putting Jews down.'

Stereotypes or Something Else

Jews are rich, Jews are brash – stereotypes are often picked up by lost Jews. Janet Schuman once lived in a Jewish area 'with many rich Jews that fit the stereotype'. Fellow New Yorker Erica Ferszt speaks of her boyfriend's dislike of his Jewish mother and her family: 'These have all the Jewish stereotypes and you tend to pick on that and you don't think it gets to you but eventually it sort of sets a stereotype in your head.' Laurence Spicer explains how antagonism towards Jews can arise: 'When Jews are wealthy they wear their wealth in a wonderful, ostentatious way. The problem is other people get jealous and don't like it.'

Claire Calman tried to nip such stereotyping in the bud when she was told by a Bengali girl at school who had bought her something, 'Just have it, I'm no Jew.' Claire, who had asked how much she owed, made a calculated reply. 'It might have made her think twice about saying it again. Whether it would stop her thinking it I can't say. I thought there was an advantage to people not saying it at that level. Otherwise it becomes accepted, other people hear it, maybe young people, and they repeat it.'

Any characteristic can be exaggerated until it becomes a caricature. For example, British Telecom's highly rated television advertisement featuring actress Maureen Lipman as an archetypal Jewish mother offended some Jewish viewers. Claire Calman can understand why: 'It is this kind of fretting, worrying, over-anxious character – yes, we all know middle-aged Jewish women who are like that but we all know middle-aged non-Jewish women who are like that.'

The counterpart of negative stereotyping is the trendiness that attaches to a minority group. Julie Clare recalls feeling 'I'm different, I'm special' and using that 'as a point of attraction'. Claire Calman observed that at Jewish assembly at school, 'most people who went to it were not Jewish. It was like you always get loads of non-Jewish kids wanting to go off to *kibbutzim* and it's some kind of trendiness to be associated with. It's a kind of identifying with maybe just otherness or maybe with the underdog.' It was also trendy to be Jewish at Isabelle Reims' *lycée* in Paris: 'On Saturday morning everyone was saying, "Have you been to the *syna*(gogue) yesterday?" just like it was the fashion to wear the Star of David on a chain.' And as a teenager, Martin Daltrop wanted to be part of a minority group: 'I think for a time I felt that by being Jewish I might be part of a minority. Now I don't want to hang onto a label like that.'

MARKERS

I think the main way of getting a response from Jewish people today is either through Israel or antisemitism.

John Davies

How true of 'lost Jews' is this observation?

Antisemitism

If you forget you're a Jew, a gentile will remind you.

John Davies

Antisemitism is quite useful in a sense because it defines you.

Mel Calman

Many Jews, even the most indifferent, are sensitive to antisemitism. Nigel Harris, for example, 'bridles' when he hears an antisemitic remark and admits that 'certain situations, including antisemitism in literature, awaken the Jew in me'. John Davies was 'dumbfounded' when he came across an antisemite during the Gulf War who 'outlined to me the perfect conspiracy theory – Jews controlling the financial media, political networks, Zionists causing the Holocaust and so on', things which Davies had 'only learnt in textbooks as fantasy'. David Casper coolly appraised an antisemite he had once lived with who believed in the world Zionist banking conspiracy and was also an avid racist. 'He never had to confront his beliefs in terms of interaction with other people so for him it was a kind of fantasy. He didn't hold it against me that I came from a mixed background but also you treat a dog well.'

Casper feels racism is an inherent human quality – 'I can feel the racism of different parts of myself towards each other' – but sometimes experiences a more 'gut level' response: 'Is that a threat in any way? How does it affect their attitude toward me as a half-breed?' But while many lost Jews react very strongly to antisemitism, Casper, like others, is less affected and admits to taking antisemitism 'musingly' in contrast to his wife, a Jewish atheist, who takes it 'personally'.

Claire Calman is conscious of antisemitism but feels she reacts to it less strongly than her father. They both told me about having lunch in a restaurant and overhearing a conversation between two businessmen about 'chaps with long noses who wear funny hats on Saturdays'.

Mel: Claire and I looked up and stopped our conversation and looked at each other. Afterwards when they'd gone I said, 'I felt like throwing wine over them,' and she said, 'Why didn't they come out and say "He was a dirty Jew?" '

Claire: It really was so pathetic, the way they said it was like a schoolboy code. I think my dad was more angry than I was and I think he was thinking of saying something and we were both annoyed and I thought, 'Am I being pathetic and a coward not to say anything?'

Michael Palmer keeps a low profile on hearing antisemitic remarks: 'The reaction is to tend rather to deny the origins just simply for a quiet life. You always feel a bit ashamed afterwards but you also think, "What's the point of just fuelling a bully's bigotry?" ' Laurence Spicer has come to a similar conclusion: 'At one stage in my life I used to say "I'm Jewish because my mother is" but it didn't help so now if it happens I just let it ride over, accepting the fact that there are people misguided enough to be against something and theirs is the loss.' He recalls getting 'ridiculed' for being half-Jewish at his Roman Catholic school in Nairobi. 'There were great cries, "Get back to Tel-Aviv", which rather startled me.' Stephen Bloom was also 'taunted' at school with being Jewish. 'It bothered me briefly but not significantly.' Bruce Bart, too, recalls his experience of Catholic parochial school: 'I hated it, they mistreated me, sort of antisemitism but I never thought of it as antisemitism till this very minute.'

Bart's children react forcefully to antisemitism. Even his son, 'this blonde, beautiful kid', who identifies much less with Jewishness than his daughter, will always say 'You didn't know I was Jewish?' if he hears an antisemitic remark. Tanya Alfillé admits to getting very upset. 'I probably show it less nowadays but when I was a teenager and maybe even at university I'd get quite argumentative, I'd say my father was Jewish. I think people do pick out Jews for particular criticism or comment. I don't know whether I'm more sensitive than someone who's more Jewish.' Jacqui Burke, with memories of her father and other Jewish shop-owners boarding up shop-windows when there was a National Front march through the Gants Hill area of Essex where she lived, 'always feels a pang' when she hears about neo-Nazism in Germany or tombstones getting vandalised. 'That's something I feel is affecting me as somebody who has a Jewish background.'

Kim Kraft has come across antisemitism from Blacks. She deals with this in different ways:

> Sometimes I'd say I was Jewish quickly if there was an antisemitic remark, just to hit them and make them deal with it quickly. Sometimes I don't tell them for a while, just so there can be a bond created, and then I let them know when they are faced with deeper feelings and have no choice but to deal with it.

While Kim Kraft feels that Blacks have been 'programmed that Jews are the money grabbers, the money lenders', without being made aware of the historical background, John Witt believes that some extremist attitudes he has come across, for example from *chassidic* Jews, invite antisemitism. Similarly, many lukewarm Jews or lost Jews cringe at the sight of black coats, side-curls and unkempt beards. Michael Palmer is one. In contrast, Palmer's brother, who has converted to Catholicism but looks the perfect Sephardi gentleman, feels that these Jews 'are bearing witness'.

Antisemitism may leave some lost Jews indifferent but can also produce the 'self-hating Jew'. Stephen Bloom cites the Russian politician, Zhirinovsky, as an example. 'He is trying to distance himself from his presumed Jewish antecedents, having wanted a few years ago to go to Israel. So he's an example of perhaps an antisemitic Jew.'

Israel

> I tend to associate with Israel whilst occasionally decrying its excesses. I never have much more than a bit of sympathy for the Palestinians and a wish that the remainder of the Arab world were a little more helpful, but the automatic view is to come down on the side of Israel.
>
> Michael Palmer

Few lost Jews who are as lukewarm about their Jewishness are so supportive of the Israeli cause. Francesca Kaye, who is more involved, has a similar reaction.

> On an emotional level I would never want anything to happen to Israel. If somebody said Israel shouldn't be there I'd say, even though I don't really know the situation, 'You don't know what you're talking about.' You are allowed to attack Israel but if somebody else does it, you feel you're being got at.

Martin Daltrop, who has been on a kibbutz, is more detached. Although his interest in going was fuelled by having a Jewish background, he was irritated by the fact that *kibbutzniks* showed more interest in him if he brought up his background, 'wasn't particularly drawn to the culture' and was alienated by the political situation. Baroness Blackstone, too, who speaks of a 'love–hate relationship' with Israel, has a pragmatic outlook uninfluenced by any ancestral feelings.

> I have always been very sympathetic to the Palestinians and I identify very strongly with those Israelis who have been very critical of past Israeli governments and the way they've handled all that. That's the hate side. The love side is that I hugely admire the way this country's been built up from very little, I love the informality of it and the sort of democratic aspect of it.

For many lost Jews, Israel does not have the same emotive force as anti-semitism. Claire Calman, half-Jewish and half-Scots, feels quite 'Celtic' when she is in Scotland but has never been to Israel. 'I don't know whether I would feel: I have a connection here.' Jacqui Burke has 'no particular reactions' even though a cousin of hers was killed in the Israeli army. Her genealogical interests draw her more to Eastern Europe where her family came from. Donatella Bernstein felt at home in Israel's cosmopolitan atmosphere. 'They accepted me as Jewish and I felt very comfortable because everybody speaks several languages and everybody's from five or six different places.' But she disliked the intransigence and tendency to quarrel she found in Israelis.

Sidney Tuck, a freemason who has researched into the Old Testament, the Talmud and the Dead Sea Scrolls, also felt comfortable in Israel. Masonic lodges, he believes, break down barriers. 'In Israel you get Muslims and Jews mixing in the same lodges. The Grandmaster of one was a Muslim and the one before him was a Jew.' An equally individual approach is that of Robert Beecham, who also enjoys visiting Israel and practising his Hebrew there. A devout Christian, he is fascinated by the

> Element of fulfillment of prophecy, the Jewish return from the diaspora, the *galut*. It is an amazing thing by any reckoning that the words of Moses are so exactly fulfilled that they would be scattered throughout the world and afterwards they would return, which I don't think any other race has ever succeeded in doing, reclaiming its homeland two thousand years on.

NOTHING LEFT?

Some lost Jews, often very young, show almost total indifference to their Jewish heritage. Sandra Olivetti, for example, remarks that her children 'absolutely couldn't care about their roots'. Sonia Ezekiel, younger sister of Laurent and also educated in the cosmopolitan environment of the French *lycée* in London, identifies as 'nothing', but did comment, 'We couldn't be Jewish anyway.' At one stage she sported a Star of David on a chain, as a trinket rather than a sign of identification. Hannah Abraham, daughter of Penelope, agrees that with her name she is, in a way, 'labelled' but in the multi-racial, secular environment she has grown up in, 'nobody cares who is what'. Her response to my question as to whether she would want something to 'show' for her name, was characteristically reluctant: 'I suppose I wouldn't mind knowing about it but I wouldn't start, I don't think, unless something really big happened to me and changed me a lot.' Leah Friedlander, in her early twenties, had a Jewish father but no religious upbringing and glories in being 'nothing'. 'Sometimes', she concedes, 'I feel I've missed out because obviously to have a religion is a way of who you are, what you are, but all the people around me, they're not into any religion either because that's how they all are and I don't seem to have missed out on anything, neither have they.' People apparently take her surname to be German and her first name is usually associated with *Star Wars*, rather than anything Jewish.

An American Scenario

Lindsay Rothschild, a student at Michigan State University, has a more relaxed acceptance of her Jewish – and Christian – backgrounds despite being equally indifferent to organised religion. Meeting her with her paternal grandmother in a restaurant on New York's Upper West Side was an eye-opener into the dynamics of America's mixed heritage culture.

Grandmother Claire, turned off by her orthodox background, wanted her children to have some experience of Jewish history and culture, but was deterred by the high cost of 'temple' membership. 'You've just lost a Jew,' she told officials at a Los Angeles synagogue. Lindsay's father, with no religious education or bar mitzvah, met his Episcopalian 'flower child' wife-to-be and asked Claire to make a Passover dinner: 'He wanted her folks to see it.' To accomodate her future daughter-in-law's wish to have a religious marriage, Claire, with the backing of her future 'in-laws', found a reform rabbi to officiate: 'They broke the glass but it wasn't orthodox.'

Now, on the initiative of Lindsay's mother, the family do more than what Lindsay's father did as a child, something he goes along with because 'he doesn't want to be bombarded with Christianity. We light the *Hanukah* candles, my dad has a tape of songs my mum bought, and we do Christmas–*Hanukah* with five families in our street, all mixed marriages.

We have *latkes* and matzah-ball soup and we have *dreidls.*' Lindsay and her brother went to church when they were younger 'to feel like the other kids' but she doesn't like church. 'We never went to "temples" or anything but we had Passover dinners and some of our friends had bar mitzvahs. I enjoy the Passover dinner. We do it with a progressive group of people.'

At university Lindsay has been welcomed at the Jewish Student Union and at Hillel, but is not deeply involved. She would like to learn more about things Jewish, not so much for herself but 'just because when people ask me questions they think I should know'.

REMNANTS OF JEWISHNESS

> I sometimes wonder whether we have already assimilated the Jewish tradition and whether the Jewish culture is already inside us. Do we need to keep this culture alive and together or is it a kind of blood that is already in ourselves?
>
> Sandra Olivetti

It is clear that Jewish traits survive where Jewishness is remote or non-existent and that remnants of Jewishness are likely to mark increasing numbers of people in the foreseeable future. While this is obviously not enough to ensure the continuity of Jewish communities, lost Jews like Olivetti may also be saddened by such a prospect and 'miss a culture that is completely integrated in the individuals'.

10

To Be or Not to Be

THE MARGINALS

At the crossroads of Jewish life are young Jews who acknowledge that they are Jewish but remain outside any official communal structure. These 'marginal' Jews come from a variety of backgrounds, from relatively traditional to completely secular. Is their 'aloofness' a reaction against the established Jewish community? Or are these young Jews negating any form of religious authority like their counterparts throughout the Western world in a prevailingly secular culture? Has their level of Jewish awareness been shaped by their background or have outside factors played a greater part? Are marginal Jews committed to the continuity and survival of the Jewish people and does this concern influence their relationships? How many of today's marginals will become tomorrow's lost Jews?

These questions were discussed when I interviewed a selection of young Jews, all highly educated and from middle-class backgrounds. Most lived in London, others were from Manchester and one from New York. I was interested in this very specific group because I believe any religious or cultural denomination needs to retain intelligent and independent-minded young people. Yet it is precisely such people that Chief Rabbi Sacks has labelled 'indifferent to Judaism' because they are not, at present, concerned with 'a search for community or building structures of Jewish life'. Are marginal Jews irrelevant, then, to the Jewish future? Or should the Jewish world find creative ways of exploiting what they may have to offer?

The Mating Game

'Love and marriage go together like a horse and carriage,' claims the 1950s pop song. 'Not if you're Jewish, they don't,' might be the retort of many young Jews. Despite parental pressure to marry within the fold and, in many cases, their own reluctance to 'break the chain' of Jewish continuity, these young Jews are unwilling to socialise exclusively with others of the same faith and are likely to meet more gentiles than Jews with whom they may fall in love.

Andy, dark-haired, good-looking, with a laid-back South African manner, is the creator of Fantasy Football. He would meet the most exacting standards of any Jewish – or gentile – girl looking for a mate and spoke with feeling of the premarital ritual followed by many young Jewish men:

> We went through a phase, my male friends and I, when we were all going out with non-Jewish girls because we were not very challenged by Jewish girls – we found them unintellectual and uninteresting. This was until our early twenties when marriage was still not really an issue. We're shifting our emphasis now and we're trying that much harder to find Jewish girls. I'm not saying we're lowering our standards but we're trying harder.

Like his friends, many of whom attended a Jewish secondary school, Andy does not wish to 'marry out' – 'except under extenuating circumstances like when you're madly in love with someone. There could be a lot of people that we're meeting that we could potentially fall madly in love with but we're not letting it develop that far.'

He admits to having 'got quite far down that line', after being involved with a non-Jewish girl for two years.

> I had to separate in my mind my feelings why I was ending the relationship, whether it was because of my feelings for her as a girl *per se* or whether it was purely because of religion. I don't really know if I got myself in a similar situation and I was totally in love with the girl and she wasn't Jewish, what I'd do. But I'm not prepared to face that dilemma again.

Nevertheless, he professes an uncanny respect for those who do not care about their partner's religion:

> I'm almost in a funny sort of way jealous that they can be that true to themselves and they're not worried so much about their parents or their kids or their religion and they believe that 100 per cent in love conquering all barriers. I think it's great, it's quite brave in a way, given all the outside pressures we have against marrying out.

Andy seems to have a stronger commitment to the Jewish future than many marginal Jews. But contrary to statistics which indicate that more Jewish men than women 'marry out', the importance of finding a Jewish partner was of greater concern to the young men I interviewed, irrespective of their upbringing.

Tom, a lawyer and Oxford graduate, is an atheist with a secular upbringing who expresses strongly positive views about Jewish identity. He wishes to marry a Jewish partner, or, at least, to have Jewish children. This would involve a prospective non-Jewish partner converting to Judaism. While not everyone I spoke to viewed conversion as a viable option, some are unable to, even if they wish. Ari, a student from a traditional Jewish background, is still reacting against an overdose of strictly orthodox Judaism doled out during his 2 years at a Jewish secondary school. He has had a series of non-Jewish girlfriends and strongly resents the fact that his status within Jewish law as a 'Cohen' or 'priest' prohibits him from marrying a convert. 'I have to be that much purer,' he explained, not without bitterness. 'I feel I cannot marry someone who is not Jewish as it would break my parents' heart.' Guy, a student from an ostensibly traditional Manchester home, has also been out primarily with non-Jewish girls but opposes intermarriage both for personal and family reasons. Nick, an Oxford graduate from a reform synagogue background, who has recently emigrated to Israel, is spared the problem as he hopes to marry 'a sexy Israeli'; otherwise, he would have no hesitation in 'marrying out'. Indeed, as a Zionist, he feels that the identity problem of diaspora Jews is becoming increasingly acute with each succeeding generation and he wouldn't want to impose this on his children.

Of the girls, only one, Melissa, a soft-spoken student who attended a reform synagogue, has put head before heart in restraining herself from getting too emotionally involved with a non-Jew. Clare, tall, handsome-featured and articulate, with an unashamedly Bury accent, is a student from a so-called 'middle-of-the-road' orthodox family. She, too, does not intend to 'marry out' but has never been out with a Jewish boy. In common with many marginal Jewish males, her ideal as a marriage partner is the 'non-Jewish Jew'. To date, her choice of boyfriends has spanned a gamut of Christians: the vicar's son, the born-again Christian, the lapsed Catholic. Both Melissa, a 'daddy's girl', and Clare, whose father emerged as a reclusive and almost antisemitic figure, were convinced that nobody they brought home would satisfy 'daddy'.

While acknowledging the advantages of marrying within the faith, most of the other girls stressed the importance of 'love' or 'happiness' or 'the right person'. Debbie, an Oxford graduate whose Jewish background was minimal, saw Jewishness as a bond, but no more than, say, a taste for the same music. Michelle, a postgraduate studying psychology from a more traditional home, has recently become immersed in her familial and historical roots, in the hope of forging a strong Jewish identity of her own which she can pass down to her children. She sees another side to the argument.

Sometimes I feel I will only marry a Jew, mainly because every ancestor from the year dot has managed to maintain that. At other times I think there's so much assimilation that it's ridiculous to say 'I'll only marry a Jew', because the world is moving on to a new millennium, it's a very different world from fifty years ago, even ten years ago, and it's a multi-ethnic, multi-cultural world and maybe we should all reflect that.

The feeling that the world is changing was shared by Sophia, a New Yorker studying town planning at the Massachusetts Institute of Technology: 'I'd want to live my life and try to raise my children understanding that they have to get along in the world. How Judaism fits in in that I don't know. It's a matter of not losing your identity and being proud of it but being able to get along.' Petite and blonde, Sophia does not feel that marrying out would threaten her Jewish identity: 'Growing up in New York, it's not difficult to be Jewish. Everybody eats bagels on Sundays and everybody goes to Passover *seders*, so it's not a big deal to hold on to your heritage because you take it for granted. So marrying outside of Judaism really doesn't change your life very much.'

When I spoke to her, Sophia was in a relationship with a committed Catholic and saw the difference in religion as no more significant than holding different beliefs about anything. 'I'd make a very big effort to get to learn a lot about Christianity and I assume he would learn a lot about Judaism so that becomes something you share and learn about. Just because he believes in a different version of history, there's no proof in my life to say he's wrong.'

Did the fact that a child of a Jewish mother is considered *halachically* Jewish enable these young Jewish women to take a more relaxed stance than their male counterparts? Hardly anyone was prepared to acknowledge this as a major factor. Sophia was concerned that her children should grow up with a spiritual environment she feels unable to provide herself. Like many others, she would want them to learn about their Jewish heritage and also about their father's religion, if it was different. Andrée, a sculptress, felt similarly but would insist, unlike some of the girls, that any son of hers should be circumcised, as Jewish tradition dictates.

A few would accept any religious identification their children might choose. 'As far as I'm concerned, my kids could tell me that they were Hindu and that would be fine,' said Sara, a graduate from a reform synagogue background, who admits to 'sometimes feeling quite Jewish' herself.

The Shadow of Persecution

Some of the young women accepted, often against the grain, that were a World War II situation to repeat itself, it would be a comfort to face the ordeal with a Jewish partner. Andrée, with a gentle, distracted manner, was particularly sensitive to such an eventuality:

> When people talk about racist uprisings, it sends an absolute shiver down my spine. Antisemitism is the only thing that really frightens me. If you feel that you might be hounded for who you are, what you believe, you need to have a partner who can understand that anxiety. That's a tall order for someone who is not Jewish to comprehend.

Tom expressed a more global perspective: 'The overriding factor for someone Jewish of my generation is the Holocaust, whether or not it's on their consciousness on a day to day level. The Holocaust and the very real possibility that it could happen again are the great cloud that hangs over every Jew.'

On the whole, those whose families had suffered directly under the Nazis and who had grown up with a sense of defensiveness, fear and even guilt, acknowledged the connection between the Holocaust and their Jewish sensibilities. As Andrée, who comes from a traditional background, put it:

> I consider myself to be culturally Jewish and I associate that mostly with my grandparents. Both sets of grandparents were affected in the Second World War and because of their histories and particularly because of the number of people that were killed in my family, it's of extreme significance to me that I am Jewish. When I walk into a synagogue I'm always incredibly aware of my family's history and I go out of a respect and a duty to them and when I don't go, I feel like I'm trying to forget what they went through.

Sometimes a journey into the past arouses strong feelings of Jewishness, as Alex, a student recalls.

> The one time I felt most Jewish was visiting the town my grandparents had lived in in Central Europe. The town had had 500 Jews and there was one gentleman and one lady left. They had built this memorial stone because the Jewish cemetery had been completely desecrated and on it was every single name of every Jew from that town who had been killed, including members of my family that I hadn't known. The woman had been in Theresienstadt as a kid and she had this postcard

from her mother which said, 'By the time you get this I'll be dead but I want you to know that I love you.' And it's so upsetting to be in that sort of context and in terms of being Jewish you come out feeling very angry and that made me think about it a lot more.

That Alex needed an experience of this nature to be reminded of her Jewishness was surprising as with her dark hair, strong features and emphatic manner, she comes over as decidedly Jewish and admits being dubbed by gentile boyfriends as 'my little Jewish girlfriend'.

A distinction between the impact of the Holocaust on young American Jews and their counterparts in Britain was made by Nicole, also dark and somewhat exotic-looking, who had recently returned to Britain after several years in the States and whose paternal grandparents made a last-minute escape from Nazi Europe. 'One of the differences between Jews in America and England is that, for the Americans, the Holocaust and the concentration camps were not only forty years ago, they were like a whole world away. It wasn't the same feeling, it wasn't the same threat.'

Some young Jews appear to remain personally detached from the Holocaust despite the suffering of their families. Ari's paternal grandmother was a survivor of Auschwitz. But not having experienced antisemitism himself, he shared the tendency of many to deplore it as just a racist phenomenon. Only the mention of neo-Nazism drew a stronger reaction, mingled with a certain Jewish pride: 'Neo-Nazism I can't stand, because they killed most of dad's family. I'm proud that I'm in a minority that the neo-Nazis hate, because I look down on them.' Ari may have been 'cushioned' by generations of maternal ancestors who had never known persecution or his detachment may be the result of his experience at a public school with a high proportion of Jewish students: 'We had superiority in numbers and picked on them. So if there was a fight between Jews and non-Jews, the Jews always came out on top.'

Further evidence of the curious imbalance between Jews and non-Jews at this particular school was provided by Tim, a stocky, dark-haired school-leaver: 'On the Jewish holidays, when a lot of the more religious Jewish boys took more days off than I did, the non-Jews actually quite liked it. They could express themselves, they didn't feel so restrained. They were quite intimidated, I think, a lot of the time.'

Others who had attended public schools were not so fortunate. Tom, also dark, with quite semitic features, faced 'a measure of public-school type antisemitism' at Westminster where the number of Jews are restricted by a 'non-Anglican' quota.

> One would expect it among other schoolboys because schoolchildren are bullies but what's much more important was a comment by the deputy-headmaster at the time when he told me to 'Go back to Golders Green' or words to that effect. I didn't react to it in any way really but it was a remark I remembered. I also remember a remark from other people to the effect that 'One day we're going to get you all.'

Nick, tall, slim and sensitive-looking, would not fit any antisemitic stereotype. After attending a London preparatory school which was predominantly Jewish, he decided, 'unlike anyone else', to go to Charterhouse, the well-known public boarding school, whose alumni include the novelist, Frederic Raphael, who has made no secret of the antisemitism he encountered there. Nick's decision was to shape his life.

> Whilst I was there, I got hassled a lot for being Jewish. It was a complete case on my part of the mystique of it. They treated me like some sort of outsider; they beat me up, abused me, drew swastikas on my door and this went on and on for about 2 years. I learnt karate and then towards the third year I started tackling the issue face on.

At the same time, he was studying for his bar mitzvah with an Auschwitz survivor and was deeply affected by his teacher's recollections.

Nick's experiences at Charterhouse made him look at what it is to be a Jew in Britain and he was not 'all that impressed with the image'. His perception of the prototype British Jew led him to reject the diaspora Jewish identity *in toto.*

> There's very much an identity, a persona which has developed, built on values that I find almost pathetic. Judaism is 'just a religion', so then a persona and an identity based on 'just a religion' will generate pretty groundless values, and characteristics such as Jewish jokes, Yiddish words interspersed, certain looks, certain poses and so on. Judaism's moved from being just a religion to being a national identity. I see diaspora Jews as in a transitional period from being 'just a religion' to either completely rejecting it or taking upon themselves the national characteristics.

Tom, in contrast, attempted to evaluate the nature of antisemitism. 'Is antisemitism such a virus world-wide that people who aren't even obviously antisemitic have been infected by it? I think it is.'

Where Nick has turned his back on the equivocations and ambivalence that often characterise life in the diaspora, Tom is able to come to terms with this: 'Many Jews are neither going to feel totally comfortable in a gentile society, nor do they necessarily want to, because they take pride in their Jewishness or Judaism, but on the other hand they do not want to be in an exclusively Jewish environment where they feel ghettoised.'

Several others may not have experienced antisemitism at school but were conscious of belonging to a minority. Guy, very Italian-looking with flashing dark eyes, has a dreamy manner of speaking with the remains of a barely-discernible Mancunian accent. His account of his schooldays traced a progression from the self-image of the outsider, embarrassed at being 'different', to the self-image of someone comfortable with his religious and ethnic distinctiveness and yet able to integrate within the majority culture.

> When you get older, people learn to accept each other's differences. By the time I had come to terms with this, not my own Jewishness because I had always come to terms with that, but by the time I let people know that *I* know I'm Jewish, *they* know I'm Jewish, everybody knows I'm Jewish, it's not a problem.

Choosing when and whether to make their Jewishness known to outsiders was a factor many were very conscious of. Whether or not the decision to impart or withold the information is conditioned by fears of residual antisemitism, the prevarication is characteristic of marginal Jews or, from the perspective of a Zionist like Nick, part of the diaspora Jew's perennial crisis of identity. In London, Guy was confronted, like many Jews who may look more 'Mediterranean' or 'Continental' than 'English', with the question 'Where are you from?' Michelle, who, with her light brown hair and pale olive complexion, also looks indefinably 'Continental', has the answer: 'Now that I've got this sort of awakening, I find the best answer is "I'm Jewish". I like to see people's reactions. A lot of them think that we're just a different species, a lot of them have got Jewish blood or Jewish friends.'

For someone who doesn't look 'English', being 'Jewish' can be preferable to some alternative identity. Ari, who at the time of the interview was sporting a beard that would have done an Islamic fundamentalist proud – or alternatively earned the envy of a less hirsute *Yeshiva* student – conceded that the fact that he was often identified as an Arab made it easier to state openly that he was Jewish.

Some admitted to making a point of coming out and saying 'I'm Jewish' as a protective mechanism, to ward off anything they may not want to hear. Debbie, light-complexioned with a perky, somewhat 'Jewish' look, takes that line. Others tend to keep a lower Jewish profile, because of their fear of antisemitism or their sensitivity to negative Jewish stereotypes. Andrée is one of these.

Abroad, both girls adopted a different approach. Andrée has spent periods in Prague, as a gesture of solidarity with her Czech ancestry.

> I was quite amazed that when I worked in Prague I made it pretty obvious that I was Jewish. There is definitely quite a strong feeling of antisemitism over there, it's the sort of thing that if you mention to people that your family's Czech, they know that you are Jewish and it's generally treated with a kind of silence.

Debbie, in contrast, was less up-front about her Jewishness when she was studying in France, where she found antisemitism far more prevalent: 'I was quite reluctant to tell people I was called "Deborah" because there nobody's called "Deborah" unless they're Jewish. And I didn't want to be put into that stereotype straightaway.'

Many believed Jews have less to fear in Britain than elsewhere in Europe because other 'whipping boys' stand out more. Annie*, an attractive twenty-five year old actress, is not so sanguine. 'I'd be the first to say antisemitism is rife in this country as well as everywhere else. It may be out of ignorance or reasons like jealousy or resentment. I think it abounds, it always has done and I really do think that history repeats itself.' Annie's sensitivity to antisemitism is tempered by the fact that her family has been in England for many generations and her somewhat mysterious demeanour, while not typically English, is unlikely to label her as Jewish. 'I probably feel more angry than uncomfortable, which is quite a good sign. I'm so many generations along the line that I don't have a chip and I don't feel very insecure. I do feel happy that this is my home.'

Sometimes an antisemitic episode can trigger more than just anger, as Clare describes:

> In the tube station there were these two foreign people and they were very, very *frum*, side curls, the works, but they didn't understand English and they couldn't work the ticket machine. I could hear this man muttering under his breath and then he just swore a lot and said something like 'You Jews go back to Jerusalem. Why are you always getting away without paying?' I didn't realise I'd do it but I just took on another self. I was swearing myself, going 'What are you doing?' and I was getting very, very mad. Apparently, I grabbed him by the collar and I nearly thumped him and I've never been violent with anyone in my entire life. It's just that these people were so defenceless, they didn't even understand that he was slagging them off and I was so angry, I couldn't believe it.

Experiences of Judaism

Clare's instinctive reaction to stand up for the defenceless outsider could be seen as classically Jewish. In stressing the defencelessness of the two ultra-orthodox Jews she was, unconsciously and in a somewhat dramatic manner, reinforcing Judaism's traditional precepts of justice and protection for the fatherless, the widow, the stranger. These basic values are not what most marginal Jews would associate with Judaism, however. As Ari explained 'I learnt about those things at my primary school but I associate them with the Judaism of the past, not of today.'

In contrast to the strong impact of the Holocaust and antisemitism on Jewish identity, the impact of Judaism was negligible. At best it had little negative influence. Most accepted that religion offered a moral code but felt that belief was a personal matter and that the formal practice of Judaism, like any religion, was outdated and irrelevant in todays's world, an attitude reflecting indifference to religion among young people in a prevailingly secular culture. Andy pointed out that while religion provided a valuable framework in which to be raised and in which to raise children, it was low on the priority list of young people from the mid-teens onwards until marriage and children came on to the horizon.

I found a striking degree of alienation among those who had had contact with orthodox Judaism without being brought up in a strictly orthodox environment. This is in line with the observations of Todd Endelman, who finds Anglo-Jewish religious institutions unresponsive to the needs of their constituency: 'Jews in Britain are no more religious or secular than Jews in America, but in Britain it's religious institutions with a very right-wing cast which have the prominence and it simply does not match the mood of the people in the community and it's very off-putting.'

There was one exception to this somewhat negative picture: Tim, who has become much more religously involved.

> Recently I've been going to synagogue every Saturday and getting to learn more. There are so many young Jews of my age who know absolutely nothing about the religion and aren't even being bothered to investigate and I think it's a tragedy because there's so much there. People who are Jewish should at least give religion a chance.

A key factor which has enhanced Tim's experience of synagogue participation has been the informal seminars, run by the rabbi of the orthodox Spanish and Portuguese synagogue he now attends, for young, mainly marginal Jews, who find they are able to question and challenge aspects of the religion without being made to feel 'blasphemous'.

Tim was brought up in a reform synagogue. While this did not 'turn him on', it was probably a reasonable entry point into Judaism for a young person from a traditional but not orthodox family. While no-one from a reform synagogue background was particularly enthusiastic, no-one was hostile. Marginal Jews accustomed to an orthodox service which is long, all in Hebrew and largely incomprehensible, have found a reform service, part of which is in English, far more 'sincere', 'down to earth', 'spiritual', 'friendly' and 'enjoyable'. But Sophia, who was raised in a prominent reconstructionist congregation in New York, felt the dogma-challenging environment had provided her with intellectual stimulation but without religious belief.

Like several others alienated by being coerced into attending an orthodox synagogue, Nicola, a graduate, might have benefited from a reform service. 'If I'd been sent to a synagogue where I could actually understand what's being talked about, if there were songs that one could participate in or at least recognise tunes, if there were sincere people, I think I'd actually be more Jewish than I am now.' But much of Nicola's overt hostility to things Jewish comes down to resentment against her father, with his inconsistent attitudes to Jewish observance and his reluctance to acknowledge his own Jewish roots in India – not to mention the attention he had lavished on her elder brother at the expense of her sister and herself. In reaction Nicola dresses plainly, in common with many of the other girls I spoke to, rather than in the designer clothes 'daddy' would have preferred. Her final act of rebellion was to move in, shortly before the interview, with the non-Jewish boyfriend her father rejects, whose obvious fascination with Judaism has, ironically, sparked an interest in her that years in an ostensibly Jewish home failed to do.

Memories of orthodox synagogues and of *cheder* or Sunday School where teachers were often ultra-orthodox, were invariably off-putting. Michelle perceived the synagogue she had attended as 'sort of cobwebby with quite an oppressive atmosphere'. Others, unable to follow the service in Hebrew, spoke of the absence of prayerfulness or spirituality. Indeed, the failure of Judaism to provide them with the spirituality they were seeking was a complaint common to many of these young Jews. Another turn-off factor voiced virtually unanimously was 'the fashion parade', whether in the ladies' gallery of the various north London synagogues the girls had attended or 'the Giorgio Armani runway' in the forecourt of Guy's synagogue in Manchester. Guy, himself, responded to some more stirring moments of the ceremonial but felt that the orthodox service in his synagogue 'needs sorting out and modernising'. He also stressed the importance of attending synagogue with a parent, in order to understand

and feel comfortable with the service. His father never accompanied him but just made him go.

Ari, in contrast, sometimes attended a strictly orthodox synagogue with his father. But by the time of his bar mitzvah, he had acquired a deep-seated antipathy to Judaism – and Jews – from the orthodox secondary school from which his parents removed him after two years. While his reaction might have been extreme, it was in line with the findings of a survey conducted in 1985[1] which suggested in a section on 'Concern for Israel and fellow Jews' that Jewish secondary schooling could have a negative influence. Religion in the home and a good Jewish primary school often mitigated the negative trend but not in Ari's case.

Andy had attended a well-balanced Jewish primary school in South Africa and succeeded in maintaining a more reasoned attitude while criticising the same orthodox school's 'sledgehammer approach'.

> There was too much ramming of the religion down your throat. There was never any discussion about why you believed, did you perhaps feel you didn't want to believe. I've probably got a bit of an animosity towards the people who are very religious, I found them quite bigoted against other Jews who weren't as religious. For example, they used to actually punish us for not wearing *tsitsit*, which is not the way to get religion into people.

Like several others, Andy felt that some of the Jewish festivals which 'stressed bonding with the community and family' were the most attractive aspects of Judaism. This positive approach, however, had not been developed at his school: 'There was so much stress on what you can't do, on the hundreds of ways of breaking the Sabbath, rather than on ten or fifteen festivals a year and how much warmth and good feelings you can get out of them.'

Many agreed that religion had been 'thrust down their throats'. Nicola was clearly riled at being prevailed upon to attend an orthodox synagogue on the Day of Atonement, the most sacred day in the Jewish calendar.

> It's the one thing my father asks me to do, half an hour on this particular day to sit in a synagogue, and that is a chore and a half for me. I suppose it is Jewish respect. My mother says to me, 'Please, Nicola, just this one day, don't argue with your father, go to the synagogue for half an hour, don't let him see you making coffee . . .'

Observing *Yom Kippur* is the bottom line for Jews who have not totally renounced the practice of their religion. Many will take the day off, put in an appearance in synagogue and, probably, fast. Breaking *Yom Kippur*, for young Jews who have been brought up to observe it, is a means of rebelling, asserting their independence. Alex, while not observing it the conventional way, at least finds some meaning.

> *Yom Kippur*, I've been brought up to believe, is to do with assessing your year, questioning the relationships you've had with people. In a way it's just a landmark like New Year's Eve. You're looking at 'Where am I now? Where do I want to be?' without religious sentiment. I don't necessarily take the day off. I just think about it when I'm on my own.

Most made it clear that the Judaism they had experienced had diminished rather than enhanced their sense of Jewishness. In contrast I discovered that a secular upbringing with a stress on Jewish cultural values may indeed produce young Jews proud of their Jewish heritage. Michelle believes strongly in the cultural route to a strong Jewish identity.

> It's very much a cultural thing that I'm feeling. What's really important is being in touch with your roots and your history. That passes through your blood like your genes are passed through when you are born. I think I would do things differently with my children, I would teach them as much as I could about their ancestors and their culture rather than just send them off to Sunday School in the hope that they pick up a few things and come out with a bar mitzvah.

Then there was Tom, brought up without synagogue or a bar mitzvah but with an intensely Jewish *weltanschaung*. He now attends synagogue twice a year and while remaining an atheist, is prepared to 'defend the Jewish God'.

At the other extreme is Nikki, a nineteen-year-old student from south London, who has received virtually no Jewish input, either religious or cultural, beyond being told that she was Jewish.

> I'm sort of in limbo at the moment. It's very difficult. People say, 'Well, what religion are you?' So I say, 'Well I'm Jewish, sort of,' but I don't know if I can say that I really am because I don't know the first thing about it. I would quite like to have had the upbringing, the education.

Nikki's light brown hair and pale features contribute to an impression of anonymity. While she affirms that she is quite capable now of existing without religion, it was difficult when speaking with her not to pick up an overwhelming sense of deprivation. Unlike others with a similar background who might welcome a relationship with a more committed Jew as an opportunity to 'catch up' on the Judaism they had never practised, she asserts that it is too late now to start learning what she was never taught as a child and that she would find it difficult to pass on anything to her children. 'I don't think it's right for me to have a religion where you've got the laws set down because I'm not used to it. I think it's important to preserve something Jewish but obviously I don't feel it's important enough to go into it myself.'

The Promised Land

Is Israel the key to a stronger Jewish identity as many community officials claim? Some marginals have reservations about enlarged Jewish communities and are reluctant to visit Israel for this reason. Andrée feared that Israel would be like 'an enlarged synagogue or Golders Green'. The majority, however, found Israel quite interesting and enjoyable and agreed that the experience had helped to strengthen their Jewish identity; some plan to spend time there in the future to learn more about their Jewishness. Coming face to face with Jewish history, in particular, perhaps, at the Western Wall in Jerusalem, made an impression on many, though some saw a certain irony in the Jewish State being the repository not only of its own history but that of Christianity and Islam as well.

I detected a degree of ambivalence between acceptance of the need for a Jewish state and awareness of the problems the existence of Israel had brought in its wake. Tom was one of a minority who were quite unequivocal: 'Jews have no choice but to support the state of Israel. Had it existed fifty years ago, six million people wouldn't have died.'

I was more surprised to discover that responses to the media image of Israel were influenced less by Jewish commitment than by knowledge of the subject. As well as Nick, who as a Zionist had no difficulty in finding arguments to defend Israel's actions, a few, like Tom, were able to see beyond what is often served up in the media. Several marginals, however, expressed disappointment when Israel's behaviour fell short of 'Western standards' and would have wished, somewhat naïvely perhaps, for more skilful media manipulation by Israeli authorities. Others who were more streetwise or mediawise were able to distinguish the reality, however unpleasant, from the footage presentation which dramatised the most unpleasant details. Overall, several who were embarrassed by various Israeli actions admitted to feeling 'protective' and 'concerned' when Israel receives bad press.

At university, where there was strong sympathy for the Palestinians, Alex felt obliged to defend Israel in circumstances where she might have been openly critical in the company of other Jews. Nicole contrasted the all-powerful 'Goliath' image of Israel she had grown up with with Israel's vulnerability in many areas which she later recognised. Nicola, on the other hand, had been influenced by her research for an assignment representing the Palestinian cause in an international students' forum.

Most acknowledged the importance of Israel being there for Jews, though some felt slightly guilty that they didn't want to live there. As Alex explained: 'You talk to Israelis and they feel quite resentful and you can understand it because you feel they're slogging away and I sit back here and say "Well, I think it's very good that there's a place for Jews to go but I'm staying here, thank you." '

Nick, who feels an outsider in Britain, found Israel the answer to what he perceived as the diaspora Jew's identity problem:

> All these questions, the importance of how comfortable you feel as a Jew with the identity given to you through the various rituals and institutions like bar mitzvah, for me, it's all answered in Israel. Rather than being Jewish as a religion, you become Israeli and being Israeli means that *Hanukah* and *Rosh Hashana* become national festivals, national holidays like Christmas. I'm sure I'll be happy coming back to England after maybe five years in Israel as an Israeli. I'll feel completely solved as to my Jewish identity.

Nick sees a philosophical – and practical – necessity for the religious perspective to be replaced by or at least to co-exist with a nationalistic vision. In his opinion, Judaism, which sees its fulfilment in the coming of the Messiah, is essentially future orientated whereas Zionism offers answers for the here and now: 'Zionism, as Herzl put it, is like a normalisation. It completely solves all these questions, all this insecurity of identity, all this having a problem with saying I'm Jewish.' His views were supported by a few others, like Tom, who suggested that 'ethnic solidarity with Israel' might have replaced Judaism as a marker of Jewish identity.

Not everyone was able to accept the 'nationalisation' of Judaism Nick advocates. Guy was shocked to find that Friday night, observed through much of the Jewish world as a consecration of the Sabbath with blessings on bread and wine, was 'party night of the week' for most Israelis. This was similar to what Nicole had found in the United States where a secular Jewish culture is widespread, far more so than in Britain. Tom, however, felt that the existence of a Jewish state which is largely secular vindicated a more diverse form of Jewish expression: 'As far as I'm aware, Israel is thoroughly unreligious apart from those who are orthodox Jews. It's certainly not a Jewish state by any religious definition. If Israel as a state was a person in Anglo-Jewry, it's far from certain whether Israel would be counted as Jewish!'

What Is It To Be Jewish?

So what is it to be Jewish? Nicola had no problem in answering. 'It's two things, it's a family thing and a thing that has been imposed on me through blood. It's a genetic thing if you like. It doesn't play any part in my attitude towards life, morals, principles, any of that.' Nevertheless, she acknowledged a certain 'irrational Jewish pride'. Clare's definition was equally unenthusiastic: 'It's something that has been imposed on me, it's a blood thing, I can't escape from it.' Sophia defines her Jewishness in a similar way, but with much more acceptance and pride: 'I feel Jewish, out of history, my blood and it's just like a nationality.'

Many marginals were uncomfortable with the connotations of racial purity evoked by the concept of 'Jewish blood'. As Guy explained: 'Entertaining any idea about racial purity just stinks of Hitler but it is an issue. I feel all sorts of people have some pride in their roots and they feel racial mixing dilutes your heritage. I think I might feel that. It frightens me.'

Nick had a similar view. 'All these connotations of racial purity are quite revolting but mixing does dilute culture.' He argued that the Israeli experience was necessary to avoid the question of blood, purity and culture.

> Israel is developing its own culture, its own traditions, based primarily on Judaism. Ultimately, I hope, anyone would be welcome to that country and anyone from that country would be welcome in other countries. Now that Israel exists, I believe there is a solid structure there that can look ahead to the future.

The concept of Jews as 'chosen' also provoked mixed feelings. While Ari admitted to having enjoyed the idea of being 'chosen' and therefore superior in his more arrogant younger days, the prevailing opinion was that Jews were 'chosen' for their responsibility to humanity. Alex found this difficult to reconcile with Jewish exclusivism: 'How do you put that into practice? Judaism is very insular, it doesn't happily bring people in, so if you're supposed to be setting an example yet you keep everyone out, that's contradictory.' Some felt, however, that being Jewish had made them more open-minded and tolerant.

Most acknowledged that being Jewish was being part of a culture, a heritage and a religious tradition. Some felt it was not necessary to practise the religion. As Guy argued: 'I don't think that's an issue here in Judaism. In other religions it might be. You don't have to practise to be Jewish because it's a duality.' Ari compared a non-practising Jew to a non-practising Catholic. Both had a heritage to fall back on. 'You have your heritage and you have your actual belief within your heritage. The good thing is that the heritage is always there for you.'

Tim, like many others, would emphasise that being Jewish was much more than the religion itself. 'There's so much that remains unsaid, the impact of the persecution over the years, family attitudes.' He is convinced, nonetheless, that 'the hub of being Jewish is the religion. I'm considered a Jew but I don't feel worthy yet. I think it should be judged on your Jewishness and how much you know.'

Others were glad to be Jewish for different reasons. Melissa enjoys 'the affinity, the bond' which a Jew feels when meeting another Jew in a situation where there are not a lot of them around. Michelle sees her Jewishness as a path to self-understanding: 'In a negative way my Jewishness pushed me out so that I was on my own and had to find my own belief and my own philosophy of life. Now I'm coming back because I want to understand my past and understand myself better.' Nick finds it 'endearing just to be told you're Jewish and therefore to be inscribed in that incredible history.' Tom's pride in his Jewish heritage, however, is mingled with the angst of the perennial outsider:

> Jews should recognise they're lucky to be part of an incredibly rich tradition. Equally they will recognise that the position of the Jew in any society is not an entirely comfortable and stable one; also it is too early to tell whether Israel will survive as a state. Both the positive and negative points co-exist for anyone who feels Jewish.

Conclusions

Have marginal Jews, who challenge established Jewish social and religious 'norms', a role to play in the Jewish future? The detachment they displayed, brought about by ignorance as well as alienation, was not necessarily a step towards losing a sense of Jewishness. In many cases, I discovered, it could lead to a strengthened Jewish identity.

While remaining highly individual, these young marginal Jews shared many attitudes and perceptions. I was surprised that so few of the young women cared whether or not their children would be raised as Jews, while the young men were virtually unanimous in wishing to have Jewish children. Were these attitudes representative, it would suggest that the children of Jewish women, although technically Jewish, may well receive less Jewish input in their upbringing than the children of a Jewish father. In contrast, most surveys carried out in the United States show that more Jewish women than men who 'marry out' bring up their children as Jews.

Antisemitism appears to remain a marker of identity for many young Jews in today's multi-ethnic, multi-cultural society. A hesitation to 'come out' as Jewish, perceived by Zionist thinkers as endemic to the diaspora Jewish identity, may equally well reflect the individual marginal Jew's reluctance to make a commitment to his or her Jewishness. It may also be far more prevalent in Britain than in the United States, as Todd Endelman explains:

> In Britain the larger culture is simply not as welcoming to Jews and it makes Jews much more self-conscious about being Jewish in a way that was true for many American Jews up through the 1950s. America's becoming more diverse and that has had a profound effect on how people view Jews and how Jews view themselves and how they can operate. Britain's cultural ideals are still mono-cultural. British Jews are reticent and unaccustomed to operating in an open way.

Significantly, Sophia from New York says she has never witnessed antisemitism, but acknowledges it is more likely to exist in small-town America.

Attitudes towards Israel were more complex. Jewish commitment in itself appeared less likely to generate understanding of Israel's actions than knowledge of the Middle-East situation. And despite frequent references to 'Jewish blood', hardly anyone spoke of Jewish ethnicity.

As to the perpetuation of Judaism and a more positive Jewish identity, there is no magic formula, no infallible blend of religious and cultural ingredients guaranteed to attract and hold a varied group of independent-minded young people to a tradition 3500 years old. Some pointers, however, did emerge. An education, both within the family and outside, focusing on an awareness of roots and history, on Jewish social and cultural values many Jews are unaware of; more accessible forms of worship – one young man suggested a compromise between the orthodox and reform service; participation in traditions in which enjoyment and family feeling are emphasised more than ritual, all these factors would undoubtedly help to strengthen the Jewish identity of marginal Jews.

What came over most strongly throughout the interviews was the openness of these young, marginal Jews, the majority of whom had friends of many different races and denominations. Does this suggest that they can make no contribution to the survival of Jewry? Surely not. Marginal Jews would be eminently suited as emissaries in intercommunal relations; they could also be encouraged to find modes of Jewish expression which are meaningful to them personally and which could be communicated to the next generation of young Jews. In this way, marginal Jews would be helping to shape the Jewish future, a challenge that Michelle, for one, would be ready to seize:

> With religion having to adapt itself to the reality of today, this is something that we, the awakened people, may be able to influence and build. We understand that in today's world it's the individual that's paramount, and building a life or a culture with that philosophy is something I would like to think of as a goal.

COMMUNITY OR GHETTO?

An Outside View

Ask the average marginal Jew about the Jewish community and the words 'narrow-minded', 'insular', 'inward-looking' invariably pour out. Unlike other young Jews who may be affiliated to some communal organisation and who tend to fraternise exclusively with Jews, marginal Jews wish to 'open up', 'branch out' and explore friendships and relationships with a wide variety of people. Even Melissa, who was less 'turned off' than most marginals by the Jewish crowd she spent time with, made a conscious decision to go to a university where there would be very few Jews. Unlike many marginals, she flaunts her Jewishness among her fellow students: 'People absolutely adore me being Jewish. In a way I play on it, because I find it quite funny, only with people that know me well and wouldn't take it the wrong way.'

Rejection of close-knit Jewish communal structures is not unexpected, since what defines a 'marginal Jew' is his or her separateness from organised Jewry. But marginal Jews are not alone in noticing the clannishness and exclusivism of many Jews. Nor is this a purely British phenomenon, although Todd Endelman echoes many observers within Anglo-Jewry and outside, who criticise the long tradition of Anglo-Jewish anti-intellectualism which has alienated many of 'the best and the brightest': 'The organised Jewish community seems narrow, it seems uninteresting and many of its institutions are simply not welcoming.'

In France, Carole C, Déborah Lévy and Isabelle Reims were often irritated by the behaviour of Sephardi Jews from north Africa. Isabelle could ask one of the Jewish girls in her class for a cigarette and they would say 'no'; if another Jew asked, they would say 'yes'. 'They create a union, they want to be together. I think it's normal because of the wars and all.' Carole confirms this: 'If you say, "Okay, I'm Jewish", okay, all the doors are open. If you say, "Okay, I'm not Jewish", they say, "Okay, we can accept you", but when you do something wrong, they say, "Oh, it's because she's not Jewish." ' Madame C has heard such attitudes advocated by some rabbis: 'They shouldn't speak of "Let's keep ourselves together, we're Jews." I find they're very sectarian. They are very afraid of assimilation, of mixed marriages, that all the Jews will disappear.'

At Michigan State University, Lindsay Rothschild has observed the same phenomenon.

> The Jewish students, they're really into their religion because they're the minority in the college so they cling together and they talk about it together. It doesn't turn me off but I notice it's really cliquey. It's worse at the University of Michigan where there's a higher Jewish population than at Michigan State. They get a lot of people from out of state from upper-class families and they get that JAP (Jewish American Prince or Princess) reputation. I think some people could get turned off by them.

Both 'marginals' and 'lost Jews' believed Jews sticking together tended to fuel antisemitism and that shutting out people of other religions was 'really dangerous'. As Carole C explains: 'It's this closed attitude. "We will reproduce among ourselves and create a community in the middle of a community. It's just to stay among ourselves and to be different from others." All the time they need to be together in gangs or clans. They try to make a ghetto.' Gabriel Solomon also sees the danger:

> A lot of people would say, 'They keep to themselves, they don't look you in the eye.' It's as if they thought the 'ghetto people' were treating them like complete dirt. It's ignorance on both sides. The ghetto isn't actively provoking antisemitism but it's passively contributing to it. When you have a group that's self-perpetuating and doesn't pay much heed to its neighbours, naturally the neighbours are going to be a bit suspicious.

While he sees that the 'ghetto attitudes' may be self-destructive, like Isabelle Reims, he feels they may be provoked by a history of persecution.

More concretely, Melissa received an uncomfortable insight into gentile resentment at what may be perceived as Jewish exclusivism, the nearest thing to antisemitism she had ever encountered, when she turned down a gentile boyfriend who had previously been rejected by another Jewish girl. 'You think you're so special, you hang on to this persecution, you cling to the Holocaust as something which keeps you together, it's sick, it's perverse . . .' And Annie gave an example of a Jewish child not being allowed to go to a non-Jewish friend's party:

> I think it's so rude saying 'You can't go to Joanna's party because she's not Jewish because I don't want you meeting people who aren't Jewish.' If Joanna had not been allowed to go to the Jewish child's party because her parents didn't want her to mix with people who weren't Protestant, there'd be an absolute outcry with letters to every national newspaper.

Instead, many felt that Jews should share their customs with people of other faiths and cultures in order to promote tolerance and understanding in a multi-cultural society. As Andrée put it, 'Jews don't actively invite Christians to go to synagogue services or participate in a Friday night dinner or any of the traditions and I think there's a lot of room for that kind of sharing.' Alex agrees: 'I feel you should invite people to see the nice side of your culture so they ask about it and it's demystified. It's not this thing they're not allowed to be a part of.' An example of sharing was provided by Claire Rothschild, Lindsay's grandmother, who recalls the Passover dinner to which she invited her future daughter-in-law and her parents: 'They said, "This is beautiful", and they read, everybody read, and they really enjoyed it.'

'The Jewish scene' was an experience many marginals had been through, either belonging to some Jewish youth organisation or just hanging out with crowds of other young Jews in certain areas. Most had become disillusioned with 'the scene' and left in their mid to late teens. Criticism abounded of the expensive clothes, phoney mannerisms and limited horizons of 'this little collective group'. Ben Selwyn, more of an outsider, was equally critical:

> If God came down he would say they're definitely not what the 'chosen people' are supposed to be. The 'chosen people' are about sharing their ideas and integrating themselves. Not losing themselves, keeping yourself and integrating at the same time. These people stay in a group of Jews. They're so stupid and paranoid.

Whether the strong sense of revulsion expressed by so many would merit the scorn of a Julie Burchill, who argues that Western Jews are self-loathing and always knocking themselves,[2] is debatable. In Nicole's more balanced view, the 'ghetto' was a double-edged sword:

> There's something comforting about numbers and community. I personally feel it's a bit of a cop-out, in the sense that it's a very easy way of life, you're with your own which, in a way, is a really nice thing. On the other hand you're not experiencing life. Ghettos create a balance. As much as they are keeping Jewish identity strong by being together, they're also alienating Jews outside the ghetto.

Ivan Ezekiel has personal experience of this.

> Before I was married I lived in Finchley and tried to do whatever I could to get into the Ashkenazi community. I do find them ghettoised. I think that within their own sphere they're actually fine but they can't operate outside of it. I had one or two Ashkenazi girlfriends and I met their parents and so on but they stick together a lot and they don't move out of it and you have to make a conscious effort to break in. I met a lot of others through the one or two friends I did have but it was a difficult community to penetrate. It wasn't worth the effort, definitely not, that's why I just gave up.

Not surprisingly, Ezekiel 'married out'. As a young man, Air Commodore Wober also felt that 'a lot of the Hampstead Garden suburb lot were like the Jewish princess stereotype but not all Jewish girls were like that'. He admits that it wasn't so much that they 'turned him off' as the alternative, the outside world, 'turned him on'.

The cliqueyness they find so objectionable, many conceded, was not exclusive to Jews but equally characteristic of other minorities or groups like Blacks or Sloanes. Laurent Ezekiel, for one, is not bothered by Jews sticking together. 'It's just like some areas are Black, some areas are Indian. You can compare Golders Green to Southall or to the St Paul area and the Marais in Paris.' He admits he has never tried to get into such a community. 'I don't know what it's like. Maybe I would be rejected and maybe I'd start to hate them. I don't know how they react to people from the outside, people not from the same religion.' And while others voiced blanket criticism of the 'Jewish scene', Annie noticed a self-critical element among the group insiders themselves. 'They can make antisemitic comments about themselves like, "Do you think my friends are really flash or really *Jewish*?" '

Young Jews who had not grown up near predominantly Jewish neighbourhoods were more tolerant of the 'ghetto' phenomenon. Tom defended the right of Jews to live in 'self-imposed ghettos', while Debbie and Nikki, who had grown up in what was virtually a Jewish cultural desert, perceived the north London Jewish scene as some sort of nirvana. They could not conceive how an intensely Jewish social life could lead to alienation and were convinced that had they lived in an area like north London, their Jewish identity would have been much stronger.

An Inside View

> The 'ghetto' if you like is not necessarily some manifestation of religiousity. In my view it's a manifestation of selfishness. People are selfish, they're afraid of the unknown and they're incapable of projecting their thoughts, their care, their compassion, beyond their immediate society. The 'ghetto' in this sense has no religious connotation at all but we do suffer a lot from it.
>
> Dayan Isaac Berger

> There are those who maintain that Jews and Judaism can only exist in a spirit of isolation. Jews must settle in self-imposed ghettos that insulate them from the adverse effects of secular culture and contamination.
>
> It is fair to say that Jewish history has been dominated by this philosophy and spiritual outlook. Far more frequently than wicked antisemites forcing the Jews to live in ghettos, Jews have chosen them of their own accord. Jews found spiritual and physical security in numbers. Their co-religionists who were of similar mind and conviction were the only ones to be trusted with exposure to their children.
>
> Rabbi Shmuel Boteach[3]

> Why are so many people alienated from the Jewish community? One reason is the 'gilded ghetto'. You have to realise that some of these people are very unattractive.
>
> Barry Kosmin

I put some of the charges made against close-knit Jewish communities to media personality Vanessa Feltz and received short shrift:

> The terms 'self-imposed' and 'ghetto' are so mutually exclusive as to render the phrase absolutely nonsensical. The whole point of a ghetto was you weren't allowed to leave it and it was effectively a slightly larger than usual prison.
>
> I've never met a Jew who has a social life exclusive of non-Jews. That's fantasy, it's fallacy and an arid stereotype of absolutely no worth

whatsoever. There's a certain derogatory tone in your voice that there's something wrong or unduly sectarian in choosing to live near people of similar ilk. It makes perfect social sense. People tend to live near other people who share similar station or situation or aspiration so there's nothing sinister to be derived from this concept of Jews living near other Jews.

One of the reasons we do it is because it makes life more convenient on a purely practical and pragmatic level in terms of access to a synagogue, a kosher butcher, to a place where you can buy your *lulav* and your *etrog* when you need to and access to people who won't regard you as a bizarre anthropological study but will regard you as a human being.

You'd be hard pushed to find an area which isn't mixed. I would put it to you that there are more Indians in Golders Green than Jews. I live in 'Jewish' Finchley, literally ten seconds from a synagogue, and my next-door neighbour's a Nigerian. I would say *if* an area *were* to be exclusively Jewish, which of course you could never achieve and I wouldn't think anyone would ever want to achieve, but if they did I would think nothing wrong in that.

There are lots of Jewish people who, as you so unpleasantly put it, 'hang together'. They're people of all different kinds. Some of them are 'becks' who hang out on a basis of a mutual interest in clothes or pop music or whatever. Others are left-wing pioneering types whose primary reason for 'hanging together' is Zionism or a wish to implement a Utopian world; other Jews attend seminaries or study weekends; some, you know the Jewish union of students, are political activists, some are genuinely religious, so yes, there are Jews who decide to keep company with other Jews for a myriad of different reasons.

Anybody who finds *that scene*, as you put it, intimidating or a turn-off has to be lacking in discernment because there is no *scene* that you subscribe to hook, line and sinker, it's an incredibly divided scene, divided just on the face of it between orthodox and *chassidic*, reform and progressive, lesbian and gay, and intellectual Jews and sporty Jews and various other different Jews. If the entire *scene* turns you off, then there must be either just a genuine desire not to go with the flow or you're rebelling against your parents or grandparents or something you didn't like in your upbringing or you're a pioneer spirit and would like to become a Hare Krishna because it's so different from your upbringing in Golders Green – or there's something vaguely wrong with you.

The thing people must remember, and that includes you with these statements, is that Jews are individuals. We are Hitlerian if we allow ourselves to deal and dabble in these stereotypes for anything but the purposes of comedy or light social chit chat and really there is no *scene* which is a cohesive entity which ought to turn every single young Jew off. That's just bollocks if I might say so.

11

The Establishment Voice

THE ORTHODOX WORLD

> If I were writing a script for history and my wishes were to be fulfilled and I had an option saying, 'Here you've got a whole tribe of patrilineal Jews, would you write into the script with a happy ending: all of them have suddenly embraced Judaism and decided to convert to be true to the God of their fathers? Or alternatively, they realise that Judaism rejects them in a way and therefore, without animosity and without hate, decided to embrace the culture in which they were surrounded?' I would be quite matter of fact and say,'Let them stay the way they are.'
>
> Dayan Isaac Berger, London

> In some very deep sense they are Jewish, in another sense they are not Jewish. Their sense of themselves, their own way of looking at the world and their whole sense of identity is Jewish so what we have to do is just have the law catch up with their own consciousness. The law should catch up, the law should enable them to enter in as easily, as warmly, as lovingly as possible.
>
> Rabbi David Hartman, Jerusalem

To probe orthodoxy's stance towards children of Jewish fathers became a burning quest as I researched this book, leading me to speak to 20 prominent orthodox rabbis in five countries, as well as several of other denominations.

I sought recognition that the Jewish ancestry of these patrilineal lost Jews differentiated them in some way from gentiles, despite the strictures of *halacha* and hoped that a patrilineal's desire to throw in his lot with the Jewish people might kindle some spark of gratification. As the extracts cited above indicate, I was often frustrated but occasionally heartened.

I also tried to gain some understanding of the legal anomaly which accords Jewish status to lost Jews of the most remote matrilineal descent, notwithstanding the total absence from their lives of any facet of

Jewishness and denies it to the most committed patrilineal lost Jew. What did patrilineals have to do, I wondered, to be accepted as Jewish by the orthodox world?

'They are Gentiles'

To satisfy the orthodox establishment in Britain – and France – patrilineal lost Jews, like gentile converts, are required to testify to exemplary standards of observance. Both Dayan Berger and Dayan Berel Berkovits, formerly registrar of the London *Beth Din* and now with the Federation of Synagogues, told me of ultra-orthodox *yeshiva* students who discovered some 'fault' in their lineage and were converted the same afternoon. Similarly, a patrilineal boy denied Jewish schooling but sporting the *kipah* and *tsitsit* worn by orthodox Jews was seen by Dayan Berger to be on the right track: 'That will all stand him in good stead. When he comes of age and leaves the parental home, if he is to the standard he will be converted the same afternoon.'

Failing these standards, patrilineal lost Jews are gentiles and have no part in what Dayan Berger sees as the 'mysterious body of the Jewish people'. 'I don't regard these people as Jewish at all. Since it's a mystical sort of perspective I believe that somehow God has installed Jewish souls in those who are of the Jewish line and those who are not of the Jewish line are none of our concern.' In contrast, the most remote matrilineal lost Jew counts. 'In my view the Jewish people are like a homogenous body and even if the furthest item or the furthest limb hurts, the whole body hurts. So it's some sort of mysterious link between the Jewish people and one has to reach out to any Jewish soul.'

I was surprised to find solid support for Dayan Berger's perspective from a new breed of dynamic rabbi engaged in outreach work among disaffected Jews. South African-born Rabbi Shlomo Levin, for example, renowned in Anglo-Jewry for revitalising a dying north London community, also takes a mystical view. 'Judaism is not defined by the way in which you feel. What defines a Jew is one single factor, the fact that they have a soul which is connected to God in a particular kind of way through the mother's line.'

Others, like American-born Rabbi David Orlofsky, who trains rabbis in Israel for outreach work in the diaspora, and Canadian-born Rabbi Israel Roll, who has injected new life into a venerable west London congregation, describe the Jewish people as a family. As Roll puts it: 'You're either born into that family or not born into that family. If you want to join that family, there are very strict rules of how one can belong.' Orlofsky sees the commitment an outsider has to make as 'even more than a family member himself'.

The family analogy was used particularly effectively by American-born Rabbi Shmuel Boteach, founder of the successful L'Chaim Society at Oxford University, to justify his assertion that the most remote, indifferent matrilineal was as Jewish as the late Lubavitcher rebbe: 'Imagine you have five children. One treats the parents like a king and queen, the other abuses them publicly, destroys their reputation. You could say one child is more appreciative of the parents but that doesn't make him any more of a child.'

Like Berger, once a member of the notoriously strict London *Beth Din*, none of these younger rabbis admits to the slightest gratification if a patrilineal Jew wishes to join the Jewish people. All emphasise that there is nothing superior in being Jewish since a key precept of Judaism is that 'the righteous of all nations have a share in the world to come'. Their approach is to encourage such people to find fulfilment as righteous gentiles, obliged to obey only the seven Noachide laws prescribed for all humanity rather than the 613 commandments incumbent on the observant Jew. Where Levin claims that the London *Beth Din's* reptutation for harshness is a 'myth', Roll defends this harshness from an apocalyptic perspective. 'The *Beth Din's* restrictive because they want to take care of the person's *neshama*. The *Beth Din* seems harsh but it's out of complete love for a person's well-being in it's ultimate sense.'If a patrilineal Jew – or any gentile – converts to Judaism but does not seriously follow the commandments, Roll believes he or she has forfeited the right to the world to come that would have been theirs had they remained a moral gentile.

Something More

Other orthodox rabbis, while equally mindful of *halacha* and high standards of observance, appear less indifferent to the prospect of lost Jews returning to the Jewish fold. Rabbi Eliahu Avihail of Jerusalem, the man responsible for bringing representatives of the lost ten tribes and descendants of Marranos back to mainstream Judaism, is also a seeker of Jewish souls. He follows the Jewish mystical tradition which conceives of souls which were supposed to belong to the Jewish people but somehow got lost over the last two thousand years. Although a sincere gentile convert may possess a Jewish soul, a descendant of Jews is more likely to have one. Consequently, Avihail will not encourage a serious patrilineal to remain a righteous gentile. 'If he feels very strongly he wants to be a Jew, we have to help him more than other gentiles. Maybe he has a Jewish soul after all. We have to know it's a *mitzvah* to bring Jewish souls back.'

On a more pragmatic level, Rabbi Claude Brahami, who ministers to a large community in the Paris suburbs, also sees it as a *mitzvah* to encourage a patrilineal Jew who wants to convert and admits that he can't regard the child of a Jewish father as just a *goy*. 'Despite the wisdom of *halacha*, in every-day reality one is obliged to admit that the father is Jewish and therefore there is something Jewish in that child.' Rabbi Dr Abraham Levy, spiritual head of the Sephardi community in Britain, would also encourage a patrilineal who wants to convert. 'If a person shows interest I would bring him into the synagogue and treat him as a candidate for conversion.' He concedes that he would look 'slightly more benevolently'on a patrilineal candidate than on a gentile candidate for conversion. 'Legally a Jew is someone who has a Jewish mother but on the other hand we are part of many generations. Our parents and our grandparents are part of us.' Because of this confusion of identity, Dayan Berkovits would treat a patrilineal lost Jew applying for conversion with greater warmth and sympathy, even if he decided, at the end, that a conversion was not appropriate.

By admitting that he would be 'definitely' pleased if a patrilineal Jew decided to convert, American-born Rabbi Rashi Simon, founder of the Jewish Learning Exchange in west London, differs from colleagues involved in outreach work. He argues that 'contemporary *halachic* authorities are of the opinion that it is proper to encourage someone who has a Jewish father to convert – on *halachic* terms'. Like Dayan Berger, however, he would not encourage a whole 'tribe' of patrilineal Jews to become Jewish. Dayan Berkovits disagrees. 'If they want to do it properly, why not? They're not different from any group of people. My father remembers a whole village in Rumania which converted to Judaism *en masse*. They were all farmers. Every afternoon they would stop and *davven mincha*.' A mass return of lost Jews is something Rabbi Dr Jacob Schacter of the Jewish Center in New York would welcome: 'The best scenario would be to have all these people coming and converting according to the *halacha*, going through a process, so we are now supplementing the ranks of the Jewish people with people who are really serious.' Similarly, Rabbi Dr Jeffrey Cohen, a pioneer of women-only services within the United Synagogue, like Chief Rabbi Dr Jonathan Sacks (Chapter 1), values the contribution lost Jews can make even before conversion.

> I regard them as a source of great support and numerical support for Israel, I recognise the contribution they are making towards fostering the ethical, moral and spiritual values of Judaism and I would recognise these people as potential converts to orthodox Judaism, if not them then their children.

On an individual level, Berkovits and former Chief Rabbi of Paris Alain Goldmann, see the return of the 'lost Jew' as some compensation for defection in a previous generation. As Berkovits explains: 'Somewhere along the line somebody in their family married out so there was a dilution of their Jewishness. To that extent when they come back several years later and want to rejoin the Jewish people, that gives me satisfaction.' Goldmann who speaks of 'the joy of seeing the ones who find again the path of the Torah from their father or from their mother', admits that his satisfaction is tinged with regret when he sees 'so many Jews who don't practise and that it is often the non-Jews who are the best examples for the continuity of the tradition'. Similarly Chief Rabbi Sacks experiences 'a sense of discrepancy that we demand so much of converts and apparently so little of born Jews'. He explains the return of the 'lost Jew' in the context of 'a personal spiritual search which, since the mid-1960s, has affected everyone in the western world but in particular and dramatically it's affected Jews and people who see themselves as Jews'.

'They See Themselves as Jewish but They're Not'

> What people are is not decided by the *halacha*. People are what they are. It's all a question of exercising power. The authorities need to exercise power in order to stay in power and run other people's lives for them and one of the most potent weapons that remains in the hands of the orthodox rabbinate is a power of definition. They define who you are and this is very potent indeed. It affects your whole life.
>
> Rabbi Dr Norman Solomon, Koerner Visiting Fellow at the Oxford Centre for Hebrew and Jewish Studies

> The fact that the Jewish ancestry is calling to them, the fact that they consider themselves as Jews, the fact that a lot of them have a great deal of knowledge about Judaism, the fact that even more so a lot of them have a great deal of warmth towards Judaism goes without saying.
>
> Rabbi Dr Jacob Schacter

> *Halacha* is one aspect within Judaism. Some people will understand it as the controlling aspect. There is a contemporary orthodox myth that Judaism is *halacha*.
>
> Rabbi Dr Norman Solomon

The clash between personal and *halachic* definition was acknowledged by many orthodox rabbis – and lay figures – as the source of much human tragedy. While lay leaders like Eldred Tabachnik, President of the Board of Deputies of British Jews, and Rosalind Preston, former vice-president of the Board and the first woman to hold the position, called for courage and vision from the rabbinic leadership to resolve questions of conversion and Jewish status which, given the very different stance adopted by progressive Judaism, threaten to tear the Jewish world apart, the impression I gained from the rabbis themselves ranged from powerlessness in the face of *halacha* on the one hand, to an obvious sense of power and control. In some instances there was a curious blend of both facets. Former Chief Rabbi Alain Goldmann, less enthusiastic than many of his counterparts about the matrilineal ruling, stressed 'It's not me who makes the *halacha.* I am a believer and I depend on the tradition of the Pharisees. It's the Pharisees and *Beit Hillel* who fixed this *halacha.*' Nevertheless, during our meeting I was made very much aware of the power he exercised over thousands of applicants for conversion throughout France and the Francophone countries, his obsession with rejecting what he considered excessively easy conversions and his pride in bringing successful converts and their families to orthodoxy. From Dayan Berger, too, I gained an impression of the control the London *Beth Din* exercised over the lives of prospective converts. And with several rabbis stressing the awesome responsibility of 'creating Jews', Dayan Berkovits, with great humility, depicted a tribunal of three rabbis that constitutes a *Beth Din* as 'playing God with people's lives'.

Not all rabbis would 'play God' the same way. Where Déborah Lévy (Chapter 4) was excluded by the Paris *Consistoire* from the family conversion because her adult status required her to have a separate dossier, Dayan Berger was at pains to point out that the London *Beth Din* would never willingly split up a family. Goldmann, to whom I put his reaction, conceded that Berger might be right but proceeded nonetheless to justify the consistorial line, finally attributing responsibility to Déborah's father for not having taken the right steps when she was younger. Goldmann was far more forthcoming about Janet Leighton (Chapter 6), rejected by the London *Beth Din* as a candidate for conversion, and claimed he would take her if she were in his territory. Berkovits, too, expressed interest in her case.

'They're Special'

How many orthodox rabbis would subscribe to Daniel Kumermann's conversion? (Chapter 7). Although it took place under orthodox auspices and involved the key ingredients of conversion – circumcision, which he had had done previously, immersion in the *mikveh* and being called to the Torah in the synagogue – it was clearly an 'inside job', demanding no formal period of study and no detailed scrutiny of observance. Yet American-born Rabbi David Hartman, a highly regarded scholar within modern orthodoxy and founder of the dynamic Shalom Hartman Institute in Jerusalem, told me without any hesitation: 'I would absolutely subscribe to that.'

Hartman clearly sees the committed patrilineal Jew as someone special who should be helped 'with great love' to be seen as a Jew by the whole community. It was only some months after I met him that I heard Rabbi Josy Eisenberg's proposal (Chapter 1) for a ceremony of 'reintegration into Judaism' for children of Jewish fathers. Eisenberg would not demand a *mikveh* ceremony, which involves the presence of a *Beth Din* and some questioning of the prospective convert, but simply a *bain rituel* (ritual bath) which presumably would be a more private experience.

What Eisenberg has in mind is a sign of commitment similar to that undertaken by the composer, Schoenberg, after he regretted having converted to Christianity. Although reassured by Jews that in their eyes he had not changed, he came to the synagogue in Rue Copernic with Chagall as a witness and declared solemnly that he wanted to be Jewish.

> What we need to invent is a solemn ceremony of reintegration. To go up to the Torah, for example, make a blessing on the Torah, make a solemn declaration on two or three of Judaism's great precepts, for example the thirteen principles of Maimonides, a solemn declaration that you believe in the Jewish beliefs and not other beliefs, you believe, for example in the legitimacy of the Torah and the necessity of the commandments. Something vague like that without going into details.

Eisenberg's proposals are based on 'a certain number of great sages of Judaism' who were party to the decisions of the *halacha* and deemed that far fewer difficulties should be demanded of children of Jewish fathers than of others who wish to be Jewish. Consequently, he would impose no conditions about future religious practice.

A MIDDLE WAY

> I have to reassure the person with a Jewish father who comes here as if he had been dragged before a tribunal. He arrives here, I have the impression he wants to bash my face in, he doesn't know me but he says to me: 'There is someone who demands from me something while

> that thing already exists in me and I am being forced to sign a paper and go through a procedure whilst I already belong to the group.' So I have to reassure him and tell him he is not starting off from scratch, that the fact that his father is Jewish counts.
>
> Rabbi Rivon Krygier, Paris

The Masorti (traditional) movement would treat patrilineals with special consideration, within the framework of a *halachic* conversion, as would a few orthodox rabbis I spoke to. Rabbi Dr Louis Jacobs, the distinguished scholar and founder of the Masorti movement in Britain, feels a patrilineal has a religious right, as opposed to a *halachic* right, to be accepted more readily than a gentile convert. 'Although *halachically* he's not Jewish, in the eyes of God he's nearer to Judaism than someone else.'

Nevertheless he would not accept a patrilineal without a conversion. 'Since the machinery of conversion is available, why should you accept patrilineality? You can't wipe out 2000 years of Jewish tradition so you have conversion.' Rabbi Rivon Krygier, the masorti rabbi in Paris, also saw conversion as a 'solution which exists in *halacha*' for children of Jewish fathers, although he sees the process more as a 'regularisation of status' (Chapter 1). Rabbi Jonathan Wittenberg, a creative young masorti rabbi in London, admits he would not necessarily regard a committed patrilineal as a convert and require him or her to begin a process of study and preparation from the beginning

> if he or she has clearly felt throughout their life some sort of identity with being Jewish. After all one of the main features about becoming Jewish stressed in the Talmud and in our sources is that converts should be aware of the difficulties and challenges of taking upon themselves the historic lot of the Jewish people and this is something that person has already done.

Wittenberg would, of course, require such a person to complete the procedures demanded by Jewish law.

> Whether this should be preceded by a longer or shorter period of study or facilitated at once would depend on the individual in question. What matters are the motivation, knowledge and commitment of the person concerned; there has to be respect for who they are and what they have already done.

Like Krygier who sees the process as 'very serious, not in the sense of rigidity but in the sense of depth, sincerity and commitment', Wittenberg believes that serious study prepares a person to enter the Jewish community although he acknowledges that there is no requirement for a long period of study laid down by *halacha*.

While impeccably observant themselves, these rabbis did not feel they could demand the same of converts. As Jacobs explained 'The *halacha* says if someone wants to be converted, they have to show evidence of sincerity and willingness to lead a Jewish life. It doesn't say you have to spell out all the details and they are not expected surely to be more observant than the average member of the United Synagogue.'[1] Wittenberg admits he would 'like in some way to be able to say "You must keep *Shabbat* and you shall not drive" but, as with the rest of the community, one has to work through encouragement and example, rather than demands and condemnations. One has to recognise where people are coming from.' Krygier does try to tell his community that they shouldn't travel on *Shabbat* but is aware of reality. The same applies to converts: 'If someone lives thirty kilometres away, it's a constraint. I can't tell him "You can't convert." '

Jacobs believes that the London *Beth Din's* exacting standards are 'foreign to the whole Anglo-Jewish tradition', an opinion shared to some extent by Rev. Malcolm Weisman, minister to numerous small communities in Britain, who operates 'under the traditional umbrella' with the certification of the Chief Rabbi but independently of the London *Beth Din*.

> Once you survive a *Beth Din* conversion course you're more royalist than the king and more Catholic than the Pope. Whether that's a good thing or not I don't know. Many feel there ought perhaps to be a relaxation. If the orthodox community reverted back to the standards they had before the war when virtually nobody went to the Reform or Liberal movement, it would help stop the outflow to the reform and liberal ranks.

In recent years Weisman has found the *Beth Din* more sympathetic and helpful than in the past. Wittenberg would also 'much prefer a more tolerant attitude on the part of the London *Beth Din* so that we could work together'. Like many lay figures including former Board of Deputies Vice-President Rosalind Preston, he would like to see some sort of consensus procedure on conversion.

Mindful of the huge losses the Jewish world has incurred as a result of the Holocaust and assimilation, Rabbi Dr Jeffrey Cohen confesses that in his 'early days of rebellion' he used to be very critical of the *Beth Din* and 'strongly believe we should make as many converts as possible which I still do believe'. He can now appreciate the *Beth Din's* cautious approach since he wouldn't like to have on his conscience the responsibiblity of a convert turning round and kicking 'in the teeth all that *halacha* holds sacred'. Rabbi Menachem HaCohen, a former Member of the Knesset, the Israeli parliament, and a pioneer of the conversion *ulpanim* in *kibbutzim* in Israel, agrees that 'it is not easy for the conscience of an orthodox rabbi to convert' but believes

> that was the way of all the rabbis in Jewish history. In all the stories you read the rabbi used to say, 'I don't want to let a human being suffer.' Who says being a rabbi you shouldn't take some responsibilities on your conscience and if you go to hell in the world to come at least you know what for.

HaCohen deplores the fact that 'in Israel and anywhere else' today the rabbinic establishment 'have not the spirit of great men. They are not living among the Jewish people, they are isolated from the Jewish people and their problems. They are not challenging the *halachic* problems of our times.' He, himself, is very aware of the changes in the post-Holocaust Jewish world and, if faced with a committed patrilineal, would 'do everything to bring him into the Jewish people by *halachic* criteria'. Like demographer Barry Kosmin, HaCohen feels many rabbis 'are using the *halacha* in terms of the eastern European communities of a 100 years ago'.

In Prague, too, Sylvia Wittmanova, co-ordinator of *Beit Simcha*, a controversial progressive community, sees a group of *yeshiva*-trained Holocaust survivors from the eastern regions of pre-war Czechoslovakia exercising undue influence on the mainstream Jewish community. This is a factor Czech Chief Rabbi Karel Sidon, himself a patrilineal convert (Chapter 7), has to contend with. Where Wittmanova seeks the religious pluralism Prague Jewry enjoyed in pre-war days, Sidon feels the community today is too small for splinter groups. He would like *Beit Simcha*, for example, to be a centre for information about Judaism rather than a reform synagogue with its own approach to conversion and Jewish status. Conversions, he believes passionately, must be orthodox so that the convert will be accepted as Jewish anywhere in the world. 'That's the reason I want all conversions to be according to the *halacha*. As for how the convert will behave after that, I can only hope!'

Sidon, not surprisingly, is sensitive to the problems and dangers faced by prospective converts, both from the outside world and within the Jewish community. While he is open to all who approach him and is keen to help anyone who is serious about becoming Jewish, he does not want to proselytise among gentiles or even among young people from mixed families. He realises he is faced with a dilemma:

> Of course I feel for these kids. Many of them have problems and don't know which side they belong to. That's also the reason they want to convert – the problem of identity – and that's their motivation. But I also think conversion is a religious process, I don't want there to be Jews here who don't believe in the religion. Of course that's a problem but what can I do? If there was a different *halacha* it would be easier, but the *halacha's* the *halacha*!

THE PROGRESSIVE SCENE

Seen from the Outside

Orthodox rabbis I spoke to generally took the very lenient standards of some congregations and rabbis within the American Reform movement to exemplify progressive Judaism. The criticism I heard most frequently was that standards of practice – or the lack of them – demanded for progressive conversions were only good for one generation and were unlikely to ensure a transmission of Judaism. Chief Rabbi Sacks put the argument this way:

> In the diaspora, Judaism as a religious way of life is the only viable and transmissable form of Jewish identity there is. That's why, surrounded by a non-Jewish culture and a very invasive and intrusive culture, any *Beth Din* in the diaspora would want to know that any prospective convert has immersed himself or herself for a period of time in a very intense form of Jewish existence.

Needless to say, the acceptance of patrilineal Jewish status by some movements in progressive Judaism was universally condemned.

But not every comment was negative. Within Anglo-Jewry, Rabbi Dr Abraham Levy could see that the Reform movement had helped many Jews although he deplored their interpretation of Judaism. Rabbi Dr Jeffrey Cohen felt Reform was doing a service to the Jewish community in increasing the number of Jews whom he saw as potential orthodox converts: 'The Reform is a good source because they're starting them off in stimulating them Jewishly.'

Chief Rabbi Sacks, too, observed that converts might find this 'two-stage process' a 'natural process of evolution'. More positively Sidney Corob, a London businessman and philanthropist prominent in the orthodox community and in Christian–Jewish relations, recalls a discussion he had with the late Rabbi Shlomo Goren, a former Chief Rabbi of Israel: 'I said we ought to thank the Almighty that we have such a thing as a Reform and Liberal movement. Because of that a lot of non-Jews who enter our faith or Jews who marry out can be retained as part of the Jewish people.'

The acceptability of conversions was the subject of some disagreement. While Rabbi Dr Louis Jacobs would accept reform conversions in Britain as *halachic* because they now include the *mikveh* ceremony, Rabbi Menachem HaCohen felt it was more a matter of who was performing the conversions.

> If the rabbi and the *Beth Din*, if these three rabbis are not observing anything, I wouldn't accept them but if they are traditional rabbis, if I knew they were *shomrei Shabbat*, observing *kashrut* and they're based on the *halacha* it would be acceptable. But if somebody's denying the *halacha* it doesn't mean if he sends somebody to the *mikveh* that that's an acceptable conversion.

Uneasy Within

Mikveh and *halacha* provoke fierce contention between different branches of progressive Judaism. Progressive movements like the Reform in America (UAHC) and the Liberals in Britain (ULPS), who accept the patrilineal principle, are openly 'non-*halachic*'. The use of the *mikveh* for ULPS conversions is optional and often depends on the predilection of the individual rabbi. However, Collette Kessler, director of education for the Mouvement Juif Libéral de France (MJLF), which accepts patrilineals but uses the *mikveh* for conversions, believes that 'no liberal Judaism, including that of the USA, can be defined as non-*halachic*. On the other hand there's a conception that *halacha* has to be made to evolve.' Non-orthodox movements like the Conservatives in America and the Reform (RSGB) in Britain, which seek the middle ground within a *halachic* framework, have reintroduced the *mikveh* ceremony as an essential ingredient of the conversion process. This was not the case when Michèle Charkham had to 'convert' (Chapter 4), nor was it part of the conversion of Anita Fox and her children (Chapter 6). And the grandmother of Jane (Chapter 4) is unlikely to have gone to the *mikveh*; otherwise her daughter, Jane's mother, would have been 'dunked' with her.

Both Rabbi Mark Solomon, a one-time orthodox rabbi who has moved to the ULPS and Rabbi Rodney Mariner, co-ordinator of the RSGB *Beth Din*, see the *mikveh* as a powerful symbol. For a patrilineal who has had 'quasi-status', Mariner considers the *mikveh* 'the last stage of a homecoming. If somebody has felt psychologically that there are a lot of barriers, people saying "You are Jewish","You're not Jewish", the *mikveh* in a way becomes a confirmation of a mini-death and a rebirth.' He would require committed patrilineals to have the *mikveh* ceremony but rather than issue a document of conversion, would give them an 'intermediate certificate' which would say the candidate had 'come before this *Beth Din* to be recognised as Jewish'. Solomon agrees that the *mikveh* is 'a psychological and spiritual symbol of rebirth and renewal' but only for someone who sees himself as entering a new phase in life. 'Someone who believes himself to have always been Jewish will see this as a token conversion. It might only be token but it's still a conversion. The very act of going to the *mikveh* signifies that.'

Solomon supports the patrilineal principle for reasons of justice. 'There're many cases of fathers who struggled to give their children Jewishness even though they knew very well that their children wouldn't be accepted by the Jewish community and this deserves recognition and the Jewishness of their children deserves recognition.' Mariner sees the division between the RSGB and the ULPS on patrilineality as 'more apparent than real. Whereas Reform does not accept patrilineality as an automatic basis for being Jewish, by the same token it recognises there's a difference between someone who's come from completely outside the magic circle and somebody who's had a foot inside.' ULPS director Rosita Rosenberg considers the *mikveh* requirement 'not in accordance with the true spirit of progressive Judaism. We should be welcoming Jews and if someone feels himself to be Jewish we should not put any hindrance in their way', while liberal rabbi Helen Freeman feels the RSGB approach sends mixed messages:

> It's like saying 'We do accept patrilineal Jews but you've got to convert.' The Liberal movement doesn't muddy the waters or look *halachic* when it isn't. I think if you're not a *halachic* movement you should say you're not a *halachic* movement and then people know where they stand, whereas the Reform movement says it is *halachic*.

The battle over *mikveh* and *halacha* has been extended to the progressive European *Beth Din* dominated by the RSGB with the ULPS as runner-up. Its primary function is to help Central and East European Jews who, as Mariner puts it, have 'hung on to their Jewish identity with their fingertips' through decades of intermarriage and assimilation under communist rule. Many of these Jews are patrilineals or of more remote Jewish descent. While Mariner envisages using his *mikveh* and 'intermediate certificate' formula, this is a red rag to many in the ULPS. Rabbi Danny Rich, a liberal rabbi on the extreme left of the spectrum, whose community is twinned with the Jewish community of Olomouc in Moravia, threatens to opt out if the formula is finally adopted.

> If faced with somebody who wishes to convert or have some certificate of affirmation I will bring them to England through the ULPS. I'm not prepared to work through the European *Beth Din* if it isn't prepared to operate according to the principles of the vast majority of progressive Jews in this world.

While the Reconstructionist movement in America favours the patrilineal principle, Rabbi Edward Feld of the Society for the Advancement of Judaism in New York opposes it for pragmatic reasons.

> Since the UAHC decision to accept patrilineals, there is a decline in conversions so that the practical outcome of the decision has been negative. It's clearly an unacceptable position for at least 50 per cent of Jewry and that means you create a great deal of identity confusion. I think that's a greater problem than the problem it comes to solve.

Feld would not consider a patrilineal who had chosen to be Jewish as a gentile convert and prefers to use the word 'affirmation' for the process involved.

Common Ground

Despite the gulf that divides the various branches of Judaism on questions of Jewish status, each branch assesses the patrilineal 'lost Jew' according to his experience of Judaism. For orthodoxy, of course, a patrilineal would have to prove he was fully observant to be spared the rigours of a long conversion process. But in cases like that of James Moses (Chapter 7) several orthodox rabbis, including Rabbi Dr Abraham Levy, would have effected a regularisation of status with a *mikveh* ceremony and a declaration of acceptance of Judaism's principles.

Among the non-orthodox, a candidate well-versed in Judaism though not necessarily fully observant would also be processed very quickly. British-born Rabbi Michael Williams of the Copernic synagogue in Paris told me of a girl who had accumulated certificates in Judaism, spoke perfect Hebrew and had studied at a girls'seminary in Jerusalem. 'She's not accepted at the moment at the *Consistoire*. We're going to accept her *miad* and shove her in the *mikveh*.' Usually Williams requires 6 to 9 months of study for patrilineals with some Jewish background, according to the level of their knowledge and practice, while someone who had never studied would be prescribed the same course as a gentile convert.

Similarly, conservative rabbi Stephen Lerner, founder and director of the Centre for Conversion to Judaism in New Jersey, sends patrilineals raised in the UAHC movement who had always thought of themselves as Jewish to the *mikveh*, while someone with a Jewish father who has been raised as nothing would need to have a formal conversion.

A three-tiered strategy is also followed by the ULPS in Britain. A patrilineal child raised in the synagogue's religion school and active in the community would be considered automatically Jewish while someone with a fair if patchy Jewish background would be asked to study for 6 months to fill in the gaps in their knowledge and then undergo a ceremony of affirmation of their Jewish status. Adult outsiders who come in with a strong Jewish background but no formal education would be interviewed by a rabbi to see whether or not they needed the affirmation process. Patrilineals who have come to discover and value their Jewish background later in life are required to convert.

Is a Mother Enough?

> In the twentieth century in central Europe when we have ladies who are definitely Jewish according to *halacha* but they are influenced by Christian philosophy or are deeply believing Catholics who milk their child with Jesus and not with Moses, I don't know what *halacha* is talking about.
>
> Sylvia Wittmanova

The ULPS would, in principle, treat a 'lost Jew' of matrilineal status exactly the same as a patrilineal; in practice such candidates are usually advised to apply to the nearest reform or orthodox synagogue. And Rabbi Lerner would require a matrilineal raised in another religion to undergo a formal conversion. But while many rabbis I spoke to would have liked to be able to impose some course of study on a matrilineal without any Jewish background who came forward, for example, to be married, most felt it was not feasible. However, Dayan David Caplin, a member of the London *Beth Din*, and Dayan Berger informed me that someone of more remote matrilineal ancestry would be required to undertake a course of 'reintroduction to Judaism' and a symbolic immersion in the *mikveh*. This is possibly what the Jerusalem *Beth Din* had in mind for Lindsey Taylor-Guthartz (Chapter 7) though it was patently absurd since she had been living an observant Jewish life for several years.

Former Chief Rabbi of Paris Alain Goldmann went one better in cases when two generations of women, a mother and a daughter, had married out. 'At that point there is a *halacha* applied by certain rabbis that the child born of the daughter must himself convert even though he is born to a Jewish mother because there is an influence from two generations of non-Jewish husbands.' Re-introduction to Judaism, Goldmann emphasised, was not sufficient!

A logical solution would be that Jewish status should not be accorded on matrilineal lineage alone but only where both parents are Jewish. This was mooted by both Rabbi Rivon Krygier and Rabbi Karel Sidon. Krygier, in fact, was greatly in favour of such a ruling, though he emphasised that 'this can only be decided by a collective organ like a *sanhedrin* which has collective representation'.

WHATS WRONG AND CAN WE PUT IT RIGHT?

> At the end of the day we will only keep Jews if they are knowledgeable, if they have a sense of pride, of commitment, if they understand Jewish history, Jewish prayer, Jewish ethical values, the importance that Judaism attaches to the family, to community, to collective responsibility. Until they've really understood what Judaism means, people will continue to disaffiliate because it has no particular significance. We have to make that significant, that's the challenge.
>
> Eldred Tabachnik

Many rabbis and lay figures I spoke to had strong views about the decline in Jewish numbers and the threat to Jewish continuity posed both by the prevalence of a powerful secular culture and by inadequate or even negative exposure to Judaism and Jewish culture. Rosalind Preston's question: 'Why should people want to be Jewish, what's the motivation?' echoes Tabachnik's theme and voices the concern of many community leaders.

The Intermarried: What Shall We Do with Them?

The dramatic increase in intermarriage throughout the Jewish world is often perceived as a manifestation of indifference to Judaism and Jewishness. Rabbi Shmuel Boteach would concur. 'The only thing that fuels intermarriage is if you don't have any reason to be Jewish you don't choose to marry a Jewish partner.' While it used to be quite common to hear that Jews who marry out are 'doing Hitler's work', this charge was universally rejected by both the religious and lay leaders I spoke to. As Rabbi Dr Jeffrey Cohen put it: 'If the only justification for remaining Jewish is not to give Hitler his posthumous victory, then there's no justification for remaining Jewish.'

There were conflicting views as to whether attitudes to intermarriage and those who intermarry had changed since the beginning of the decade. Eldred Tabachnik cited the review *Women in the Jewish Community*,[2] instigated by Chief Rabbi Sacks, to indicate that 'public opinion (in Britain) is much more sympathetic than it used to be to people who've married out'. This was certainly true of the lay leaders I spoke to, including those who are orthodox, who supported what has generally been seen as a progressive Jewish stance that intermarried couples and their children should be welcomed into the Jewish community.

Nevertheless there remains a hard core of opinion that sees 'Thou shalt not marry out' as virtually the only commandment worth observing. Vanessa Feltz, aged thirty something, spoke of friends who 'don't keep anything of the religion and they're certainly not cultural Jews because they really have no culture but they would never have thought of marrying out'. Dayan Berger believes that 'the more peripheral people are, the more they're concerned about intermarriage'. He would like Jewish women who have married out and their children to be welcomed into synagogues and Jewish life[3] but has found resistance to this from ordinary Jews who are not particularly observant. Rosalind Preston has observed 'a bit of a phobia' about intermarriage. 'There's a feeling on the part of parents that they have failed. It's a sort of rejection'. This feeling operates in the community, too, as Preston explains: 'We are obsessional about it because we are so few in number so we feel "another lost person". Instead of trying to reclaim or hold onto those people we're letting them go.'

Ostracism has long been the orthodox way to deal with intermarriage. Rabbi Boteach, who challenges this stance, has faced censure in ultra-orthodox circles. 'I object to those who ostracise Jews who intermarry because they think it will curb the tide of intermarriage. Firstly that tactic has proved a colossal failure and secondly it's a non-Jewish tactic. The *halacha* doesn't say a person who marries a non-Jew should be ostracised.' Another 'tactic' has been to ignore the problem of intermarriage. That, now, has changed dramatically in Britain with the setting up of Jewish Continuity and the publication of Chief Rabbi Sacks' book *Will We Have Jewish Grandchildren?*[4] Rabbi Dr Jonathan Romain, who, since 1988, has pioneered a series of annual seminars for couples in mixed-faith partnerships under the auspices of the RSGB, claims credit for 'bringing out into the open a subject that was totally taboo. There was an enormous denial that it was a problem.'

Apart from helping people feel less isolated, Romain believes his seminars have brought benefits to the Jewish community.

> It has helped people in mixed-faith relationships get back into the community by showing them a warm welcome. 50 per cent of these people come from orthodox synagogues. Seeing real-life rabbis has helped the non-Jewish partner's relationship with Judaism. It has made them understand why certain things were so important and why this lapsed Jew was still enormously attached to his or her roots.

While Romain has faced criticism from the orthodox for facilitating mixed-faith relationships, according to Rabbi Helen Freeman some couples from liberal synagogues have found the seminars too judgemental. Rabbi Shlomo Levin, who counsels many couples in this situation, appreciates Romain's initiative but thinks 'there's a quieter way to do it'. He believes 'orthodoxy ought to be less forbidding' and would like the orthodox community to set up a counselling service for mixed couples before they marry so that all alternatives and outcomes can be explored. He is looking for a team of people who are sufficiently objective and non-judgemental to talk the important issues through. Levin is aware that 'guilt remains the big stick. It is clearly less effective than it used to be.' Nevertheless, he doesn't believe the 'big "no", still a very important word in the realms of intermarriage', should be removed altogether.

Religious and lay leaders I spoke to in Anglo-Jewry felt the community had brought the problem on itself. Sidney Corob speaks for many: 'In a sense we are all responsible for it. There's very little to give a Jewish child a real desire to maintain their Jewishness. Jewish education was poor and still is and we didn't give our children enough facilities to enable them to mix with other Jewish kids.' Barry Kosmin berates the Anglo-Jewish community for focusing on primary school education rather than facilities for young adults.

Both Rosalind Preston and Clive Lawton, chief executive of Jewish Continuity, believe young Jews should receive messages about the desirability of finding a Jewish partner at an early age. Lawton would suggest twelve to thirteen as the best age for

> relationship education – before they get really into the business of playing around. We have to engage young people in thinking about

what are the sane ways of looking at your future, making key choices. Parents have to do it at a point before they start becoming hysterical about how the choices are to be made.

Preston also strongly advocates the modern equivalent of a *shadchan.* This would take the form of an international computer introduction service. 'As you reached the stage in your life when you were looking for a partner you would register; you could then be supported and helped to find that partner. It's got to be generally affordable and it's got to be presented as the "trendy" thing to do.'

In the end, finding a Jewish partner has to be seen as something of personal benefit. Rabbi David Orlofsky is one of many who believe that the message young people usually hear is 'We've lost so many so you have to stay Jewish. People want to hear a positive message. "How would it add to my marriage, how would it add to my life-style? I stand to gain in my marriage. I stand to have a partner who understands me more." That's the message that has to be put across.'

Lost Jews: Do We Take Them In?

> There are so many different ways to identify as Jewish, some of which are profound and some of which are shallow that that is a problem to be addressed but not in the political arena of who your parents are or how many Jewish parents you have.
>
> Jerry Raik, director, Chavura School, New York

> There is a hinterland of three-quarter grandparent Jews or whatever it is who are sort of members of our people, part of our people, not part of our religion or could be part of some of our religion.
>
> Matthew Kalman, Editor of *New Moon*, London

> I think the community's task is to try to respond appropriately and facilitate the journey for those who wish to come towards it. We need to avoid alienating people; instead we must try to be supportive and encouraging.
>
> Rabbi Jonathan Wittenberg

The overwhelming majority of lay leaders I spoke to, as well as some rabbis, would wish to put lost Jews 'on the Jewish map', to borrow a phrase coined by Rabbi Rodney Mariner. Opinion was divided as to whether it was necessary to instigate any particular institution or network for the purpose or whether lost Jews who came forward should be welcomed into existing communal structures. Sir Sigmund Sternberg, a businessman and philanthropist involved in Christian–Jewish relations, is 'very glad that people who have been turned away have a home they can go to' at the progressive Sternberg Centre for Judaism in north London, the largest Jewish cultural centre in Europe.

> At the Sternberg Centre we encourage people who say they're Jewish and want to identify with the Jewish people. We never turn anyone away. I think it is in the Jewish people's interest. We've lost so many people and the more people we have who want to identify must be to the advantage of the whole Jewish faith.

Despite the achievements of the Sternberg Centre, of which he is the patron, Sternberg sees it as 'a drop in the ocean' and believes there should be more communal outreach to people of Jewish descent. Rosalind Preston agrees.

> There're just thousands of people like that out there and if there is some way of reaching out to them, so that they can taste or experience their Jewishness, we must make every attempt to do so. Even if they decide not to, their children might choose to come back. We'd be able to achieve more if we had Jewish community centres, or alternative attractive venues, where people could come without feeling they have to show their Jewish identity card.

Ned Temko, editor of the *Jewish Chronicle*, the voice of British Jewry, feels strongly that 'our definition of "Jewishness" *vis-á-vis JC* readers and *vis-á-vis* the community is: as long as you, whoever you are, feel Jewish for whatever reason, that's good enough for us and it's a Jewishness we want to connect with at some level.' He is not convinced, however, that there is a 'crying need' for some special structure for lost Jews. 'Rather than the need for yet more institutions, what we would like to see is a wholly different atmosphere.' This would allow orthodox Jews to engage in dialogue 'with half-Jews, non-Jews, progressive Jews' without feeling threatened. As he sees it the *JC*'s agenda is to broaden 'the sense of community and the sense of Jewishness, not necessarily in *halachic* terms'.

Author and journalist Chaim Bermant is an orthodox Jew who admits his attitude to patrilineal lost Jews proud of their Jewishness is 'not in accordance with the *halacha* as it stands. My own instinctive feeling in regard to anyone whose father is Jewish and has received a Jewish education and likes to think of himself as Jewish and performs Jewish usage, as far as I'm concerned he is Jewish.' Bermant doesn't believe in proselytising to the intermarried and their children. 'One shouldn't go consciously after them but people should know that you're there to welcome them.'

Matthew Kalman is also orthodox and can understand

> why orthodox Judaism simply cannot tolerate the idea of patrilineal Jewish identity. At the same time I completely sympathise with those people, including friends of mine, who find themselves in this absurd situation of being brought up as Jews, encountering antisemitism, their parents are refugees from the Holocaust and we don't accept them.

New Moon, the alternative Jewish monthly, was created to 'feed the obsession' of Jews 'in the hinterland', including lost Jews, for the 5 per cent of the time that their Jewishness was important to them. 'It's a very deep thing. I discovered this because people coming to our dinner table had non-Jewish wives, haven't had the children circumcised, all this kind of thing but they'd kind of let it all come out over our *Shabbes* dining table.'

Unaffiliated Jews: How Do We Keep Them?

> I believe today we have to market Judaism, market God and I think a rabbi in outreach has to be in the business of marketing religion as relevant and dynamic. The marketing we do is just as professional as any Revlon or Lamborghini ads.
>
> Rabbi Israel Roll

> The message I give out all the time is it's never our place to judge a person. The best we can do is to present ideas and if people think they'll add meaning to our lives they'll incorporate them.
>
> Rabbi David Orlofsky

> The only way to prevent Jews being lost is by creating a Jewish environment that is so vibrant and so exciting that it becomes palpably clear to secular Jews that it's more fun and more value living an orthodox way of life.
>
> Rabbi Shlomo Levin

> I always say to these young people that a rabbi in our position has to be unshockable. The moment we are shockable we can't do anything. The

main thing is whether we can give a religious dimension to their lives. They are searching for something and we are there to help them.

Rabbi Dr Abraham Levy

I think there's a lot of internalised antisemitism and resentment and that's stuff we have to name and deal with. I think a lot of the young Jews who are angry are hating themselves. I think one has to address the fact that people who purport to be open-hearted, open-minded, unprejudiced, only carry a prejudice about their own group.

Clive Lawton

Being Jewish is a kind of web of identity. There are all kinds of points of entry into the web and what we're looking for is improvement in the quality and variety of points of entry so that there are different kinds of contexts in which people can hook in.

Clive Lawton

My main point is to try and chase to find Jews wherever they are, even to pick up Jews who are originally hostile and try and make them less hostile. I make myself the protagonist of Judaism in the wider sense of the term. I don't go along and talk about Religion with a bit 'R'.

Rev. Malcolm Weisman

Away from the metropolis and the other main community centres, Rev. Malcolm Weisman has for years ferreted out unaffiliated and lost Jews in provincial towns and villages and organised some form of Jewish life for them. While his has been a one-man mission, he has worked closely with all sections of the community, including progressive rabbis. One of his most successful projects has been Quest, the development of regional conferences for small communities. Weisman is also Jewish chaplain to the forces; his presentation of Judaism has been attractive enough to inspire a former Anglican naval chaplain and his wife to convert to orthodox Judaism with the London *Beth Din*.

The ULPS also runs an 'outward development' project, going into areas not known to be Jewish and founding small congregations if Jews or lost Jews are discovered. As Rosita Rosenberg explains: 'In each of the areas we have done intensive market research, taken the roadshow out, put on programmes. It's very much looking for Jews. We have found quite a lot of Jews who have married out and thought that Judaism had rejected them.' It was one of the newly established liberal communities that gave Aslan Devere (Chapter 6) his first experience of Judaism.

With the advent in Britain of foreign-born 'outreach' rabbis and the obsessive concern about intermarriage, there has been a mushrooming of educational, cultural and social programmes designed to attract unaffiliated Jews, some under the auspices of Jewish Continuity, as well as some new-look synagogues. Two organisations which have made a particular mark in this sphere are the Jewish Learning Exchange (JLE) in London and the L'Chaim Society in Oxford.

The JLE has programmes geared specifically to marginal Jews on the outer fringes of Jewish life. Patrilineal Jews sometimes enrol but are not encouraged to continue studying unless they are involved in a process of conversion. The JLE's director, Rabbi Rashi Simon, is clean-shaven and scholarly looking. This, he feels, is important.

> In religious terms every person has a *yetser ha ra* and he or she is looking for an excuse not to get involved with Judaism, not to approach the rabbi, and any kind of intimidating imagery or any kind of imagined confrontation or hardship that result from approaching that rabbi is sufficient to get the person to run the other way.

Rabbi Shmuel Boteach, founder of L'Chaim, is bearded but immaculately dressed. Still in his twenties, he has created, in the words of Eldred Tabachnik, 'an enormously interesting and challenging environment and students do find it exciting and they do respond'. L'Chaim has succeeded by bringing in speakers of note from all over the world and fostering a warm, informal atmosphere. With a large proportion of non-Jewish members L'Chaim seems to hold some secret ingredient that attracts a number of recalcitrant young Jews.

Despite the widely differing approaches of the establishment figures I spoke to, a motivation they share is to engage and involve the Jewish periphery with Jewish values in a very secular world. Boteach's success in creating a microcosm in which Judaism can flourish in a gentile environment indicates that this is not an impossible dream.

12

A Way Forward

> At a time when the Jewish community is spending time, money and tears on trying to counteract assimilation and loss of Judaism, at the same time with the other hand they're pushing people out who, if they were to accept, would both increase and enrich the community they are striving to preserve.
>
> Jean Pato

> Doors could be opened to people like me. I think the Jewish community could do with some new blood. For the Jewish community to isolate itself and keep itself in a little island of its own is a great loss to them and to the rest of us.
>
> Penelope Abraham

> The Jewish establishment hasn't really decided whether it feels it should proselytise, even proselytise after its lost people, a different kind of diaspora.
>
> Richard Cohen

> It depends if you regard a child who marries outside the community as a child lost or an opportunity. The Catholics perhaps regard it as an opportunity.
>
> Stephen Bloom

Would the Jewish world benefit from an infusion of new life? Have lost Jews a role to play in determining the Jewish future? Does the continuity of the Jewish people serve any larger purpose? These questions which emerged from discussions I had with over a hundred lost Jews as well as marginal Jews and communal leaders, both religious and lay, will form the basis of this final chapter. Since conditions in different countries may determine some of the answers, it is worth focusing briefly on how lost Jews fare in the diaspora communities I have visited in the course of researching this book.

WHERE AND HOW?

The Land of the Free

> While you want a degree of vibrancy in the periphery, if you get too far from the sun it's just cold. In America it's so diverse and fragmented that I don't really know what a Jew is in some instances.
>
> Air Commodore Antony Wober

America today offers lost Jews the greatest opportunity to enter and influence the Jewish world. Two studies of conversion (1979 and 1992) by conservative rabbi Stephen Lerner[1] indicate a considerable thaw in the climate towards the intermarried and their children. But the very freedom that facilitates the reabsorption of lost Jews into Jewish life encourages a large degree of disengagement. The fluidity of the American religious scene, touched on by Erica Ferszt (Chapter 8), also affects Judaism. As demographer Barry Kosmin explains: 'Certain people are leaving Judaism because of their own spiritual search but equal numbers roughly are coming in to Judaism.'

Kosmin believes religion flourishes better in the strongly secularised United States than in western countries with an established religion. 'Religion can operate in a free market, religion becomes flexible and adaptive and, to some extent, counter-cultural, which makes it attractive to people.'

For people of Jewish descent, the key question is 'what are the incentives for being Jewish?' Within the free-market context, these people, together with intermarried couples, are the target of numerous outreach programmes; major communal funding is earmarked for the periphery and a report published in September 1994 by a task force established by the Council of Jewish Federations on 'Jewish community services to the intermarried' concludes with a vision of 'a vital Jewish community which retains the allegiances of its members and is attractive to others who may wish to join'.[2]

How far-reaching are these initiatives? Reform rabbi Daniel Bridge, director of Hillel at the University of Washington in Seattle, acknowledges that there are places to welcome those on the periphery, 'but there are not enough places and they do not always welcome people in the way they think they need to feel welcomed'. He believes in a 'supermarket approach' to create and publicise social opportunities for lost Jews: 'People should know it's out there for them and that nothing is expected of them when they come.' University Hillel branches, Bridge feels, are good places for newcomers. When reconstructionist rabbi Edward Feld was director of Hillel at Princeton, 50 per cent of Hillel members were from unaffiliated or mixed families and became interested in Judaism at college.

Would-be converts to Judaism are spoilt for choice, although the ludicrous mini-conversions referred to earlier in the book are not the rule. The average reform conversion programme, according to conservative rabbi Stephen Lerner, lasts 14–18 weeks. Some conservative programmes are similar but most last 30–50 weeks. Lerner's own programmes are from 9 months to a year. Because of the pressure of competition, the conversion process is bound to be shorter in America than elsewhere, he acknowledges: 'Non-orthodox conversions in Europe take longer because they're operating in a ball game where no one else does it.' With no centralised *Beth Din*, even orthodox conversions in America are easier to come by and far less lengthy than in Europe.

While a progressive Jewish educator like Jerry Raik of the Chavura School can express confidence in the survival of Judaism 'because Judaism is strong and powerful and Judaism works', Kosmin is 'willing to accept that Judaism is not doing very well in America'. The non-orthodox ascendancy, it would appear, is a double-edged sword.

Revolution from Africa

> If we had remained *frum* from the beginning we wouldn't be 15 million, we'd have been 300 million.
>
> Léon Masliah, Director-General, *Consistoire*, Paris

With non-orthodox Judaism totally marginal and an increasingly hardline orthodox establishment, large numbers of lost Jews in France who wish to return to the Jewish fold have been forced to remain in the cold.

The situation is one result of the post-war North African immigration which, in the words of Henri Bulawko, Vice-President of the lay representative body CRIF, 'shattered the image of French Jewry. They brought more religion, more traditions, more superstition.' Certainly the *Consistoire,* traditionally 'middle-of-the-road' like the old United Synagogue in Britain, had taken a relatively tolerant line on conversions. This changed with the retirement in 1980 of the late French Chief Rabbi Jacob Kaplan, the last Ashkenazi to hold the position.

While North African Jewry may not have had experience of the enlightenment and of the intellectual and psychological challenges of the modern world, it had been characterised by a spirit of understanding and pragmatism. Masliah, a suitably urbane spokesman, told me of a synagogue in Tunisia which held two services on Saturday mornings, one at six for people obliged to work on *Shabbat*! But the encounter in France between the East European-inspired Lubavitch and North Africans with orthodox aspirations[3] produced an ultra-orthodox hybrid which, in line with the increasing rigidity of orthodoxy elsewhere, assumed the most stringent stance towards the erosion of Jewish numbers. In what Rabbi Michael Williams of the fashionable but marginalised Copernic synagogue refers to as 'a return to ignorance, prejudice and tribalism', the number one casualty was conversion, with lost Jews the prime victims.

The rapid integration into French society of North African Jews, familiar with French language and culture, led to a high degree of intermarriage accompanied by a desire to retain some form of Jewish life. Strong family ties reinforced the North African's 'deeply sentimental attachment' towards Judaism, as Rabbi Claude Brahami explains: 'The North African Jew can't stand being detached from his family by a marriage that makes his children and descendants no longer Jewish.' Brahami himself, clean-shaven and professorial, exemplifies the breadth and tolerance of the best of the Sephardi tradition.

Where 'old regime' rabbis criticised by former Chief Rabbi Goldmann as excessively 'flexible' used to 'regularise these situations', conversions with a view to marriage have become virtually impossible. The pressure then built up for conversions at bar mitzvah age but by the early 1990s, a virtual moratorium was imposed on conversions.

The *status quo* was challenged in November 1993 at a gathering of French Jewish intellectuals by Rabbi Josy Eisenberg, the one-time secretary of former Chief Rabbi Kaplan and, according to Rabbi Williams, 'the most famous rabbi in France'. His speech describing the difference between the old *Consistoire* and the new was 'like Moses coming down from Mount Sinai and smashing the tablets'.

In a series of new moves, Eisenberg was chosen to head a rabbinical governing committee working with French Chief Rabbi Josef Sitruk, while Goldmann was replaced by Rabbi David Messas, formerly of Geneva. Messas, in a long telephone conversation, refused to be drawn on his policies, but stressed the need to be humane. 'It is very painful when one has to reject someone,' he told me. The 1500 lost Jews and others who apply annually for consistorial conversion now have a new man at the helm. Might French Jewry be at the dawn of a new era?

Decline versus Continuity

As indicated in Chapter 1, Anglo-Jewry has suffered a dramatic decline in the last decade and a half. The following quotations assess the decline and what is being done about it.

> In Britain the decline is much more real. British Jewry believed that by becoming stricter it would preserve itself. The concept here is that if the core is more firm, the stronger the magnet at the centre will be and then the peripheral situation will be better. But does the magnet attract or repel? Statistics seem to suggest that the movement into a more rigid stance, far from strengthening British Jewry has polarised it.
>
> Barry Kosmin

> I think Anglo-Jewry is too busy trying to be English. The consequence is that it's allowed some of the really special qualities of Jewishness to lapse. There are many elements in the culture in England which run counter to natural Jewish instincts and have not been helpful in promoting strong Jewish feelings.
>
> Rabbi Shlomo Levin

> England has to go through a real re-energising of its intellectual resources and create a public debate, a theological debate.
>
> Rabbi David Hartman

> We're dealing with the cutting edge of Jewish culture. We're saying this development of Jewish comedy is a significant new form of Jewish cultural expression and it's absolutely central to the way people of my generation are expressing their Jewishness. They're not going to synagogue, they're not keeping kosher, they're not members of Jewish organisations, they're not giving money to Jewish charities and they are obsessed about their Jewish identity.
>
> Matthew Kalman

> Nothing has been done in any diaspora community which remotely compares to Jewish Continuity. It aims to promote and sponsor a whole range of open-ended initiatives to try and make Jews, especially Jews on the margin, feel they have access to Jewish experience and Jewish belonging.
>
> Chief Rabbi Dr Jonathan Sacks

I'm not happy with this 'wanting to be Jewish', all this thing about optional identity, this entire disruption of the continuity of identity. You don't choose who you are. If you are half this and half that then your problem is not that you're both but that you're neither. Now if the traditions allow you to be one – your mother is Jewish and the tradition is saying 'From our point of view you can count yourself as a Jew' – that to some degree gives you permission to resolve the dilemma of your identity.

Clive Lawton

Museum or Trailblazer?

The Prague community will not be the same community as before the *Shoah* but also the present of the community does not resemble the future. I don't just have expectations, I know it will be different.

Rabbi Karel Sidon

Most of us would like to rebuild what Prague used to be in smaller numbers and Prague was always a cosmopolitan, very tolerant city and the only way to make it again a cosmopolitan, tolerant city is not to educate exclusively Jews about Jewish topics but also educate gentiles about Jewish topics.

Sylvia Wittmanova

Everyone in our country has a 'Jewish grandmother'. In Prague, especially in cultural circles, among the intelligentsia, people like me or Jewish people are something extraordinary, special and interesting.

Jana Smidova

If you have a small community like here you haven't a division between community and synagogue which means synagogue actually rules the community and that's the trouble. We can only have members of the community who are Jewish according to *halacha*. All the rest are people who are somehow adjoined to the community who can participate in a lot of the activities but they can't be members.

Daniel Kumermann

> What I can do is to give them education, give them correct information and, if they want, to receive them, not to throw them away. But the process, the transition, is a matter for each individual.
>
> Rabbi Karel Sidon

Within the ferment that is post-Communist Jewish Prague, lost Jews play a crucial role in the struggle to determine the shape of the future. As in other communities in central or eastern Europe, Jews are defined according to two criteria, *halacha* and the Law of Return. The latter may dominate many communities, for example Sofia in Bulgaria, as Zionist leader Arie Wolf explains: 'The non-*halachic* Jews are even more active, they go around with big *Magen-Davids*, they identify strongly and are very enthusiastic about their identification – not as a religion, they are not religiously involved, you won't find religious Jews in Sofia.' But the advent of the dynamic and newly orthodox Rabbi Sidon has given the Prague community a different stamp.

Sidon's desire to promote a Judaism which is acceptably orthodox yet open to all is challenged by progressive elements in Prague and progressive rabbis from the West who seek to bolster struggling communities in Central and Eastern Europe. Ironically, it was the progressive forces which put into effect two of his dearest wishes: to involve the relatively numerous Jewish ex-pats from America and other Western countries in Jewish activities and to hold services in the High Synagogue, one of the synagogues incorporated after World War II into the Prague Jewish museum. On the Jewish High Holy Days in September 1994, services were conducted in the High Synagogue by an English reform rabbi.

Without wishing to impose religious demands on his non-*halachic* flock, Sidon is aware that to ensure a future for communities eroded to the bone, a rabbi must work hard with whatever material he has:

> Here in Central Europe there was assimilation already before the war, that's the reason for today's situation, together with the *Shoah*, with the Communist regime. The same problem exists all over Europe but in all the other places they don't yet need to do something about this and we have no other way.

NEW BLOOD: THY PEOPLE SHALL BE MY PEOPLE

> I've always felt particularly warm towards converts because my very first teacher in *yeshiva* was a non-Jew who had converted to Judaism.

Jewishness is a covenant into which some of us are born and some of us enter of our own free choice and those who enter of their own free choice excite our imagination.

Chief Rabbi Jonathan Sacks

You can show as much interest in Judaism as you want till the cows come home but you simply can't become a Jew.

Nicola, Chapter 10

At one time we all felt what a wonderful world it would be if everyone was Jewish and kept the Jewish values. Now there seems to be a feeling among some that Judaism is only for the people who are Jewish and being born Jewish gives some special rights over being converted to Judaism. I find this not only obnoxious, I find it a betrayal of Judaism.

Rabbi Sidney Brichto, ULPS, London

If anybody feels Judaism is compelling and interesting and would like to join Judaism, we welcome them.

Rabbi David Hartman

Three times a day devout Jews pray for *gerei ha-tzedek* to be blessed together with the most respected members of the people of Israel. And however reluctant to proselytise, the most orthodox rabbis I met spoke almost with reverence of converts who matched up to their standards. Yet many Jews are anything but welcoming towards those who choose to enter their faith community. Some go so far as to flout the requirement in Jewish law that a convert should never be reminded of his origins. Dayan Berger told me of a London community who had openly humiliated a pious woman convert who had become the mainstay of that community, while Sylvia Wittmanova in Prague sensed that some orthodox Jews of the older generation tried to exert control over Rabbi Sidon by reminding him he had not always been a Jew. This lack of acceptance of converts at gut level was reflected in the reservations expressed by some marginal Jews and even a few lost Jews I spoke to.

Rebekka Weddell admits: 'I can be as exclusive as the next Jew, all my prejudices come out.' As a lost Jew of patrilineal descent who has struggled to hold on to the Jewishness many deny her, she fears converts may invade her sense of identity. Lydia Howard, a matrilineal Jewess, takes another view.

> It's to do with what Jews have been through and what Jews have endured and what Jews are more than what Jews believe. Jews have had a hard time over the centuries and therefore having Jewish blood is actually being a part of this people who have been persecuted and you can't be a part of that if you don't have any of their blood.

David Matthews, another matrilineal Jew, finds a convert puts him in an anomalous position: 'Someone like that who I don't think of as intrinsically Jewish can convert, can learn far more than I know about the religion. Something in me says she's not really Jewish whereas I think of myself as Jewish while I know none of those things.'

Overall among marginal Jews, there was more support for converts. Tim, the most religiously committed of the 'marginals' interviewed, felt people who converted 'because they love the religion can be more faithful and more useful than people who are just Jewish by birth'. He was convinced that 'one of the major downfalls of the Jewish religion is that they just do not accept new people'. Stephen Bloom took a similar view: 'Lack of proselytising is a failure in Judaism. Currently Judaism is becoming less and less important and the number of Jews smaller and smaller as a percentage of the world population.'

Another, equally pragmatic reason given for welcoming converts was to 'strengthen the gene pool', as Rabbi Rodney Mariner put it: 'One of the most important factors in the survival of Judaism has been the capacity to renew itself by new genes. We would have died off long ago through general diseases if we'd continued to marry among ourselves.' Rosalind Preston, too, spoke of the 'danger of inbreeding', while evidence of this was provided by Rabbi Menachem HaCohen who played a major role in rediscovering a community of Marranos in Belmonte in Portugal. 'I found them a very ancient, crippled and disabled people, physically, because they have been marrying among themselves for so long.'

Ultimately, attitudes towards conversion are influenced by attitudes towards Judaism itself. Those rabbis who believe that Judaism is a way of life prescribed for those who are born into the faith community and that any outsider has to win his spurs by proving more knowledgeable and observant than most born Jews are, necessarily, reluctant to convert. Others, like Rabbi Rodney Mariner, who believe that 'Judaism has something to offer' are more inclined to welcome converts for their own benefit. As Rabbi Dr Louis Jacobs put it, 'If we believe, as I do, that Judaism is a good thing then why shouldn't as many people as possible be Jewish? I wouldn't favour going around in this day and age and making mass conversions or engaging in missionary activity but if someone wants to be Jewish, why not?' While mass conversions might smack of soul-saving, something which is quite alien to Judaism, to welcome and encourage gentiles who see the benefit of the Jewish way of life can only strengthen the Jewish people.

LOST JEWS: WHERE DO THEY STAND?

Outside Perspectives

> I think there must be thousands, probably tens of thousands, lost in the gentile world who could be brought back at least into a social bonding with the Jewish people. It's the responsibility of the Jewish leadership to have a vision to care and have compassion for those who are, as it were, waiting to be found.
>
> Dr Margaret Brearley, Fellow in Jewish–Christian Relations, Institute of Jewish Affairs, London

> I would fight on every level. You do not know if you going to be able to reclaim people and I think you will reclaim people if you reach out to them and make them feel there is a place for them.
>
> Rosalind Preston

Viewed from the Inside

A definite majority of lost Jews I spoke to would appreciate some overture from the Jewish world. As Air Commodore Wober explained: 'A chance to be welcomed into some sort of fold would be an added dimension. I can't answer for how my children would have responded but had there been something from birth, that would have been nice.' Gabriel Solomon also believed there would be a positive response: 'I feel this would bring other people out into the open who perhaps have some Jewish heritage or are just inquisitive about Judaism.' Martin Daltrop, however, speaks for a sizeable minority when he says he would not wish to find out more about his background. Within today's Jewish climate, Jessica Greenman's feeling that the exclusion of half-Jews by Jews is unfortunate, in view of what Jews have suffered from persecution, is shared by many lost Jews. Claire Calman, however, can understand that the Jewish community might not want 'a whole lot of people all claiming some sort of kinship'.

Most lost Jews disagreed with the *halachic* ruling on status, as did the majority of marginal Jews I met, believing that self-definition and upbringing were more important than lineage. Baroness Blackstone who has the key ancestor, the maternal Jewish grandmother, feels 'it doesn't make much sense to say I'm Jewish because I had one Jewish grandparent who wasn't a practising Jew anyway and three who were gentiles and I was never brought up as Jewish'. Michael Palmer put it this way: 'It's a matter of the person's attitude rather than the accident of birth. I think the idea of one grandparent or perhaps two grandparents is enough.' If he had a Jewish name, Palmer believes, he would 'tend to have a much more Jewish life. Everyone would assume I was Jewish and I might find I had a greater circle of Jewish friends.' Julie Clare sees the decision whether or not to be Jewish as a question of adult choice: 'If you want to be Jewish, then be Jewish, whatever that means for you, and there shouldn't necessarily be obstacles placed in the way of that.' However, she concedes, some obstacles might be necessary in order to ensure a certain level of commitment.

An 'open door policy' in line with what is advocated by secular, humanist Jews and also by progressive rabbi Dr Dan Cohn-Sherbok[4] was put forward by Ari (Chapter 10): 'Anyone who wants to be Jewish should be welcome to be Jewish and anyone who's Jewish and doesn't want to be ought to be welcome not to be. You'll go through phases but if you converted out of Judaism and then you felt in the end that Judaism was the right thing you ought to be welcome back.' Within a more traditional framework, Lindsey Taylor-Guthartz, who acknowledges she can't 'remake *halacha*', advocates a 'quickie' process for committed patrilineals: 'They should say "Fine, you've got a Jewish father, you want to commit yourself? Okay on Tuesday you come and dunk. There we are, finished." '

A Personal View

One proposal I put forward at the beginning of the book was to see patrilineal and matrilineal lost Jews treated in the same way. The most reasonable proposition I came across in this respect was Rabbi Rivon Krygier's preference for Jewish status to require two Jewish parents. Within that framework, both a patrilineal and a matrilineal lost Jew would need a process of *tikkun* (repair), in order to be accepted as a fully fledged member of the Jewish people. This concept of 'repair' was compared, by Rabbi Josy Eisenberg, to the curing of a sexual disease: 'The Torah forbids a man to marry a non-Jewish woman. I don't want to make the comparison but if a man has a sexual disease, he knows he is taking a risk for his child. Afterwards something has to be done to cure the child.'

Although the *Beth Din* and rabbis are formally called upon to repair the situation, Chief Rabbi of Paris David Messas regards the process of 'repair' as something the individual has to undergo internally.

I also suggested that the Law of Return definition of Jewishness should be taken as an entry point to Jewish status, backed by an adequate level of background knowledge and commitment. While this is not as radical as the 'open door policy' referred to earlier, my research in the course of preparing this book has forced me to question how effective my proposal would be in reality. Would any religious Jewish body accept it? And would it enable a lost Jew of non-*halachic* lineage to marry an orthodox girl whose one stipulation was that she must marry a Jew? (Chapter 4).

While a Jewish grandfather might have entitled someone to be given preferential consideration for conversion by former Chief Rabbi Goldmann of Paris, no religious leader, not even the most progressive, would give *carte blanche* to a prospective Jew with a non-*halachic* Jewish grandparent. He or she would have to undergo – at least – the ULPS affirmation process or the RSGB *mikveh* and intermediate certificate package.

But would either of the above formulae, both of which I personally find perfectly acceptable, enable our lost Jew to marry the girl? Again the answer is no. As many stories in this book have shown, the division between the orthodox and the non-orthodox world has given rise to a great deal of pain. Some initiative has to come from within orthodoxy that would make any other conversion process superfluous.

Rabbi Josy Eisenberg's proposal for a reintegration into Judaism for children of Jewish fathers who have chosen their Jewish heritage, were it to be adopted within the orthodox world, would undoubtedly be the most painless means for our lost Jew to get his girl. By enabling a wide variety of committed yet not necessarily orthodox lost Jews to find a place within the Jewish world, this process of initiation would strengthen the Jewish people from its own sources. While it does not cater for lost Jews of more remote ancestry, a climate of orthodox opinion that accepted the reintegration process would probably approach conversions in a far more sympathetic manner than at present.

WHY BE JEWISH?

As Judaism has again become an *or le-goyim,* a light to the nations, it has also brought a new light and spirit to all Jews.

Rabbi Stephen Lerner[5]

One wants to say to a person thinking of marrying out, 'You may not feel it now when you're 25 but when you're 35 where you come from will matter to you enormously with a profundity and depth and with a grip on your life which you're perhaps not able to understand now.'

Rabbi Jonathan Wittenberg

Why it runs that deep, why it's so vital and crucial, I don't know, but I don't think escaping from being Jewish works. Even if it works for you, it doesn't work two generations down the line which is this whole patrilineal or matrilineal problem.

Matthew Kalman

Many of the Jewish traditions, especially *Shabbes*, are benign, attractive in themselves and psychologically beneficial, and there's a case to be made for preserving impalpable things as well as palpable.

Chaim Bermant

Are we being emphatic enough about the joy, the privilege, the pleasure of being Jewish?

Rosalind Preston

It depressed me to feel there were people whose Jewishness was a burden to them. I want them to feel, like me, that Jewishness is a source of comfort and happiness and fulfilment.

Matthew Kalman

A Personal View

The union of our lost Jew and the orthodox girl, the synthesis of the core and the periphery, is the ideal for a new and reinvigorated Jewish future. All too often in conversations, I was confronted with the spectre of a future that was bleak and divided. All over the world there would be increasingly large numbers of people with remote Jewish ancestry, bands of what might be called 'friends of the Jewish people', sprinklings of residual Jewish qualities within ever larger segments of the general population. And in a few enclaves, the remains of the Jewish people, sects of ultra-orthodox Jews who, if not faced with the physical problems of inbreeding which deformed the Belmonte Marranos, would be stunted by their insularity.

In a world where religion is seen to be increasingly irrelevant, is Jewishness worth preserving? I can only answer for myself and I have one reservation. If Jewishness is just a club for which membership is a special lineage and the prime club rule is 'Thou shalt not marry out', I would see no point in preserving that.

But the reasons so eloquently expressed in the quotations of the previous section and by numerous lost Jews throughout the book give a glimmer of what Jewishness is about: a sense of connectedness to a heritage and a past, a source of comfort and enjoyment and a message that has withstood the ravages of time and persecution. These qualities, so intrinsic to Jewishness, are not always apparent and, as a result, many Jews are alienated from their roots.

In the process of writing this book, I have experienced new joys which have affirmed my sense of Jewishness and which, I believe, would touch many alienated Jews. A Friday night at 'Diana's' in New York (Chapter 5), where the grace after the meal was sung with exquisite expression by an ex-pat Israeli artist; a service of rededication at the Bevis Marks Synagogue in London where the nobility of the physical environment and the beauty of the singing were overwhelming; the Friday night at the Jewish community centre in Prague (Chapter 7); a second *seder* night for lost Jews at my home in London where one of my alienated sons led the singing and admitted it was fun; an evening at Solly's, an elegant oriental kosher restaurant in London's Golders Green, with excellent food, a talented Israeli singer and a 'great atmosphere'.[6]

A Light to the Nations

> What's the point of a non-religious Jew in the Western world maintaining his Judaism unless he feels there's something special about it? And if there's something special, surely it should be shared? The fact that for hundreds of years we were a persecuted people doesn't mean our message isn't still worthy of transmission, but if we don't know what that message is and if we're keeping it to ourselves and we think our only loyalty is to maintaining our Jewishness and not realising what the depth of Judaism is, then we're lost and our purpose is lost.
>
> Rabbi Sidney Brichto

> The world is fixated about Jews. But it is necessary to put aside feelings of excess satisfaction. We must find an equilibrium, not to hide

> ourselves, not to be arrogant but not to allow ourselves to be humiliated. There is something we have brought to the world and if we remain faithful to these values we will have our place in a society which is in the process of being built.
>
> Henri Bulawko

When I started this book, my position was that if committed, open-minded Jews were convinced of the merits of Judaism and Jewish culture, they should find ways of putting forward Jewish teachings and values in the open market-place of ideas and ideologies. I also advocated the need to reach out to uncommitted young Jews in the non-Jewish contexts in which they live and suggested that Jews who have found their way back to Judaism or committed secular Jews might act as unofficial emissaries at universities, seeking out Jewish students in the bars and common rooms and engaging them in conversation together with their non-Jewish friends.

I was not aware at that time of the work of the L'Chaim Society at Oxford University, sponsored until September 1994 by the Lubavitch foundation. What distinguishes L'Chaim from other Jewish institutions is the large proportion of non-Jews who attend its functions. While this has earned L'Chaim's founder and director, Rabbi Shmuel Boteach, flak from more conservative Jewish quarters, it is a crucial ingredient of L'Chaim's success with young Jews, as Boteach explains:

> Because we're very universal, we have many non-Jewish members, a lot of famous speakers, the Jewish students who come here don't feel they have to change before they walk through our door. They can actually explore things without having to commit either way and to me that's the most beautiful way of being Jewish. It's like becoming Jewish without choosing to be; it means there's a substructure of Jewishness within you which you may not consciously be aware of but you sort of tap into when you come here.

Boteach is also aware that 'the non-Jewish world has always had a fascination, sometimes even an obsession with Jews', and that the Jewish people serve a unique purpose to be a light unto the nations.

> The special message entrusted to them by God is to teach the world godliness and goodness. Therefore if Jews lead godly and goodly lives and go out into society instead of shackling themselves up in ghettos, then their message begins to rub off on the non-Jewish nations. So I would hold the observant Jew who leads a Jewish life but lives in a

ghetto and only mixes with Jews as accountable for not spreading the message as the completely secular Jew who has no Jewish identity whatsoever. Both are not executing the reason for the Jewish people's existence.

Notes

Notes to Chapter 1: Where Have All the Jews Gone?

1. Stanley Waterman and Barry Kosmin, *British Jewry in the Eighties* (Board of Deputies of British Jews, 1986) p. 8.
2. Cited in Egon Mayer, *A Demographic Revolution in American Jewry* (Jean and Samuel Frankel Center for Judaic Studies, University of Michigan, 1992) p. 14.
3. Chief Rabbi Dr Jonathan Sacks, *Studies in Renewal 2: The Crisis of Continuity* (Office of the Chief Rabbi, July 1993) p. 1.
4. Personal communication, July 1993. In future where authority figures express opinions as opposed to providing information, these will not be footnoted and should be assumed to be personal communications unless stated otherwise.
5. Barry Kosmin, 'The Demographic Imperatives of Outreach', *Journal of Jewish Community Service,* vol. 66, no. 3 (Spring 1990) p. 211.
6. Jonathan Sacks, op. cit., p. 7
7. Kosmin (personal communication, July 1993) gave an alternative breakdown of the religious upbringing of children of mixed marriages in the USA: '25 per cent are raised as Jews in Judaism; 35 per cent are raised as nothing; 40 per cent are raised in Christianity of some mixture, some other religion or syncretism – Jewish and something else'.
8. Kosmin, op. cit., p. 211.
9. Another theory ascribing the matrilineal ruling to rape finds support in various quarters – but the rapes in question are presumed to have taken place in the Middle Ages, for example at the hands of the crusaders.
10. Several rabbis, notably Dayan Berger.
11. For this information I am indebted to Dayan Berel Berkovits of the Federation of Synagogues.
12. Instant conversion – immersion in *mikveh* or ritual bath – is offered in very rare cases when someone who has been leading an irreproachably orthodox life is suddenly discovered to be *halachically* non-Jewish.
13. Berkovits, personal communication, December 1993.
14. Speech on induction as Chief Rabbi, September 1991.
15. S. J. Prais and Marlena Schmool, 'Statistics of Jewish Marriages in Great Britain: 1901–1965', *The Jewish Journal of Sociology*, vol. IX, no. 2 (December 1967); Marlena Schmool, 'Synagogue Marriages in Britain in the 1980s', *The Jewish Journal of Sociology,* vol. XXXIII, no. 2 (December 1991).
16. *Radical Assimilation in English Jewish History 1656–1945* (Indiana University Press, 1990). Comments by Endelman are taken from a personal meeting in June 1993.
17. Goldmann, personal communication, February 1994.

18. Cited in an article by Patricia Har-Even in the Literary Supplement, *The Jewish Chronicle* (19 February 1993).
19. 11 May 1993.

Notes to Chapter 2: Immigration to Assimilation

1. For the link material in this chapter I am indebted to Todd Endelman's *Radical Assimilation in English Jewish History 1656–1945* (Indiana University Press, 1990).
2. Endelman, op. cit., pp. 10–11.
3. Ibid., p. 15.
4. Robert Barrett, personal communication, March 1994.
5. Article by Lydia Collins, *SHEMOT: Journal of the Jewish Genealogical Society of Great Britain,* vol. 1, no. 3 (Summer 1993) p. 9.
6. It was also not unknown for Jews in the United States and in Italy to rebury their ancestors in a Christian cemetery so as to hide the stigma of their Jewish origins, as I learnt from the social historian John Cooper.
7. Robert Barrett, personal communication, March 1994.
8. *Moses Gaster Memoirs*, edited and collated by Bertha Gaster (London, 1990).
9. Endelman, op. cit., pp. 34–5.
10. Ibid., pp. 35–6.
11. Christine Wagg, personal communication, September 1993.
12. Ibid.
13. Endelman, op. cit., pp. 34–5.
14. Ibid., p. 39.
15. Ibid., p. 42.
16. Paul H. Emden, *Jews of Britain* (London: Sampson Low Marston, 1940), p. 146.
17. Margaret Brearley, personal communication, January 1994.
18. Endelman, op. cit., p. 43.
19. Sabine Doust, personal communication, September 1993.
20. George Rigal, lecture to Jewish Genealogical Society, November 1993.
21. Endelman, op. cit., pp. 73–4.
22. Robert Barrett, personal communication, March 1994.
23. Endelman, op. cit., p. 74.
24. Ibid., p. 92.
25. C. Russell and H. S. Lewis, *The Jew in London* (1901), cited by Rabbi Dr Anthony Bayfield in his Cardinal Bea Memorial Lecture, May 1993.
26. Endelman, op. cit., p. 173.
27. Michael Brandon, personal communication, December 1993.
28. George Rigal, lecture, November 1993.
29. Endelman, op. cit., Chapter 6.
30. S. J. Prais and Marlena Schmool, 'Statistics of Jewish Marriages in Great Britain: 1901–1965'.

Notes to Chapter 3: Intimations of Decline

1. The experience and integration of German refugees from Nazi Europe is included in *Second Chance – Two Centuries of German-speaking Jews in the United Kingdom,* Co-ordinating Editor Werner E. Mosse (J.C.B. Mohr, Tubingen, 1991).
2. Anton Gill, *The Journey Back from Hell* (Grafton, 1989).
3. The Horst Wessel liede, a Nazi marching song, opened with the words: *Wenn Judenblut unter'm Messer spritzt – When Jewish blood spurts from under the knife.*
4. Robert Barrett, personal communication, March 1994.
5. Ibid.
6. Lubavitch Chassids are a sect of ultra-orthodox Jews who owed their allegiance to the late Lubavitcher *rebbe* who died in 1994.

Notes to Chapter 4: Who Says I'm Lost?

1. Jerry Raik, personal communication, July 1993.
2. There is also a small but expanding Masorti (traditional) movement with a few congregations in the London area and the provinces, affiliated to the Masorti group in Israel. It observes the *halacha* on Jewish status.
3. Le Mouvement Juif Libéral de France founded in 1977, as a secessionary movement from the synagogue in Rue Copernic in Paris. Until then Copernic, founded in 1906, was the only outlet of non-orthodox Judaism in France. The Masorti movement has also recently started a congregation in Paris.
4. Shlomit Levy, personal communication, January 1994.
5. *Liberal Judaism and Jewish Identity.*
6. From a debate on conversion recorded in *L'Arche*, the French Jewish monthly, September 1994.
7. Dayan Berger and several other orthodox rabbis in Britain justified this by explaining that the minor living at home with a non-Jewish mother would not have the facilities for eating kosher food or leading a Jewish life.
8. The practice of conversion at approximately bar mitzvah age in France was explained to me by former Chief Rabbi of Paris, Alain Goldmann, orthodox rabbi Claude Brahami and Léon Masliah, director-general of the *Consistoire*. In contrast to orthodox rabbis in Britain, Goldmann emphasised that the teenage child was capable of feeding himself. In an off the record telephone conversation, Goldmann's successor, Rabbi David Messas, then in Geneva, confirmed that he would continue with bar mitzvah-age conversions.
9. This practice was explained to me by the convenor of the RSGB *Beth Din*, Rabbi Rodney Mariner and by reform rabbi Dr Jonathan Romain. The Talmudic precedent on which it is based was also cited by the American conservative rabbi, Stephen Lerner. A child converted in these circumstances may reverse the conversion at bar mitzvah age.

Note to Chapter 8: The Promise Spurned

1. Asphodel Long's research has appeared in journals and essays and in her book *In a Chariot Drawn by Lions – The Search for the Female in Deity* (The Women's Press, 1992).

Notes to Chapter 10: To Be or Not To Be

1. Survey on 'The Impact of Jewish Education on the Religious Behaviour and Attitudes of British Secondary School Pupils' conducted by Dr Stephen Miller, Department of Psychology, City University, London 1985.
2. Interview with the author in February 1993, part of which was published in *New Moon,* April 1993.
3. *Moses of Oxford*, vol. 1, pp. 444, 445 (André Deutsch, 1994).

Notes to Chapter 11: The Establishment Voice

1. The Kalms Report on the United Synagogue (1992) revealed that only 10 per cent of members observe *kashrut* and *Shabbat* fully.
2. *Women in the Jewish Community*, survey report by Marlena Schmool and Stephen Miller, 1994.
3. In the summer of 1995 the Community Research Unit of the Board of Deputies was seeking out Jewish women married to non-Jews to take part in a postal survey of social attitudes.
4. Chief Rabbi Sacks, *Will We Have Jewish Grandchildren?* (London: Vallentine, Mitchell & Co., 1994).

Notes to Chapter 12: A Way Forward

1. *Gerut: An Approach for Our Time* (1979) and *Choosing Judaism* (1992).
2. Reported in *The Jewish Chronicle*, 23 September 1994.
3. I gained this impression from M. Henri Bulawko, personal communication, February 1994.
4. *The Future of Judaism* (T. & T. Clark, 1994).
5. *Choosing Judaism* (1992).
6. Same expression used in *New Moon*, December 1994.

Glossary

Adonai Hu haElohim: The Lord, He is God.

Aleph, Bet, Gimel: First three letters of Hebrew alphabet.

Aliyah: Immigration to Israel.

Ba'al Teshuva: Born-again orthodox Jew.

Bar mitzvah: Religious ceremony marking boy's coming of age as a Jew. Also **bat mitzvah** for a girl.

Beit Hillel: The followers of Rabbi Hillel, renowned for his lenience.

Benching: Grace after meals.

Beth Din: Religious court.

Bracha, brachot (pl.): Blessing.

Brit mila: Ritual circumcision. Also **hatazat dam brit**: drawing a drop of blood.

Cachère: French for kosher.

Challa: Plaited bread eaten on Sabbath and festivals.

Chanukah/Hanukah: Festival of lights, usually in December, commemorating the liberation of the Temple by the Maccabaeans.

Chassid: Follower of certain ultra-orthodox sects. Also **Chassidim** (pl.), **chassidic** and **chassidism**.

Cheder: Religion school.

Chupa: Canopy used in marriage ceremony.

Chutzpah: Cheek, nerve.

Cohen: Descendant of the ancient priestly caste.

Davven: Pray.

Dayan, Dayanim (pl.): Religious judge who sits on a **Beth Din**.

Davka(ish): Wish to be contrary, being contrary.

Dreidl: Spinning top used in **Hanukah** celebrations.

Etrog, lulav: Citron and palm branch used during the festival of Tabernacles.

Frum: Orthodox or ultra-orthodox.

Galut: Dispersion, diaspora.

Ger: Proselyte; also **Gerei ha-tzedek**: righteous proselytes.

Goy: Gentile; also **goyim** (pl.) and **goyische**: gentile manners or ways.

Hadassah: Jewish women's organisation.

Haftorah: Readings from the later books of the Hebrew Scriptures read after the reading from the **Torah**. In traditional synagogues, the **bar mitzvah** boy will chant the **haftorah**.

Hagadah: The order of the Passover **seder**.

Hagim: Festivals.

Haham: Literally 'wise man'.

Halacha: Body of Jewish religious laws; also **halachic, halachist**.

Hanukiah: Candlestick used at **Hanukah**.

Hashgacha pratit: The hand of providence.

Hochma: Hebrew for 'wisdom'.

Judengasse: Street in Jewish ghetto.

Judenrat: Jewish council.

Kabbala: Jewish mysticism; also **kabbalist**.

Kaddish: Mourner's prayer.

Kashrut: Dietary laws.

Ketubah: Marriage certificate.

Kibbutzim: Plural of kibbutz; also **kibbutzniks**: members of kibbutz.

Kiddush: Prayer over wine and bread said on Sabbath and festivals.

Kiddushin: one of the tracts of the **Mishna**.

Kipah: Skullcap.

Kotel: Wall of the temple in Jerusalem known as the Western or 'Wailing' Wall.

Latkes: Potato pancakes often eaten at **Hanukah**.

Ma'asim tovim: Good deeds.

Magen-Davids: Stars, literally 'shields', of David.

Masorti: Traditional.

Matzas: Unleavened bread eaten at Passover.

Menorah: Candlestick

Meshuggah: Mad, crazy.

Mezzuzah: Parchment handwritten with verses from the **Torah**, put into a container and affixed to the gates and doors of Jewish homes and institutions.

Miad: Hebrew for 'immediately'.

Mikveh: Ritual bath, also used during conversion process.

Minyan: Quorum of ten men needed for certain prayers.

Mishna: First part of the **Talmud**, divided into six tracts.

Mitzvah: Honorable deed, good deed; also **613 mitzvot**: commandments that orthodox Jews follow.

Mohel: Ritual circumciser.

Naches: Pleasure, satisfaction.

Neshama: Soul.

ÖstJuden: Jews from Eastern Europe, usually looked down on in the West.

Pesach: Passover festival commemorating the Exodus from Egypt.

Purim: Festival recorded in the book of Esther celebrating the liberation of the Jews in Persia.

Rassenschande: Crime during Nazi era of people with Jewish blood having sexual relations with Aryans.

Rosh Hashanah: The Jewish New Year.

Ruach haKodesh: The spirit of God.

Seder: Ceremonial prayers and dinner at Passover.

Shabbat: Sabbath (Hebrew); also **Shabbatot** (pl.), **Shabbes** (Yiddish) and **shomrei Shabbat**: Sabbath observers.

Shadchan: Matchmaker.

Shechina: Jewish 'holy spirit'.

Shiksas: Derogatory term for gentile women.

Shiur, **shiurim** (pl.): Lesson in Judaism.

Shofar: Ram's horn blown at **Rosh Hashanah** and **Yom Kippur**.

Shtetl: Village in the Jewish Pale of Settlement in Eastern Europe before World War II.

Shul: Synagogue.

Siddur: Prayer book.

Tallit: Prayer shawl.

Talmud: Early oral commentary on the Bible.

Talmud Torah: Religion school.

Tenach: Hebrew Scriptures.

Tikkun: Repair.

Torah: Pentateuch, the five books of Moses.

Tsitsit: Fringed undergarment worn by orthodox Jews.

Tvila: Ritual immersion in **mikveh**.

Ulpan: Institution where Hebrew is studied. Also, in Israel, an institution where prospective converts study Judaism.

Yartzeit: Anniversary of death.

Yeshiva: Religious seminary.

Yetzer haRa: Evil inclination.

Yiddishkeit: Jewish ways or lore.

Yom Kippur: The Day of Atonement.

Zmirot: Sabbath songs.

Index